FOOD AND THE CONSUMER
REVISED EDITION

FOOD AND THE CONSUMER

REVISED EDITION

Amihud Kramer, Ph.D.
University of Maryland
College Park, Maryland

AVI PUBLISHING COMPANY, INC.
Westport, Connecticut

Library of Congress Cataloging in Publication Data

Kramer, Amihud
  Food and the consumer.

  Bibliography: p.
  Includes index.
  1. Food. 2. Nutrition. 3. Consumer protection.
I. Title.
TX353.K82   1980   641   80-20085
ISBN 0-87055-339-9

Printed in the United States of America by
Eastern Graphics, Inc., Old Saybrook, Connecticut

Preface to
The Revised Edition

Just a few years ago we wrote "now that the food producer and vendor are in the minority, the consumer can dictate to the food industry. . . . (and therefore) . . . get the food that he wants." How interesting that today, while powerful voices are accusing the food industry of denying the consumer his rightful and needed nutrients, it is only now that both food producer and consumer are beginning to recognize the all-important fact that there is a huge gap between what the consumer *wants* and what he *needs*. It is recognized that many of us want more information about the food we need. This evidences itself in universities wherein non-science majors seek courses of an essentially non-technical nature covering the subject. This book is my attempt to fill this need.

During the last decade we have seen the rise of food and health advocates who proposed, on the basis of limited knowledge, frequently incomplete, at times dangerous, and usually biased and often expensive, faddist diets. Yet the outcome of this ferment stimulated a host of activities beneficial to all of us.

Goverment now no longer limits its role in this area to regulations involving fair trade and protection of consumer's health, but it is also beginning to provide consumers with information concerning their nutritional needs. Similarly, the food industry, while continuing to develop new foods that are more appealing and convenient to the consumer (what he wants) is educating him—directly and indirectly—about nutritional requirements and food safety.

Although assessments of the first results of these efforts by government-consumer-industry, which became evident in terms of more complete label information on packaged foods, have been disappointing, the efforts may yet prove to be more beneficial than one might expect.

The first edition was written at the time that the "Club of Rome" had then just published *The Limits to Growth*, which forcefully warned that continuing trends of uncontrolled population growth and wasting of

v

nonrenewable resources would result in hunger and mass starvation soon, not in future millennia. While the general theme is unfolding according to these predictions, it is not food but energy, however, which is evidently now the first constraint on growth, and the expected global exponential rate of population growth has apparently reached its asymptote. It appears that by controlling our environment in such a way as to maximize food resources, we have the opportunity for an orderly, steady progression toward a peaceful and prosperous global era that has heretofore only been dreamt of—barring man-made or natural holocaust.

Yet throughout man's long advance, food facts have always been confused with myths, and although science may become ascendant, myths associated with specific mystical powers of foods may, like the poor, always remain with us. It is becoming increasingly apparent that the overwhelming majority of consumers are not motivated to learn more about the science of food and nutrition and therefore have little use of information provided. Most consumers merely wish to have some authority (governmental?) provide them with the assurance that *any* food they *want* will not only be safe, but will also keep them healthy. Obviously such assurance cannot be provided for everything one might eat. There must be a continuous effort by scientifically-oriented institutions in government, industry and the consumer movements not only to protect consumers but to attain nutritional support for all mankind.

AMIHUD KRAMER

July 1980

Preface to
The First Edition

We all know that until the last generation or two, provision of food was the major occupation of practically all humanity. We also know that even today in the vast majority of the tribes of man, the major obsession is finding enough to eat. How many of us realize, however, that even in this most powerful and affluent society of the West, we are still occupied with the provision of food to the extent of one-fifth of our resources, and obsessed with food problems to a much greater extent?

In past and present societies, on much of the earth's surface, the food producer was also the consumer. Today, in the United States, the food and allied industries engage less than one-fifth of the consumers. The others provide other material and aesthetic goods (or are unemployed). The food industry today is drastically reduced (proportionally) in manpower requirements, but tremendously increased in quantity and variety of products. It no longer consists merely of the collection, or even production, of raw food materials, but has developed into the largest and most complex single industry providing, not only immediate nutritional requirements, but also many labor-saving, food-preserving, and aesthetic services, all of which are demanded by an increasingly more affluent society. Production of food nutrients for all mankind could be accomplished by less than 1% of the world's labor force. Yet, because of the additional services required, no less than 18% of the U.S. consumers' resources are utilized to provide food and all its ancillary services.

Thus, the food producer and vendor are now in the minority, and the consumer can now dictate to the food industry exactly what his wishes are. It is therefore an inescapable fact that the consumer gets the food that he wants. If he purchases food that does not provide him with his essential nutrients, or food that is in fact harmful, he has only his own apathy and ignorance to blame. To survive, a food manufacturer, as any vendor, must meet the specifications which the buyer dictates.

Where does science get into the act? The term implies much that is beyond common understanding when in fact science specifically is nothing more than proven knowledge. Science, or facts about food have been in existence from pre-history, but have proliferated tremendously in recent generations. At this time there is no excuse for any consumers or consumer representatives not to have available the real knowledge, that is, the science which will provide them with facts to enable them to purchase their daily bread to satisfy their need of essential nutrients, to keep them from harm, and to provide them with aesthetic satisfaction.

Although food science, that is, food facts, should be the basis of the specifications upon which the food manufacturer should design the food for consumer satisfaction, there is in the human ethos the craving for the Deus ex Machina who will make all things well so that he will obtain his unobtainable total satisfaction, not on the basis of facts, but on the basis of belief. Just as food science existed well before recorded history, so has food mythology. And why should it not? We pray for our daily bread, but at the same time we do not live by bread alone. Deeply ingrained in the human psyche is the belief that anything produced by nature cannot be improved upon, but only contaminated or desecrated, or at best diluted. This belief in the supreme quality of the undisturbed natural product is only one of the many strange and wonderfully imaginative myths divined by men of good will or evil. The main purpose of this modest effort is to sort out food facts from food fancies. If in the process we should point out that cooked soybeans are more wholesome than raw, or that it is perfectly normal and of considerable nutritive value to consume two-, four-, six-, or eight-legged animals, we do not intend in any way to offend those whose mythology dictates otherwise. After all, those of us who call ourselves scientists, including physicians, nutritionists, even Nobel prize winners, have our share in the creation of myths which we cannot defend on the basis of proven facts.

Strange as it may seem to the non-scientist, even conclusions based logically on indisputable facts may be contradictory to other conclusions similarly derived. This may occasionally result from an investigator's willful suppression of the data that do not fit his premise. More usually it is the result of practically all experimentation being incomplete in that some influencing parameters have been omitted. Data, particularly interpretation of data, are also subject to many forms of bias, not the least of them being some degree of subjectivity in the eye of the observer. The more complex the material studied, the more difficult is complete objectivity of its evaluation. Practically all food is or was living matter. Thus, in dealing with the effect of foods on the physiology and psychology of man, the most complex form of life, any experimental data are limited so that logical, yet conflicting conclusions may be drawn by different researchers who are entirely scientifically honest.

Recognizing these limitations, we shall attempt to the best of our knowledge, to sort out food facts from food fancies for the general reader. At the same time we shall attempt to provide introductory material to the student of Food Science and Nutrition. It is our hope that this volume may also serve as a summary of educational material for the general consumer as well. Our hope is that we have not attempted too much.

AMIHUD KRAMER

May 1973

Professor,
Food Science Program,
University of Maryland,
College Park, Maryland

Acknowledgments

My sincere appreciation goes to Richard A. Ahrens, Ph.D., Associate Professor of Nutrition, University of Maryland, who prepared Chapter 2—*We Eat to Live*.

I am also indebted to William L. Sulzbacher, Ph.D., Microbiologist, U.S. Department of Agriculture (retired), who contributed extensively to Chapters 5, 6, and 8.

Finally, I extend my gratitude to Clara Louise Guin, M.A., who prepared many of the illustrations.

Contents

PREFACE
1 "Earth Has Finally Made It"   1
2 We Eat to Live   18
3 We Live to Eat   45
4 Consumer Protection   75
5 Food Codes and Habits   105
6 Food Preservation   118
7 Convenience Foods   142
8 Packaging and Marketing   162
9 Waste Disposal and Utilization   175
10 Food of the Future   193
REFERENCES   201
INDEX   213

"Earth Has Finally Made It"

Judah and Israel were many,
as the sand which is by the
sea in multitude, eating and
drinking and making merry.
I Kings, IV:20

It has always been the first need of humanity to have enough to eat and drink for all. Only in this century has this need been technically attainable. It has taken a long time—some 4−5 billion years—and it has taken some doing. It was something over 2 billion years before man—who is the first form of life capable of modifying the environment to suit his needs—made his appearance. It is now generally agreed that during all these eons of time there was continuous evolution of the environment. As the environment changed, so did the forms of life.

Before man dominated the earth, as the environment changed, the various forms of life either adapted to the changes or became extinct. Along came man; and for all but very recent history he, in his own manner, attempted to adjust to environmental changes, but he usually failed. It is only during recent millennia that man has succeeded in modifying his environment to suit his needs. Through science he has learned to modify his immediate environment and to create a micro-environment to protect him from otherwise insurmountable extremes of temperature, and from other predatory competitive species. As he developed the art of weaponry and the social science of pack-hunting, he vastly improved his food resources. Thus, the beginning of food science arrived with the thrown stone or spear, the tribe, and the controlled use of fire.

The Stone Age hunter was the first food scientist. He was also the first mythologist who based his mythology on food. As a scientist he knew that the flesh and blood of the animal he slaughtered would sustain his life. As a mythologist he believed that eating the warm heart of his victim would transfer to him the beast's courage.

1

A great advance in food science was made when the kill was heated. Without knowing it, primitive man did accomplish by this heat treatment detoxification of some naturally occurring toxins and the sterilization of the product, that is, the inactivation of microorganisms that may have made him ill. At the same time the heat treatment changed his microclimate to such an extent that the smoke and other volatiles undoubtedly affected his health adversely. More millennia passed during which some tribes survived and prospered because of their greater success in overcoming environmental problems, while others perished.

New sciences were added, and the old improved. Being omnivorous, man learned through tribal experience which animals and which plant materials provided him with sustenance, and which were detrimental to him. At the same time some of these animals, and particularly plant materials, were of value not only in providing nutrients, but also appeared to have healing properties. Thus medicine and pharmacy were born, closely allied to agricultural development. The practitioners of these skills were also credited by their fellow men with supernatural mysterious powers.

THE AGRICULTURAL REVOLUTION

The sciences of animal and plant husbandry then appeared, making it possible for the first time for man to utilize other species not only as sources of food and energy to sustain his own life, but also as means of transportation and labor-performance. Although animal husbandry provided the opportunity for man to accumulate and improve his food resources "on the hoof," it was plant husbandry that made it possible for him to reduce his complete reliance on the hunt and on the nomadic type of existence. The cornerstone of all civilization to come was therefore the first person who knew how to plant a seed and eventually harvest a crop. Again, as in previous stages on the road to modern civilization, the man who knew how to fold a seed within the earth to produce a bountiful supply of food was thought to be endowed with supernatural knowledge, which he used to aid as well as to dominate his fellow man.

Thus agriculture came into being, and as it developed, it released the energies of man in other directions, permitting him to create cultures and civilizations. One of the earliest developments of agriculture, and the beginning of food science as we think of it today, was the rapidly expanding knowledge of food preservation. The beginnings of dehydration and fermentation are lost in antiquity. Drying of meat, milk, fruit, and their controlled fermentation made it possible to store substantial quantities of food supplies for an agriculturally based sedentary population, who could thus survive from one season to the next under various and frequently adverse environmental conditions. At the same time the accumulation of such granaries provided nuclei for the construction of cities and empires where the population concentrations contaminated the urban environments and made these rapidly developing, previously impossible huge populations easy victims of other competitive forms of life. Yet breaking out of the confining city walls exposed the population to the most predatory competitor—man himself.

To gain some measure of control over this abuse of nature, man had to organize his newly developed urban centers. One method of combating such problems was the development of chemicals, certainly not originally in pure form, but as components of plant and in some instances animal materials. Such "spices" not only controlled food-born diseases, but also masked the naturally undesirable putrid flavors developing from spoiled foods. Thus the ancient arts of dehydration and (largely uncontrolled) fermentation were joined by chemical additives in the form of salts, drugs, and spices to maintain and preserve the food resources.

THE INDUSTRIAL REVOLUTION

A tremendous leap forward in human development was the Industrial Revolution of the late 18th and early 19th centuries, in which mechanical energy was first exploited for the needs of man. In a comparatively short time human efficiency increased astronomically, not only in food production but in manufacturing, transportation, and related areas. Thus man's comfort and material wealth increased to an extent beyond the wildest dreams of preceding generations. Among the amazing and far-reaching industrial developments that were born within this period of less than a century—including the loom, the cotton gin, and the steam engine—was the discovery of preservation of food by heat processing.

ROLE OF SCIENCE

Science cannot state what is or is not moral or what is or is not aesthetically acceptable, however. The palatability of foods for any group of men is dictated by past habits and customs. Regardless of what new intriguing foods are devised by refined scientific techniques purportedly for their greater enjoyment, they nostalgically crave those foods dictated by their immediate cultural-ethnic leaders. Very early in life, human preferences for food become established by education or example, so that one is satisfied only with the food to which he is accustomed and which he was told was proper—at times not only for his health and welfare, but for his immortal soul. Convincing a population group that their customary food is not adequate and that they should change or modify it in any way is a most difficult problem. It applies primarily, though not exclusively, to emerging and developing populations, to whom "adventures" in eating are as rare and hazardous as other adventures into the unknown.

During the earth's history, at no time has man been at peace with his environment. He has constantly strived to achieve a modus vivendi in a changing environment. Ice ages came and went. Variations in temperature resulted in changing shorelines, as did slippages of the earth's crust and emissions of thermal and nuclear substances from within it. No sooner did one society gain ascendancy over its immediate environment than gradual or cataclysmic changes caused its destruction, movement to a more favorable location, or replacement by other groups that were more competitive under the new environmental conditions. At all times, however, the innate desire "to multiply and replenish the earth" dominated the collective effort. Each civilization and each culture had its scientists as well as mythologists who attempted to gain ascendancy over the environment, to enable man to live in an orderly way with himself, and to allay the fears of the unknown.

All science can be divided into the empirical and the theoretical—the how and the why. Gifted inventors of all ages have discovered empirically, or deduced from theoretical considerations, ways of increasing the food supplies, thereby providing man with more leisure and opportunity to multiply. It is usually after the how that the why is attempted. Thus, at every age as man becomes more inventive and the mass of knowledge accumulates, he may "prove" that the earlier theoretician was wrong and that his new interpretation of the truth, that is, the "why," is correct. At this stage in the evolutionary process we recognize that the former theories or doctrines were not necessarily false, but merely explanations, based on the best knowledge available at the time, of the nature of environmental forces as they were then observed, while philosophers and mythologists completed explanations of the "why" by ascribing mystical powers to the unknown.

MALTHUS VISITED AND REVISITED

Two centuries ago came the first prophet of global doom—Malthus (1766–1834). In *An Essay on the Principle of Population* (1798), he showed mathematically that, regardless of continuing advances in agricultural and food science, population growth would eventually outstrip food production capacity, resulting in mass starvation, pestilence, and death. The essence of his theory was that populations expand by geometric progression, whereas agricultural production can increase only by arithmetical progression. But even as he announced this conclusion, new developments were occurring. One of these was the opening of the Western Hemisphere with its vast agricultural capacity; others were the work of creative scientists, e.g., Appert, the empiricist, and Pasteur, the theoretician, who established what we now consider the science of food preservation which vastly increased not only food reserves but their safety for human use.

As is usually the case, the empiricist came first. Appert (1750–1841) demonstrated that by placing a perishable food in a hermetically sealed cannister (can) and heating it sufficiently, it could be preserved indefinitely while maintaining much of its nutritional value. Half a century later, Pasteur (1822–1895) explained why Appert's method of canning was successful by demonstratig the heat-labile nature of the microorganisms responsible for the fermentation or spoilage of foods. Pathogenic microorganisms were demonstrated to be the causal agents of most food-borne diseases. Thus, the explorers of the 15th to 18th centuries and the scientists of the 18th to 19th centuries, although not invalidating Malthus's theory, nevertheless successfully postponed its inevitability. At the same time the scientists, particularly the microbiologists, provided yet another powerful weapon, sterilization, for man to assert his control over the environment. As a result, population growth entered its grand period shortly after the mid-19th century. However, in less than a century it seemed that Malthus was essentially right, and that there are limitations to planetary resources which, if not voluntarily conserved, largely through population control, would lead to catastrophe even sooner than originally anticipated. By the middle of the 20th century the prophets of doom and despair were again in the ascendant.

Typical of such despairing statements is the following (Kramer 1966): "It is conservatively estimated that by 1986 U.S. population will be above 250 million and income in terms of 1960 dollars will increase to 1500 billion dollars. At the same time, available land is being reduced by about one million acres annually so that farming will have to continue to improve in efficiency to meet the increasing demand for food from a decreased acreage. On the basis of past performance, it is estimated by some authorities that this can be done. However, it is also estimated that food surpluses of all kinds will vanish by 1970. In 1976 total world food reserves were down to a one-month supply. Considering the food situation in the world at large, food production, although increasing annually, is not quite keeping up with population growth so that within the next 10–20 years, if not sooner, chronic hunger and malnutrition of large parts of the world's population will deteriorate to mass starvation which in turn will result in violent upheavals in many parts of the world."

Within the last two decades this pessimistic attitude has again required revision, in some measure due to a basic fallacy in the Malthusian theory which contends that exponential population growth is limited only by food resources. It has been demonstrated time and time again by many civilizations that population growth is attenuated as the standard of living is improved. The urge to multiply and replenish the earth appears to diminish as societies and individuals gain in material wealth and well-being. Their biological urge to increase is tempered by other needs that are not basic, but are recreational rather than procreational. Thus, the more comfort and security there is from want, the smaller the family. This trend to limit population growth was greatly assisted by vastly improved birth control techniques, so that by 1977 even developing countries can approach zero population growth. Globally, the "grand" period of growth seems to have ended.

The other recent development contributing to the modification of predictions of doom is outstanding advancement in food science. Much attention has been given to the "miracle" grains which, together with relatively favorable climatic conditions, very substantially increase food resources—particularly those of rice, the staple food in the most populous regions of the earth.[1] Of even greater value in ultimately increasing food resources are current developments in total utilization of plant foods, particularly proteins, with soy protein leading the way.

ENVIRONMENTAL POLLUTION

Although the dramatic energy crunch of the winter of 1973–1974 modified it somewhat, concern over environmental pollution is still one of the subjects holding general public attention today, although its presence in the microenvironment (caves) of primitive man is acknowledged to have been far more serious than any pollution today. From a global standpoint, however, the problem is only now coming into its own. As usual, it took a big dose of exaggeration and dramatization to bring to this problem the attention it deserves. The prophetess of doom in this instance was Rachel Carson (1962) and from the standpoint of bringing this most important subject to general attention, she deserves a Nobel Prize. Over the last decade, not a month has passed when new learned journals on the subject of environmental protection did not make their appearance. Add to this the many learned and not-so-learned volumes and literally thousands of articles appearing in the press, the public is by now so completely alerted to the problem that it is a major political issue. At least one major federal agency, the Environmental Protection

---

[1]In 1970, the Nobel Peace Prize was awarded to an American, Dr. Norman Borlaug, for his work on wheat.

Agency, competes and conflicts in power and authority over the food industry with the old-line agencies.

Certainly release of atomic energy and pollution of the atmosphere with radioactive substances, increasing problems of water purification, and effects of polluting wastes on the welfare of man and of his cohabitators on earth should cause great concern. The following is a relatively moderate and positive statement on this subject (Kramer *et al.* 1971): "Rapid and efficient disposal can remove the hazard of disease and pollution of the environment. Maximum utilization, particularly of food wastes, would not only reduce the waste disposal problem, but would at the same time increase the food resources available to the rapidly expanding population. Only 20–30% of the nutrients produced for human consumption are utilized directly. If the remaining 70–80% of material could be converted into nutrients for man and animals or plants as food, feed, or fertilizer, respectively, total nutritional resources could be vastly increased, and at the same time the waste disposal problem could be minimized."

At this time, therefore, our concern appears to be not so much to meet the challenge of a constantly changing environment as to stabilize it for the improvement of human comfort and welfare and to maintain existing environmental balances, simply because we are most comfortable with what we know and expect. The larger framework has been aptly summarized by Haagen-Smit (1972): ". . . the whole system seemed to have a kind of comfortable stability. Looking at an astronaut's view of the Earth, we begin to realize that the Earth is actually not so large at all, and that the stability applies only to our time period, which is infinitely small compared to the time scale of geological and evolutionary happenings. A continuous flow of events leads from the origin of life some 2–3 billion years ago to the elaborate structures that we represent. For evolutionary processes, changes in the environment were essential; however, for the continuation of an evolved species, the constancy of the environment was of great importance. Even small changes in the environment will eventually lead to the disappearance of a species, or its replacement by others more suitable to new conditions."

This wish for stabilizing the environment or even returning to simpler ways of living is certainly not new. What is new is the global concept, and the "systems" approach to arrive at a constant, balanced environment of which "zero population growth" is only a part. Serious efforts have already been made (Meadows *et al.* 1972) to demonstrate mathematically that growth for its own sake is not necessarily desirable, and that the basis for achieving a stable environment totally controlled by a stable human population is scientifically feasible. Although a good case can be made for accomplishing this on a scientific basis, the odds against this actually occurring are overwhelming when subjective, emotional, psychological and metaphysical values are considered.

From the standpoint of food science and the consumer, the parameters that need to be stabilized can be readily listed:

(1) Provision of adequate, fully nutritious, nontoxic, wholesome, and palatable foods for the total population
(2) Control of the population, assuming the near total elimination of mortality from any environmental causes
(3) Recycling of waste matter, including contamination from extra- or intra-terrrestrial sources.

And over all this looms the specter of vanishing nonreplaceable energy resources before new technologies produce unlimited solar or other inexpensive sources.

If we should limit our perspectives largely to this century, the big problem is still that of providing sufficient subsistence; this falls into two general categories, one for the United States and other developed countries, and the other for the emerging developing countries. For the developed countries the major problem is to provide better quality convenient food products in the face of rising labor and energy costs. For the less developed countries, the problem is to provide for adequate nutrition by means of endemically acceptable foods, though they may be nutritionally fortified, to eliminate malnutrition. In both these areas, maintenance of quality and avoidance of waste by appropriate processing, storage, distribution, and recycling, must play an everincreasing and vital role.

PROBLEMS OF DEVELOPED COUNTRIES

Labor Reduction

Some future historian will contend that the great contribution of Egyptian civilization was not the pyramids but leavened bread. He will also argue that the great contribution of American civilization was not the internal combustion engine or some similar mechanical device but the land-grant college system. It is largely to the credit of these institutions that labor-saving devices were invented which freed the masses of humanity from the daily drudgery of production, preservation and preparation of their food supplies. For the greater part of our history as a nation, every succeeding generation of farmers underwrote the efforts of many of their sons who could not or would not stay on the farm to create a vast array of new food and nonfood products, while at the same time amply providing nutrition for all. As yields and mechanization improved, the size of farm units increased, thereby releasing the less successful farmers and the younger sons of all farmers to create new food and nonfood products.

The steady rise in labor productivity eventually resulted in increasing labor costs to the point that it is now no longer feasible to produce any food requiring substantial amounts of hand labor. Thus the major problem in the development of new and improved foods for the developed areas of the world is to do this with the use of less rather than more labor. It can therefore be safely predicted that farming as well as processing, storage, and distribution operations will all be done on continuously increasing levels of size and skill, and with an increasing degree of automation. The anticipated volume increase will be largely in prepared foods and institutional services. Although some of the new, prepared foods may be freeze-dried or dried by other methods, and irradiation may be a relatively common practice for certain materials that cannot be handled more easily and cheaply by other techniques, it is not expected that more than a small proportion of all food products, particularly ready-to-eat prepared foods, will be so treated. The bulk of these products will be held in cool or freezer storage before being further processed, heated, and eaten, or consumed directly. Increasing use of cold storage will be made not only to maintain stability, but also to prevent disease and insect infestation, and to preserve nutritive value.

While energy costs have increased two to fourfold over the last five years, a substantial part of the increase has already been absorbed by improved efficiency and energy savings. Major savings in energy utilization are yet to be made, not so much in the factory as in the home. Thus, for example, frozen storage in the home for one week is four times the cost of freezer warehouse storage for eight months (Rau 1978).

The use of microwave energy can be expected to expand considerably for both batch and conveyor installations. It is expected that microwave applications will be made first in commercial vending machine and restaurant operations, where labor saving is at a premium, and then in the industrial market for bulk processing, such as baking, canning, etc. Finally, microwave ovens will find a place in the home kitchen where in a matter of minutes or less they will prepare whole frozen or otherwise pre-prepared and properly packaged meals to be served to the family. The reason for these predictions is that the cost of microwave ovens has come down while labor costs have gone up.

Is the Natural Product the Best?

Most of us are still of the opinion that we cannot improve on nature, so that the best we can do is to approach as closely as possible the natural product which (since it is natural) must be best. In the past when innovations such as freezing preservation were not available and food materials spoiled rapidly, it was possible to mask undesirable, even repulsive, flavors and odors by the use of strong spices, and to consume such spoiled food if sufficiently spiced. Such practices are no longer necessary; however, flavors resulting from spoilage became accepted and desirable traits of the product. It is only now that, with the help of new physical-chemical instrumentation, we know what these flavoring substances are, so that we can produce them and combine them in such a way as to simulate all kinds of flavors—not by chance combination of natural substances but by a scientific blending of chemicals. It is therefore anticipated that old familiar foods will now be flavored synthetically and that new interesting "gourmet" types of foods will be developing rapidly to add an increasing variety of taste experiences to our sophisticated palates.

The potential of enzymes in food technology, although used to some extent for many years, has only now begun to be fully understood. The use of proteolytic enzymes to tenderize meat is not new. However, enzymatic hydrolysis of sweeteners (although the process was known for many years) has only recently begun to be used; it is proving to be a more efficient method of providing sugars than the usual acid hydrolysis method. Peptic enzymes have been used generally to clarify fruit juices, but liquefying entire fruits by the use of enzymes without the use of presses is a relatively new process. Current research will undoubtedly result in many more substantial innovations in the use of enzymes, such as the practical conversion of wood to sugar, and creation of other new flavoring, coloring, and nutritional substances at low cost.

Transportation

More perishable foods and other products are expected to move longer distances as transportation methods become cheaper. Already a military transport airplane is being produced which is capable of carrying six carloads of material across the country in a matter of hours at a cost somewhat less than rail transport.

Containerization is another development that will revolutionize transportation within our lifetime. Railcar or truck-trailer size containers are already being packed as single selfcontained units so that huge planes and ships can be loaded and unloaded in hours instead of the usual days or weeks. These units can be placed "piggyback" directly on rail or truck flatbeds upon unloading from water or air vehicles.

Packaging

Perhaps no area in the food industry is forging ahead as rapidly as packaging, which is essentially the material that determines the micro-environment surrounding a unit of food. The package may be as small as

a capsule which contains a grain or less of bitter-tasting nutrient used as an additive in a food product. The nutrient may be separately encapsulated so that its undesirable bitterness is not sensed by the taste buds. When the capsule reaches the stomach, the strong acids dissolve the package, and the enclosed nutrient is then released to perform its nutritional function. The largest packaging units are the carlot size containers described above.

The big and exciting development is undoubtedly the flexible films made by the polymerization of some common chemical substances to give such products as polyethylene and nylon. Rapid improvements in flexible film packaging are expected to continue, so that while retaining flexibility they will be practically impermeable to gases and will have great strength. There are now some chrystalline polymers that are stronger than steel. When reinforced at random with fibers (whisker composites) they become still stronger yet maintain a degree of flexibility. At this time the most successful flexible containers, which prevent moisture loss and development of oxidative rancidity, are usually laminates of several materials, with aluminum as one of the laminated materials. It is anticipated that shortly these materials will be fused together rather than laminated with adhesives. This in itself should be of real advantage, since frequently it is not the films themselves that fail but the binding material.

Such packaging materials, originally developed by the Army as "retortable pouches" have just been approved for use in the United States. These packaged foods have been available on the European and Japanese markets for years and have proven to be superior to conventionally canned foods—at times equal to frozen prepared foods. They do not require frozen storage (Sacharow 1979).

Can We Produce Enough?

As stated before, with the anticipated population growth and technological improvements in production in the developing countries, we can probably produce enough food for our own use for the balance of this century. Furthermore, we can do this with better varieties and better use of fertilizers, etc., but essentially with the conventional food materials we are now using. It is extremely doubtful, however, that the rest of the world can do the same. Thus, considering the world problem, what can we do to increase food production rapidly and dramatically?

PROBLEMS OF DEVELOPING COUNTRIES

Waste Reduction

Tremendous quantities of foods now being produced in underdeveloped countries are going to waste because of lack of adequate storage, preservation, and distribution facilities. Rapid improvement could be made very quickly by increasing cooling and cold-storage facilities in various parts of the world. This could also be aided by the use of chemicals and possibly irradiation or pasteurization of some of these products which would increase their storage life.

The concept of "total utilization" of nutrient-containing plants and animals is gaining momentum. It is the same idea as "using everything but the squeal." "Recycling," another currently popular term, to such an extent that processes are being developed which utilize the age-old process of "night soil," but extending it so that human and animal waste is not utilized as plant food, but is directly processed into human food. It is the ultimate form of waste reduction in that it not only reduces waste but eliminates it entirely, and shortcuts the usually long and elaborate natural cycle prevalent on earth under current environmental conditions (Green and Kramer 1979).

Water

Desalination of water is already a fact, with nine possible processes, some of which are already operating on a commercial scale. Water reclaimed by such methods is still fairly expensive, costing about 1¢ per 10 gallon. One of the newer more promising methods consists of freezing the water and separating the frozen water crystals from the salts in this manner. On the North American continent vast schemes for the redistribution of water have been submitted. One plan which would cost $100 billion would provide water from Canada and Alaska all the way to southwest and south central United States and northern Mexico, to irrigate 50 million acres.

Seafood

The seas cover more than 70% of the earth's surface. The upper 75 feet are exposed to enough light energy to produce 6,000 tons of plant material per year per square mile. It is estimated that 400 million tons of food per year could be harvested from the sea, while we are actually using some 50 million tons. As the total protein deficiency on a world-wide basis is estimated at 60 million tons a year, this potential harvest from the seas could take care of food requirements for the next 20 years or more. Already tremendous strides have been made in the utilization of fish flours and fish protein concentrates. Since fish account for only 3 to 6% of our food at this time, it can safely be predicted that the utilization of seafoods within the next two decades will increase substantially.

While plankton, the common microscopic animal and plant material in the oceans, is not showing hoped-for promise as human food, vast sources of krill (tiny shrimp-like animals) and squid have been discovered that may more than replace any current food deficiencies. These new sources of seafood may be used to some extent in their present form, but probably largely as whole fish, or fish protein, flour which may be used together with other ingredients as new processed foods that would be available cheaply to population masses. Tidal marshes in this and other countries provide another productive area for food production which has been almost totally neglected. Eventually such areas could support intensive aqua- and maricultural industries, producing cheaply certain species now highly prized, such as shrimp, oysters, trout, or salmon which would never need to go to sea.

Vegetable Proteins

One of the most remarkable recent advances in food technology is the development of spun vegetable proteins. These may be obtained not only from soybeans and peanuts, after the oil has been extracted, but from other vegetable products as well. The processes have already been developed, and spun protein fibers are available from which a variety of imitation conventional foods or new and different foods can be made according to any specified formula. This kind of material is just beginning to be utilized. As with fish proteins, these vegetable proteins alone have the potential of supplying the entire protein deficiency in the world at this time, although it may not be sufficient in the year 2000.

Microorganisms

Considering the cost of food production from a strictly nutritional standpoint, animal foods such as beef are by far the most expensive. Thus a pound of protein from beef costs well over $3.00. Similarly, a pound of protein from vegetable material such as spun soybeans costs 1/10 as much. It is estimated that a pound of protein from the sea will cost even less; and finally a pound of protein from microorganisms will cost still less. Of course the big question is, who wants to eat microorganisms? A partial answer is that we are already eating such products, for example yeast, and using specific extracts of other organisms, such as penicillin, for medicinal purposes. With recent giant strides made by geneticists in uncovering the basic chemistry of heredity, it is now considered possible to develop rather rapidly microorganisms that will produce certain nutrients, combinations of nutrients, flavors, etc. It is therefore possible to breed microorganisms that will have the flavor and nutritive value of beef, for example. Such microorganisms could double their weight in a period of hours instead of the months required for doubling the weight of a beef animal, and with a much greater efficiency of nutrient, water, and energy use.

Such ideas of producing microorganisms for food on a huge scale are further along than mere theoretical considerations. At the same time it is recognized that they are still a long way from practical implementation. A major limitation at this time is the high level of certain chemicals (purines) which will need to be removed before substantial quantities can be included in human diets. What is needed, if it is decided that such methods are absolutely essential to avoid catastrophic shortages of food, is to develop a crash research program in which not only cytologists and microbiologists but also biochemists, biophysicists, food technologists, and engineers would be involved. With such interdisciplinary teams working on these problems, it may be possible within the next 5 to 10 years to answer the question not only of whether it is possible to produce food by such radical methods, but also whether it would be eventually more economical to utilize these methods than to continue with the more conventional method of using resources provided practically free by nature. Before deciding that future foods will consist of microorganisms, however, it is well to remember such one-time predictions as fluid milks going off the market by 1965 in favor of dried milk, and hydroponics' soon replacing conventional farming, both of which were made by a number of experts 20 or 30 years ago.

AN AGE OF CONFUSION

As we near the end of the 20th century, we may be emerging from an age of confusion resulting from the growth in knowledge for controlling and directing our environment without parallel development of technologies for maintaining a viable environment. It is no longer sufficient to protect the individual citizen against "hidden defects" in his food supply, but worldwide measures must be taken to balance the availability of the world's wholesome food resources with population growth. A number of alternative ways are possible. The two obvious solutions are: (1) maintain, if not reduce, the population; and (2) improve, expedite, and perhaps shortcut current food waste recycling processes. We may hope that, having the knowledge to progress in both these directions, man collectively will meet the challenge, thereby enabling him not only to continue his stay on earth, but also to improve his material and aesthetic well-being.

Obviously only globally-integrated programs can accomplish this goal. Such collective programs require thorough advance planning and execution to achieve total utilization of raw materials. As recycling advances, it will become more and more difficult to determine just what the original raw material was, since a cyclic process can be entered at any point. Current public efforts to protect the consumer against adulteration of food would therefore be only a small part of the total effort.

In this unsettled period, much has been done by some individuals such as Rachel Carson and Ralph Nader and by organizations to assist and encourage public agencies to do more to protect the wholesomeness and usefulness of food supplies and to develop a stable environment. At the same time, other individuals and groups, acting at best from ignorance and at worst for personal gain, are accusing the "system" of willful negligence and exploitation of the public. One publisher, for example, distributed a chapter entitled "Unholy Alliance—Food Industry and Government." An entire book was entitled *The Great American Food Hoax.* It is recognized that some food manufacturers do attempt to cut corners, so that the food industry is and should be subjected to continuous public scrutiny. The industry must not only monitor the quality of its products, but, in addition, because of the activities of its critics, it must defend itself by informing the public of the truly phenomenal advances it has made and is making to the advantage of the consumer. Persuasion of consumers, however, is difficult because they are often prepared to believe that they are being bilked. Few politicians or others dependent on public support at election time have the courage to resist accusing the suppliers, a small minority, in order to gain favor with the consumer majority. The most unscrupulous accusations, however, have come from popular writers such as Davis (1970) and Jacobson (1972). They present interesting and informative but frequently biased and sensational books. Davis is oversold on natural unadulterated foods and her own cooking, and Jacobson is certain that his interpretation of highly controversial data is the only correct one. Deutsch (1961, 1971) gives a more balanced and yet highly readable version.

Similar accusations, both valid and scurrilously false, have been going on for centuries. Filby (1934) describes an anonymous pamphlet published in 1757 in London entitled *Poison Detected* dealing mainly with the adulteration of bread with alum, lime, and chalk, and adding that there are other ingredients "more shocking to the heart . . . it must stagger human belief; I shall only just mention it to make it abhorred . . . the charnel houses of the dead are raked to add filthiness to the food of the living . . . ." Although statements now made to discredit the food industry may not be quite as vituperative, they are relatively similar both in their exaggerations and implications. Allusions to "unnatural" or "inorganic" additives, for example, imply harmfullness without proof.

It is a relief to turn from these biased and distorted views to a publication called *An Essay on Bread*, written by H. Jackson, chemist, in

1758. In this modest volume, Jackson deals in an objective manner with the evidence for and against the bakers and millers and describes some tests for adulteration of bread and other foods. It marks the beginning of modern knowledge of the chemical detection of food adulteration. Jackson showed many of the charges brought against the bakers were fantastic. Jackson was especially bitter about earlier vague references to the use of sinister poisons ". . . this very expression betrays the subterfuge of malicious ignorance. But who can define the limits of envy? Surely the name of this material (poison) must be known. If it can be separated, why is it concealed?"

Then, as today, the food industry was much maligned. However, the controversy that arose as a result of real or imaginary abuses eventually resulted in the consumer protection we have today. Never before has the consumer been so thoroughly protected against food hazards. But we are on the threshold of another era where new and more subtle methods of handling or mishandling food materials will be used. The entire problem now is not only the assurance of the wholesomeness and adequacy of the food supply, but the very existence of life on earth. The attainable goal is emergence from the present age of confusion with new regulations and practices that will steadily improve the esthetic and nutritional quality of man's diet and protect him from harmful exposure to all environmental conditions on a global scale.

In the meantime, we are left in a state of confusion as a power struggle rages for the hearts and minds of consumers. As long as great masses of consumers—just as great masses of voters—remain apathetic and ignorant they can be won over by shrill demagogues. The scientist has an obligation to the consumer to pronounce the facts vigorously. Whether from the academic world or from industry, whether a molecular biologist, physiologist, nutritionist, or food engineer, he is most likely to perceive facts because of his training in the objective approach—although he may not be entirely without bias. Thus, despite the fact that the consumer is now receiving the best protection from health hazards he has ever received, the International Institute of Food Science and Technology in its international congress found it necessary to use as its motto "SOS/70" (Science of Survival, 1970).

The problem of survival is upon us. We have every chance for success, but as rational consumers or as representatives of the powerful consumer, we must continue the struggle of protection and enhancement of life by preventing the irresponsible critics from exploiting this platform at the expense of permanent injury to the consumer at large.

2

We Eat To Live

The forty plus organic and inorganic chemicals we must ingest to sustain life and health.

The belief that food consists of a single universal principle, called "alimentum," was held for centuries. Primitive man found his food in field and forest and pounded up for flapjacks or stew nearly everything that grows. Hunting with primitive weapons was difficult, and success was not great. Early man was probably forced to survive much as the hyena does today, living off the leavings of larger and more powerful predators. Obtaining food and shelter was a full-time job. Early explorers of the American continent observed that the California Indians often resorted to the mucilaginous film underneath ponderosa pine bark to maintain life. Malthus, describing the life of the American Indians, reported frequent cannibalism during periods of famine. Hunger and starvation were a constant threat and man's only concern with food was centered around obtaining enough of it.

Even when man began to domesticate animals and grow his own crops his efforts were inefficient. The "enlightened" civilizations of Greece and Rome were possible only by military pillaging and slavery. Many had to experience famine and squalor so that these civilizations could be maintained. Animal labor in the production of food was not efficiently used until 900 A.D. Prentice (1939) divides the history of the Western world into the distinct periods separated by the availability of the horse collar. The application of animal power to food production in the 10th century initiated the social movements which substituted serfdom for slavery. Times were better for a while, but the population increased until by the 13th century the food supply again had become critical. Famine and pestilence were so prevalent that they kept the European population at a constant level for the next 500 years.

The Industrial Revolution that began in the late 17th century brought about long-term results that were almost unbelievable. For the first time

*1980 Revised Recommended Dietary Allowances

The following tables have been approved by the National Academy of Sciences for distribution. They included tables on (a) Recommended energy intakes, together with mean heights and weights; (b) the Recommended Dietary Allowances for protein, fat-soluble vitamins, water-soluble vitamins, and minerals; and (c) estimates of adequate and safe intakes of selected vitamins, trace elements, and electrolytes.

TABLE 2.1 A.   MEAN HEIGHTS AND WEIGHTS AND RECOMMENDED ENERGY INTAKE

age and sex group	weight kg.	weight lb.	height cm.	height in.	energy needs MJ	energy needs kcal	energy range in kcal
infants							
0.0−0.5 yr.	6	13	60	24	kg. × 0.48	kg. × 115	95− 145
0.5−1.0 yr.	9	20	71	28	kg. × 0.44	kg. × 105	80− 135
children							
1−3 yr.	13	29	90	35	5.5	1,300	900−1,800
4−6 yr.	20	44	112	44	7.1	1,700	1,300−2,300
7−10 yr.	28	62	132	52	10.1	2,400	1,650−3,300
males							
11−14 yr.	45	99	157	62	11.3	2,700	2,000−3,700
15−18 yr.	66	145	176	69	11.8	2,800	2,100−3,900
19−22 yr.	70	154	177	70	12.2	2,900	2,500−3,300
23−50 yr.	70	154	178	70	11.3	2,700	2,300−3,100
51−75 yr.	70	154	178	70	10.1	2,400	2,000−2,800
76+yr.	70	154	178	70	8.6	2,050	1,650−2,450
females							
11−14 yr.	46	101	157	62	9.2	2,200	1,500−3,000
15−18 yr.	55	120	163	64	8.8	2,100	1,200−3,000
19−22 yr.	55	120	163	64	8.8	2,100	1,700−2,500
23−50 yr.	55	120	163	64	8.4	2,000	1,600−2,400
51−75 yr.	55	120	163	64	7.6	1,800	1,400−2,200
76+yr.	55	120	163	64	6.7	1,600	1,200−2,000
pregnancy						+ 300	
lactation						+ 500	

Source: Recommended Dietary Allowances, Revised 1980, Food and Nutrition Board, N.A.S.-N.R.C., Washington, D.C. The data in this table have been assembled from the observed median heights and weights of children, together with desirable weights for adults for mean heights of men (70 in.) and women (64 in.) between the ages of 18 and 34 as surveyed in the U.S. population (DHEW/NCHS data).

Energy allowances for the young adults are for men and women doing light work. The allowances for the two older age groups represent mean energy needs over these age spans, allowing for a 2% decrease in basal (resting) metabolic rate per decade and a reduction in activity of 200 kcal per day for men and women between 51 and 75 years; 500 kcal for men over 75 and 400 kcal for women over 75. The customary range of daily energy output is shown for adults in the range columm and is based on a variation in energy needs of ± 400 kcal at any one age emphasizing the wide range of energy intakes appropriate for any group of people.

Energy allowances for children through age 18 are based on median energy intakes of children of these ages followed in longitudinal growth studies. Ranges are the 10th and 90th percentiles of energy intake, to indicate range of energy consumption among children of these ages.

in human history starvation and its side effects were no longer the leading cause of death. People faced with sufficient quantities of food began to observe that not all food has the same value in maintaining life and health. It was no coincidence that the science of nutrition was born during the rise of industrial civilization. The French geologist and chemist Antoine-Laurent Lavoisier (1743−1749) became known as the "Father of Nutrition" when many of his works were published post-humously by his wife. Lavoisier was the first to show that combustion of organic matter is essentially the same inside or outside the body, with oxygen being consumed while carbon dioxide and water are produced. He correctly surmised that this respiration is the source of body heat.

Magendie, a French physiologist (1783−1855), first clearly defined the differences in the nutritive values of protein, fat, and carbohydrate. The work of Liebig (1803−1873) in the field of organic chemistry established the elementary composition of protein and the need for numerous mineral elements in the diet. In 1906 Hopkins, of Cambridge University, showed that a diet of pure protein, fat, carbohydrate, and minerals could not promote growth in young animals. In 1912 Funk found that substances which he called "vitamines" are essential to life. He coined the word from the Latin "vita" for life and "amine," designating chemical compounds containing nitrogen. We now know that not all of these sub-

TABLE 2.1B. RECOMMENDED DIETARY ALLOWANCES, REVISED 1980[a]

Category	Age (Years)	Weight (kg)	Weight (lb)	Height (cm)	Height (in.)	Protein (g)	Vitamin A (μg R.E.)[b]	Vitamin D (μg)[c]	Vitamin E (mg αT.E.)[d]	Vitamin C (mg)	Thiamin (mg)	Riboflavin (mg)
Infants	0.0−0.5	6	13	60	24	kg × 2.2	420	10	3	35	0.3	0.4
	0.5−1.0	9	20	71	28	kg × 2.0	400	10	4	35	0.5	0.6
Children	1−3	13	29	90	35	23	400	10	5	45	0.7	0.8
	4−6	20	44	112	44	30	500	10	6	45	0.9	1.0
	7−10	28	62	132	52	34	700	10	7	45	1.2	1.4
Males	11−14	45	99	157	62	45	1000	10	8	50	1.4	1.6
	15−18	66	145	176	69	56	1000	10	10	60	1.4	1.7
	19−22	70	154	177	70	56	1000	7.5	10	60	1.5	1.7
	23−50	70	154	178	70	56	1000	5	10	60	1.4	1.6
	51+	70	154	178	70	56	1000	5	10	60	1.2	1.4
Females	11−14	46	101	157	62	46	800	10	8	50	1.1	1.3
	15−18	55	120	163	64	46	800	10	8	60	1.1	1.3
	19−22	55	120	163	64	44	800	7.5	8	60	1.1	1.3
	23−50	55	120	163	64	44	800	5	8	60	1.0	1.2
	51+	55	120	163	64	44	800	5	8	60	1.0	1.2
Pregnant						+30	+200	+5	+2	+20	+0.4	+0.3
Lactating						+20	+400	+5	+3	+40	+0.5	+0.5

Source: Food and Nutrition Board, N.A.S.-N.R.C., Washington, D.C.
[a] The allowances are designed for the maintenance of good nutrition of practically all healthy people in the U.S. They are intended to provide for individual variations among most normal persons as they live in the United States under usual environmental stresses. Diets should be based on a variety of common foods in order to provide other nutrients for which human requirements have been less well defined.
[b] Retinol equivalents; 1 retinol equivalent = 1μg. retinol or 6μg. β-carotene.
[c] As cholecalciferol: 10 μg. cholecalciferol=400 I.U. vitamin D.
[d] αtocopherol equivalents: 1 mg. d-α-tocopherol=1αT.E.
[e] 1 N.E. (niacin equivalent)=1 mg. niacin or 60 mg. dietary tryptophan.
[f] The folacin allowances refer to dietary sources as determined by *Lactobacillus casei* assay after treatment with enzymes ("conjugases") to make polyglutamyl forms of the vitamin

stances contain nitrogen, and their name has been shortened to "vitamin."

Currently, evidence for the nutrient needs of the body are evaluated in the United States by the Food and Nutrition Board of the National Research Council—National Academy of Sciences. This institution uses its best judgment to make recommended daily dietary allowances (RDAs), an example of which is presented in Table 2.1B. It should be remembered that these recommendations are subjective and result from an evaluation of available research evidence. For this reason the RDAs are periodically revised. Today special attention is being given to the interrelation and correlation of the many factors involved in energy, protein, mineral, and vitamin metabolism. Multiple deficiencies are the most widespread nutritional problems.

NUTRITIONAL REQUIREMENTS

The body requires food energy for resting metabolism, synthesis of body tissues (growth, maintenance, pregnancy, and lactation), physical activity, excretory processes, and to maintain thermal balance (also, for physiological and psychological stress). Food energy values and allowances are expressed in terms of physiologically available or metabolizable kilocalories (kcal); a kilocalorie is the amount of heat necessary to raise 1kg of water from 15° to 16°C. How this energy might be expended is

Water-Soluble Vitamins				Minerals					
Niacin (mg N.E.)	Vitamin B_6 (mg)	Folacin (µg)	Vitamin B_{12} (µg)	Calcium (mg)	Phosphorus (mg)	Magnesium (mg)	Iron (mg)	Zinc (mg)	Iodine (µg)
6	0.3	30	0.5	360	240	50	10	3	40
8	0.6	45	1.5	540	360	70	15	5	50
9	0.9	100	2.0	800	800	150	15	10	70
11	1.3	200	2.5	800	800	200	10	10	90
16	1.6	300	3.0	800	800	250	10	10	120
18	1.8	400	3.0	1200	1200	350	18	15	150
18	2.0	400	3.0	1200	1200	400	18	15	150
19	2.2	400	3.0	800	800	350	10	15	150
18	2.2	400	3.0	800	800	350	10	15	150
16	2.2	400	3.0	800	800	350	10	15	150
15	1.8	400	3.0	1200	1200	300	18	15	150
14	2.0	400	3.0	1200	1200	300	18	15	150
14	2.0	400	3.0	800	800	300	18	15	150
13	2.0	400	3.0	800	800	300	18	15	150
13	2.0	400	3.0	800	800	300	10	15	150
+2	+0.6	+400	+1.0	+400	+400	+150	h	+5	+25
+5	+0.5	+100	+1.0	+400	+400	+150	h	+10	+50

available to the test organism.

[g] The RDA for vitamin B_{12} in infants is based on average concentration of the vitamin in human milk. The allowances after weaning are based on energy intake (as recommended by the American Academy of Pediatrics) and consideration of other factors, such as intestinal absorption.

[h] The increased requirement during pregnancy cannot be met by the iron content of habitual American diets or by the existing iron stores of many women; therefore, the use of 30 to 60 mg supplemental iron is recommended. Iron needs during lactation are not substantially different from those of non-pregnant women, but continued supplementation of the mother for 2 to 3 months after parturition is advisable in order to replenish stores depleted by pregnancy.

TABLE 2.1 C. ESTIMATE SAFE AND ADEQUATE DAILY DIETARY INTAKES OF ADDITIONAL SELECTED VITAMINS AND MINERALS

age group	vitamins			trace elements†						electrolytes		
	vitamin K	biotin	pantothenic acid	copper	manganese	fluoride	chromium	selenium	molybdenum	sodium	potassium	chloride
	(μg)	(μg)	(μg)	(mg)	(mg)	(mg)	(mg)	(mg)	(mg)	(mg)	(mg)	(mg)
infants												
0.0–0.5 yr.	12	35	2	0.5–0.7	0.5–0.7	0.1–0.5	0.01–0.04	0.01–0.04	0.03–0.06	115– 350	350– 925	275– 700
0.5–1.0 yr.	10– 20	50	3	0.7–1.0	0.7–1.0	0.2–1.0	0.02–0.06	0.02–0.06	0.04–0.08	250– 750	425–1,275	400–1,200
children and adolescents												
1–3 yr.	15– 30	65	3	1.0–1.5	1.0–1.5	0.5–1.5	0.02–0.08	0.02–0.08	0.05–0.1	325– 975	550–1,650	500–1,500
4–6 yr.	20– 40	85	3–4	1.5–2.0	1.5–2.0	1.0–2.5	0.03–0.12	0.03–0.12	0.06–0.15	450–1,350	775–2,325	700–2,100
7–10 yr.	30– 60	120	4–5	2.0–2.5	2.0–3.0	1.5–2.5	0.05–0.2	0.05–0.2	0.1 –0.3	600–1,800	1,000–3,000	925–2,775
11+ yr.	50–100	100–200	4–7	2.0–3.0	2.5–5.0	1.5–2.5	0.05–0.2	0.05–0.2	0.15–0.5	900–2,700	1,525–4,575	1,400–4,200
adults	70–140	100–200	4–7	2.0–3.0	2.5–5.0	1.5–4.0	0.05–0.2	0.05–0.2	0.15–0.5	1,100–3,300	1,875–5,625	1,700–5,100

Source: Recommended Dietary Allowances, Revised 1980. Food and Nutrition Board, N.A.S.-N.R.C. Because there is less information on which to base allowances, these figures are not given in the main table of the RDAs and are provided here in the form of ranges of recommended intakes.
†Since the toxic levels for many trace elements may be only several times usual intakes, the upper levels for the trace elements given in this table should not be habitually exceeded.

illustrated in Table 2.2. The "reference" man is 22 years old and weighs 58 kg (127.6 lb). Weight gained after this age is likely to be fat and is detrimental to health. Caloric allowances are adjusted upward or downward by roughly 20 kcal/kg deviation from standard weight; downward by roughly 5% per decade over standard age; upward for physical activity above that considered light (120 to 240 kcal/hr); upward by roughly 5% at temperature well below 20° or above 30°C; and upward rather substantially during periods of pregnancy, lactation, or growth.

TABLE 2.2. EXAMPLES OF ENERGY EXPENDITURES BY REFERENCE MAN AND WOMAN

Activity	Time hr	Man Rate kcal/min	Total	Woman Rate kcal/min	Total
Sleeping[1] and reclining	8	1.1	530	1.0	480
Sitting[2]	7	1.5	630	1.1	460
Standing[3]	5	2.5	750	1.5	450
Walking[4]	2	3.0	360	2.5	300
Other[5]	2	4.5	540	3.0	360
			2810		2050

Source: N.A.S. N.R.C. (1968).
[1] Essentially resting metabolic rate.
[2] Includes normal activity carried on while sitting, e.g., reading, driving automobile, eating, playing cards, and desk or bench work.
[3] Includes normal indoor activities while standing and walking intermittently in limited area, e.g., personal toilet and moving from one room to another.
[4] Includes purposeful walking, largely outdoors, e.g., home to commuting station to work site, and other comparable activities.
[5] Includes intermittent activities in occasional sports, exercises, limited stair-climbing, or occupational activities involving light physical work. This category may include weekend swimming, golf, tennis, or picnics using 5 to 20 kcal/min for a limited time.

Table 2.3 shows sources of important nutrients. Food energy is supplied by the different nutrients in approximately the ratio of carbohydrate:fat:protein as 1:2.5:1.

Carbohydrates

Starch, sucrose and lactose are the most important sources of carbohydrates in the American diet. Starch from grains and vegetables comprises approximately 50% of the carbohydrate consumption. In many parts of the world, the contribution of starch to the total carbohydrate intake may reach 75 to 80% due to the consumptin of large quantities of grain products and tubers such as manioc or potato. The intake of lactose, however, which is about 10% of the carbohydrate in the American diet, may be insignificant in some countries. The change in

TABLE 2.3. SOURCES OF IMPORTANT NUTRIENTS

Protein Sources	Amount	
Cooked meat and poultry	20−30% protein	
Fish	20−30%	
Cheese (American)	25%	
Cottage cheese	13−17%	
Nuts	16%	
Eggs	13%	
Dry cereals	7−14%	
Bread	8%	
Beans	7−8%	
Milk (whole)	3.5%	
Milk (skim)	4.0%	
Fat Sources		
Oils	100% fat	
Butter and margarine	80%	
Mayonnaise	80%	
Walnuts	65%	
Chocolate	50%	
Peanut butter	50%	
Cheese	25−35%	
Meats	20−40%	
Ice cream	10−16%	
Carbohydrate Sources		
Sugar	100% carbohydrate	
Chocolate creams	85%	
Cereals	70−80%	
Cookies	70%	
Jams	70%	
Cake	60%	
Bread	50%	
Rice, spaghetti	20−35%	
Calcium Sources	**Typical Source**	**Amount**
Cheese	1 slice—processed	150−200 mg
Dark green, leafy vegetables	spinach—1 ounce	10−25 mg
Milk	whole—1 cup	300 mg
Sardines	per fish	50−80 mg
Iron Sources		
Beans and peas	peas—1 cup	2−3 mg
Beef	3 ounce—cooked	2−3 mg
Chicken	1 slice—cooked	0.7 mg
Dark green, leafy vegetables	spinach—1 cup cooked	4 mg
Eggs	one—cooked	1−1.3 mg
Liver	cooked—3 ounce	8−12 mg
Pork	cooked—3 ounce	2.5−3 mg
Prune juice	4 ounce	5 mg
Enriched bread, cereals and pasta	bread—1 slice	0.7 mg
Whole grain cereals	wheat—1 cup cooked	1.2 mg
Niacin Sources		
Salmon, tuna fish	tuna—one 7 ounce can	18−20 mg
Liver	3 ounce—cooked	14 mg
Meats	beef—3 ounce cooked	4−5 mg
Peanut butter	1 tablespoon	2.4 mg
Poultry	2 medium slices	5−6 mg
Enriched bread, pasta, and cereals	one slice bread	0.7 mg
Peas	one cup—cooked	14 mg
Whole grain cereals	wheat—one cup cooked	1.5 mg
Peanuts	10 nuts—shelled	3−4 mg

TABLE 2.3. *(Continued)*

Vitamin A Sources		
Cantaloupe	½ melon	8000 IU
Carrots	1 carrot—medium	8000 IU
Dark green, leafy vegetables	broccoli—1 medium stalk	4500 IU
Liver	3 ounce—cooked	35000 IU
Spinach	1 cup—raw	4500 IU
Squash	Acorn—½ baked	2200 IU
Sweet potato	baked—one medium	9200 IU
Fortified butter, margarine, milk	butter—1 tablespoon	140 IU
Thiamin Sources		
Liver	slice—3 ounce—cooked	0.22 mg
Nuts	10—shelled	0.06 mg
Peas	1 cup—cooked	0.22 mg
Pork	Lean—3 ounce—cooked	0.5–0.92 mg
Pork sausage	one link—fried	0.20 mg
Veal	3 ounce—cooked	0.06–0.08 mg
Beans	snap—1 cup cooked	0.04 mg
Whole grain cereals	1 cup—wheat—cooked	0.15 mg
Enriched bread	one slice	0.07 mg
Fortified cereals	1 cup—corn type	0.11 mg
Enriched pasta	1 cup—spaghetti	0.20 mg
Vitamin C Sources		
Cabbage	1 cup cooked	40–45 mg
Citrus fruits	1 medium orange	50–66 mg
Potato	1 medium—baked	30 mg
Tomato	1 medium	20–25 mg
Green peppers	3 strips—thin	20–30 mg
Brussel Sprouts	½ cup cooked	60 mg
Orange juice	6 ounce—glass	90 mg
Fruit drinks	6 ounce—grape drink	30 mg
Riboflavin Sources		
Cheese	1 slice—processed	0.06–0.09 mg
Fish	1 cod filet	0.07 mg
Liver	3 ounce slice cooked	3.5–4.0 mg
Meats	3 ounce beef patty	0.15–0.2 mg
Milk	1 cup	0.41 mg
Poultry	2 slices chicken	0.04–0.05 mg
Whole grain cereals	1 cup cooked	0.05 mg
Enriched cereals, pasta, and bread	1 slice bread	0.07 mg
Soy flour	1 cup—defatted	0.34 mg
Spinach	1 cup leaf—raw	0.11 mg
Beans	1 cup—drained	0.07 mg
Vitamin D Sources		
Eggs	1 cooked	25–30 IU
Fish oil	cod—1 teaspoon	400–800 IU
Fortified milk, margarine, butter	margarine—1 tablespoon	20–80 IU
Vitamin E Sources		
Whole grain cereals and breads		
Oil seeds		
Vegetable oils		

Source: Labuza (1977).

sucrose intake has been one of the most notable in the American diet in the twentieth century (Friend 1967). In this period total carbohydrate intake has decreased by almost 25%, but consumption of sucrose-rich sugars and syrups has increased by 25%. This has been associated by some investigators with both the high incidence of dental caries and the current pandemic of coronary heart disease. Adaptation to diets very low in carbohydrate is possible; but, in individuals accustomed to normal diets, at least 100 g of carbohydrate per day appear to be needed to avoid ketosis, excessive protein breakdown, and other undesirable metabolic responses.

Fat

Fat is the most concentrated source of food energy, providing approximately 9 kcal/g. In 20 years the proportion of total fat from animal sources (saturated) decreased from 75 to 66%, while that from vegetable sources (polyunsaturated) increased from 25 to 34% (Friend 1967). Appreciable dietary substitution of fats rich in polyunsaturated fatty acids for more saturated fats has been found to induce a significant decrease in plasma cholesterol level in a majority of hypercholesterolemic subjects. Hypercholesterolemia has been identified as one of the risk factors in the development of coronary heart disease. Arachidonic acid and its precursor, linoleic acid, are polyunsaturated and essential for growth and skin health in experimental animals and human infants. The requirement is quite low and can be met by providing 3% of the calories as linoleic acid (human milk contains 6 to 9% of its calories as linoleic acid). Human adults contain sufficient body stores of linoleic acid to protect against deficiency.

Protein

Protein is needed in the diet to provide nitrogen and amino acids for the synthesis of body proteins and other nitrogen-containing substances. Protein in excess of these needs serves only as a source of energy. Although body proteins contain some 20 amino acids, most can be synthesized within the body. Only 8 are not synthesized in the body; these are called "essential" amino acids, which must be provided by the diet: isoleucine, leucine, lysine, methionine, phenylalanine, threonine, tryptophan, and valine. The infant also needs histidine. The requirements for nitrogen are expressed as:

$$R = U + F + S + G$$

where R = nitrogen requirements; U = loss of endogenous nitrogen in the urine; F = loss of endogenous nitrogen in the feces; S = skin, sweat, and integumental nitrogen loss; and G = requirement for growth, pregnancy, or lactation. The estimated nitrogen requirement $\times$ 6.25 (most proteins contain approximately 16% nitrogen) gives the amount of ideal protein (one rich in all essential amino acids) required, assuming complete utilization. Since utilization actually averages 70%, this works out to roughly 0.9 g of protein per kg of body weight for the reference man and woman. Protein is more likely to be a critical nutrient when its quality is not ideal (it is deficient in one or more of the essential amino acids), or when requirements are increased by growth, pregnancy, or lactation. Protein deficiency is called kwashiorkor and is found most commonly in children.

Table 2.4 shows relative quality values of protein from various sources.

TABLE 2.4. PROTEIN QUALITY VALUES

| Food | Protein Source[1] | Biological Value | |
		Growing Rat	Adult Human
Egg	100	87	94, 97
Milk (cow's)	78	90	62, 79, 100
Casein	80	69	70
Beef	83	76	67, 80, 84, 75
Fish	80	75	94
Oats	79	66	89
Rice	72	—	67
Corn meal	42	54	24
White flour	47	52	42, 40, 45, 67, 70
Wheat germ	61	75	89
Soy flour	73	75	65, 71, 81
Potato	56	71	80, 71, 81
Peas	58	48	56, 90
Cassava	22	—	—

Source: Labuza and Sloan (1977).
[1] Based on a comparison to eggs.

Macrominerals

The minerals known to be essential and present in fairly large quantities are calcium, phosphorus, potassium, sodium, chlorine, magnesium, and sulfur. Over 90% of the calcium and 85% of the phosphorus are bound together in the bones and teeth. Of the two, calcium is more often a dietary problem since phosphorus is widely distributed in foodstuffs. The richest dietary sources of calcium are milk and dairy products, edible bones, and green, leafy vegetables. The small amount of calcium in the soft tissues is critical, and its level in the blood is maintained by the parathyroid gland. When serum calcium levels get too low the usual consequence is tetany. Calcium nutrition is further complicated by the fact that vitamin D is involved in its absorption and utilization.

Over 60% of total body magnesium is found in bone; the amount in the soft tissues helps prevent personality changes, muscle tremor, lack of coordination, and gastrointestinal disturbances. Magnesium deficiency, however, seems to be rare since it is widely distributed in foodstuffs.

Sodium, potassium and chloride ion are all involved in control of body fluid osmolarity. Sodium is the chief cation of the extracellular fluid, and it is kept out of the cell by means of an active mechanism or pump. Potassium is the chief cation of the intracellular fluid; nerve transmission and muscle contraction involve a temporary exchange of extracellular sodium and intracellular potassium. The chloride ion is the major anion of the extracellular fluid and occurs for the most part in combination with sodium, as salt. A dietary deficiency of any of these three is quite rare and, in the case of sodium, there is much more concern over taking too much. Some observers feel that the high sodium intake of most Americans contributes to high incidence of hypertension and coronary heart disease. A deficiency of potassium may result from kidney failure or the excessive urination found in diabetes mellitus or alcoholism, while specific chloride deficiency may result from excessive vomiting (stomach juices are rich in hydrochloric acid).

Most sulfur in the body is found in organic form as amino acids (methionine, cystine, and cysteine), vitamins (thiamin and biotin), or related compounds (glutathione, taurine, and coenzyme A). Inorganic sulfates or sulfides are a small fraction of the total but they are essential in the formation of sulfated sugar derivatives for the formation of mucopolysaccharides (involves vitamin A) and in detoxification reactions (involve magnesium).

Microminerals

The prinipal minerals present in micro quantities are iron, copper, manganese, zinc, iodine, molybdenum, fluorine, selenium, chromium, silicon, and nickel. Iron is primarily important in the compound hemoglobin found in red blood cells and involved in oxygen transport. In iron deficiency, the lowered capacity to provide oxygen is largely responsible for the fatigue and apathy characteristics of anemia.

Copper is involved in iron utilization, and there have been some reports of anemia in children that responded to copper and not to iron. Although symptoms of manganese deficiency have been described in experimental rats, it is unlikely that manganese deficiency of dietary origin occurs in the human. Manganese toxicity, however, has been reported in miners of manganic oxide who acquire toxic levels of the mineral by inhalation of ore dust. The requirement for molybdenum in man is quite small, and a deficiency is therefore unlikely. Zinc is present in most tissues of the animal body, and a deficiency in man has produced male dwarfs with hypogonadism. A conditioned zinc deficiency has been reported in post-alcoholic cirrhosis.

Simple goiter is endemic in many areas of the world and is usually associated with a deficiency of iodine. However, iodized salt has made the problem a minor one in the United States. There is, unfortunately, a declining use of iodized salt and some cause for alarm as convenience foods, almost all seasoned with noniodized salt, begin to account for more and more of the food dollar (Anon. 1969). Fluoride ion seems to be essential for optimum hardness of the bones and teeth; 1 ppm in drinking water can reduce the incidence of dental caries and osteoporosis.

Selenium can replace tocopherol in the prevention of some vitamin E deficiency symptoms but not others. At high levels of intake it is toxic. Chromium seems to play a role in the activation of insulin, and chromium supplements have relieved the symptoms of diabetes mellitus in some people. Silicon and nickel have both been shown to have essential physiological functions in animals and are probably also necessary for optimum health in man.

Fat-soluble Vitamins

The first vitamin to be identified was a fat-soluble substance characterized by McCollum and appropriately named vitamin A. It seems to play a role in vision as well as maintaining the health of the moist tissue linings of the body and is also involved in bone maturation. Vitamin A can be formed in the body from a plant pigment called carotene. Therefore, among the best sources of vitamin A are the dark green and deep yellow vegetables.

In addition to vitamin A, three other fat-soluble vitamins have been identified. Vitamin D can be formed in the skin following exposure to direct sunlight and is often called the "sunshine vitamin." Since most milk sold is enriched with 400 international units (I.U., a designation used when a vitamin exists in more than one form) per 0.95 liters (1 qt), the risk of vitamin D deficiency seems small. However, when a deficiency does occur it is called "rickets" in children and "osteomalacia" in adults; it is characterized by bone malformations due to improper calcium metabolism. Vitamin E acts as a general antioxidant in the body and protects against free radical damage. A deficiency can interfere with hemoglobin synthesis and result in anemia. The chief sources of free radicals in the diet are the polyunsaturated fatty acids, and increasing consumption of these substances caused the National Academy of Sciences to set the first vitamin E RDA in 1968. Deficiencies are thought to be rare. Vitamin K is involved in blood coagulation, and the body's needs can be met by the synthetic action of intestinal microorganisms. A dietary source of vitamin K may be needed following antibiotic treatment which has destroyed the normal intestinal microflora.

Water-soluble Vitamins

At the time fat-soluble vitamin A was discovered, a water-soluble fraction, called B, was also isolated. It soon became evident that B was an entire complex of vitamins. The first portion of the complex to be characterized was called, appropriately, vitamin B_1 or thiamin. It seems to be involved primarily in carbohydrate metabolism, and its deficiency disease is called "beriberi." It is characterized by nervous discoordination and edema and has been found when refined cereals are eaten without their hulls. Since the flour enrichment program began in 1940, thiamin has been added back to most refined flours after its removal and the thiamin status in the U.S. seems to be excellent.

Vitamin B_2 or riboflavin is found largely in milk and dairy products and, as a result, can be lacking in diets where little milk is drunk. Peoples of Asian or African descent often are deficient in the lactase enzyme needed to properly digest milk sugar (Cuatrecasas *et al.* 1965). As a result, they consume very little milk and other dairy products. Therefore, particularly in the non-white population, riboflavin is a problem nutrient. Deficiency is characterized by cheilosis (cracking of the skin around the corners of the mouth).

Niacin deficiency results in pellagra, which is characterized by dementia, diarrhea, dermatitis, and, eventually, death. The body can meet its needs for niacin by synthesis from the essential amino acid tryptophan. Therefore, diets must be low in both niacin and tryptophan to produce pellagra. This occurred in the southeastern U.S. around the turn of the century when many poor farmers depended almost entirely on corn for food. A small amount of meat or milk in the diet prevents pellagra.

Pyridoxine, or vitamin B_6, is involved largely in protein and amino acid metabolism, and a deficiency is characterized by personality changes and hyperirritability. As vitamin B_6 is needed for the conversion of tryptophan to niacin, a deficiency can also produce pellagra. Very occasionally infants develop convulsions and other disturbances of the central nervous system which respond to treatment with doses of vitamin B_6 far in excess of normal intakes. Such infants may be said to have an idiosyncrasy which increases their need for the vitamin.

Pantothenic acid is of the highest biological importance, but in man a deficiency has been accomplished only with the aid of an antagonist. Multiple deficiencies probably exist whenever dietary pantothenic acid is lacking, so that pantothenic acid deficiency may be an unrecognized feature of nutritional debilitation. It is widely distributed in nature and its presence is assured in diets that are otherwise adequate with respect to B-complex vitamins.

Biotin is synthesized in the intestine, and a dietary deficiency is unknown. However, raw egg white contains avidin, a biotin antagonist, and diets high in raw egg white have produced the loss of appetite, muscle pains, scaling dermatitis, and other symptoms characteristic of biotin deficiency. Cooking inactivates the avidin.

Folic acid and vitamin B_{12} (cobalamine) are both involved in nucleoproteins, and a deficiency of either causes megaloblastic anemia. Megaloblastic anemia arising from folic acid deficiency occurs under four circumstances: (1) failure to absorb the vitamin, which is a common complication of chronic disease of the small intestine; (2) in pregnancy, where it is not common, but if it does occur is often severe (indeed, unless adequately treated it may be fatal, and for this reason during the last trimester of pregnancy a routine daily supplement is frequently prescribed); (3) occasionally in infants, especially in the premature and those with infections; and (4) sometimes in old age, when due to apathy, ignorance, or poor appetite intakes may be low. In contrast, megaloblastic anemia due to deficiency of vitamin B_{12} arises almost exclusively from failure of absorption which is genetically determined and quite rare. Dietary requirements are miniscule, but since the vitamin is found only in foods of animal origin, a deficiency can arise in strict vegetarians.

Ascorbic acid (vitamin C) is concerned with the integrity of connective tissue constituents, and dietary deficiency causes scurvy. The amount of ascorbic acid needed to prevent scurvy is quite small, but there have long been two views on the need for ascorbic acid. One view maintains that an amount of the vitamin sufficient to prevent signs of deficiency, and with a safety margin to allow for individual variation and for stresses of everyday life, can be recommended as a dietary intake. This has been the stance of the British, who recommend a dietary intake of 30 mg per day (U.K. Dep. Health Soc. Security 1969). The other view is based on the concept of tissue saturation. The argument is that animal species which are able to synthesize their ascorbic acid (i.e., all except primates, the guinea pig, and the fruit bat) maintain a high level of tissue saturation. For man, this requires a dietary intake of 60 mg per day, which is recommended by the U.S. National Academy of Sciences.

The richest sources of ascorbic acid are fresh fruits and vegetables, particularly citrus fruits. The fruit of the rose (rose hips) is so rich in this vitamin that is is frequently used as a "natural" source of this nutrient. Vitamin C is undoubtedly the most frequently recommended, not just to prevent scurvy, but to be taken in massive doses to prevent anything from the common cold to cancer (Pauling, 1970). While it may be of some help to "true believers," there is as much evidence to show harm as well as good from massive (1–20 g/day) daily intake of this inexpensive, ubiquitous substance.

Water

Water is by far the most critical of all nutrients. Animals will succumb to water deprivation sooner than to starvation. The water available to the animal body includes that present in liquids and solid food consumed and also water formed in the cells as a result of the oxidation of food-stuffs. This endogenous water is designated metabolic water or water of oxidation. The water of oxidation formed from the metabolism of 100 g of protein is roughly 40 g, from 100 g of carbohydrate is 60 g, and from 100 g of fat is 107 g. One can see, therefore, that metabolism of body fat in weight reduction will result quite naturally in a temporary weight gain. The data shown in Table 2.5 illustrate a typical water balance.

TABLE 2.5. DAILY WATER BALANCE

Water Intake (g)		Water Output (g)	
Drinking water	400	Skin	500
Water in other beverages	580	Expired air	350
Preformed water in solid foods	720	Urine	1100
Metabolic water	320	Feces	150
Total	2020		2100

NUTRITION IN THE UNITED STATES

Food habits in the U.S. have undergone profound change in recent years, with an adverse effect on the nutritional status of the population. At a time of unprecedented affluence, when most Americans can afford better food than ever before, there has been a decline in the nutritional quality of the diet. This was documented dramatically by the U.S. Dep.

of Agriculture in 1968 when it released the results of the 1965−66 household consumption survey. Compared to the results of a similar survey made in 1955, the percentage of U.S. households having "good" diets (per person daily intake equal to or above the full RDA for seven nutrients) declined from 60 to 50%. The percentage having "poor" diets (less than 2/3 of the RDA for one or more nutrients) increased from 15 to 20%.

In 1972 the U.S. Dep. of Health, Education and Welfare completed its final report of the 1968−1970 ten-state nutrition survey. This was the largest nutrition survey ever conducted and it was made in response to a 1967 directive from Congress. The population surveyed, however, was located in low-income areas where the risk of malnutrition was judged to be highest; therefore, the population studied was not representative of the entire U.S. population. In this survey, evidence of malnutrition was found most commonly among blacks, less commonly among Spanish-Americans, and least among white persons. Generally, there was increasing evidence of malnutrition as income level decreased. The relative importance of the nutritional problems encountered is presented in Fig. 2.1.

There was evidence that many persons made poor food choices that led to inadequate diets and to poor use of the money available for food. In particular, many households seldom used foods rich in vitamin A. Also, there was heavy emphasis on meat in many diets, rather than on less expensive but excellent protein sources, such as fish and poultry or legumes and nuts. Many diets were also deficient in iron content, but this was less a reflection of poor choice of foods than of the generally low level of iron in the American diet. The dietary data also showed that there were a substantial number of children and adolescents with caloric intakes below the dietary standards.

Poor dental health associated with low levels of dental care was encountered in many segments of the population. In adolescents it was found that between-meal snacks of high-carbohydrate foods such as candies, soft drinks, and pastries were associated with the development of dental caries. This finding illustrates the potential detrimental effect of poor nutrition on dental health.

School lunch programs were found to be a very important part of nourishment for many children (Fig. 2.2). In the low income states, school lunches contributed a substantial proportion of the total nutrient intake of many school children, especially black children.

Evidence of retarded growth and development was generally more prevalent in the low income states, and within each group of states, growth was less adequate in lower income groups. But despite lower income levels, black children generally were taller than white children and were more advanced in skeletal and dental development, indicating

| Age | 0-5 Both | | | 6-9 Both | | | 10-16 Female | | | 10-16 Male | | | 17-59 Female | | | 17-59 Male | | | Over 60 Female | | | Over 60 Male | | | Pregnant & Lactating Women |
Sex / Ethnic	B	W	S	B	W	S	B	W	S	B	W	S	B	W	S	B	W	S	B	W	S	B	W	S	
Iron																									
High income	3	2	3	3	2	3	3	2	3	3	2	3	3	2	3	3	2	3	3	2	3	3	2	3	4
Low income	4	3	3	4	3	3	4	3	3	4	3	3	4	3	3	4	3	3	4	3	3	4	3	3	4
Protein																									
High income	1	1	1	1	1	1	1	1	1	1	1	1	1	1	1	1	1	1	1	1	1	1	1	1	3
Low income	1	1	1	2	1	1	2	1	2	2	2	2	2	2	2	**1**	2	2	2	2	2	2	2	2	3
Vitamin A																									
High income	2	2	1	2	2	1	2	2	1	2	2	1	1	1	1	1	1	1	1	1	1	1	1	1	
Low income	3	2	4	2	2	4	2	2	4	2	2	4	1	1	4	1	1	4	2	1	4	2	1	4	
Vitamin C																									
High income	1	1	1	1	1	1	1	1	1	1	1	1	1	1	1	1	1	1	1	1	1	1	2	1	
Low income	1	1	1	1	1	1	1	1	1	1	1	1	1	1	1	3	3	1	2	2	1	3	3	3	

Riboflavin								
High income	2 1 1	2 1 1	2 1 1	2 1 1	2 1 1	2 1 1	2 1 1	2 1 1
Low income	3 2 3	3 2 3	3 2 3	3 2 3	3 1 2	3 1 2	3 1 2	3 1 2
Thiamine								
High income	1 1 1	1 1 1	2 1 1	2 1 1	1 1 1	1 1 1	1 1 1	1 1 1
Low income	1 1 1	1 1 1	2 2 1	2 2 1	1 2 1	1 2 1	1 2 1	1 1 1
Growth & Dev.								
High income	3 3 3	3 3 3	2 2 2	2 2 2	0 0 0	0 0 0	0 0 0	0 0 0
Low income	3 3 3	3 3 3	2 2 2	2 2 2	0 0 0	0 0 0	0 0 0	0 0 0
Obesity								
High income	0 0 0	0 0 0	2 2 0	1 2 0	4 3 0	1 1 0	3 3 0	1 1 0
Low income	0 0 0	0 0 0	2 2 0	2 3 0	4 3 0	1 2 0	3 3 0	1 1 0

From U.S. Dept. of Health, Education, and Welfare (1972)

FIG. 2.1. RELATIVE IMPORTANCE OF NUTRITIONAL PROBLEMS IN LOW-INCOME AND HIGH-INCOME STATES AMONG BLACK (B), WHITE (W), AND SPANISH-AMERICAN (S) GROUPS
High = 4. Medium = 3. Minimal = 1. Unavailable = 0.

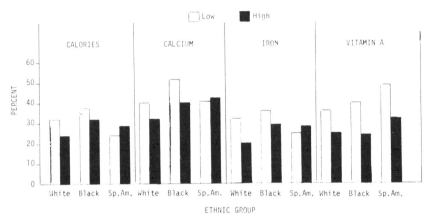

From U.S. Dept. of Health, Education, and Welfare (1972)

FIG. 2.2. PERCENT OF SELECTED NUTRIENTS CONTRIBUTED BY SCHOOL LUNCHES FOR CHILDREN 10 TO 16 YEARS OF AGE IN LOW- AND HIGH-INCOME RATIO STATES

that racially based differences as well as nutritional factors affect growth.

The 1972 HEW survey also showed obesity to be a public health concern. Obesity and other problems related to nutrition in the United States are discussed in the following section.

MALNUTRITION IN THE UNITED STATES

Despite the fact that formulation of an adequate diet from purified nutrients would require the addition of well over 40 different ingredients, practical malnutrition problems affecting large numbers of U.S. residents are relatively few.

Anemia

The most widespread problem amenable to dietary treatment seems to be anemia—the lack of adequate hemoglobin levels in the blood, leading to weakness and lack of stamina. The low level of iron in the American diet is the basis for most of the trouble, and in 1971 an FDA proposal was made to triple the iron level in all enriched flour (Anon. 1972B). Despite the overwhelming endorsement of this proposal by most nutritionists, it has drawn some spirited opposition from physicians and there has been considerable delay in its implementation. Those who oppose the FDA proposal are concerned primarily about those individuals who are susceptible to iron overload for any one of several reasons. These conditions include hemochromatosis, liver cirrhosis, genetic conditions which involve high rates of iron absorption, and anemia due to hereditary iron-storage diseases such as sickle-cell disease and thalassemia (Anon. 1971). The richest dietary sources of iron are liver, eggs, lean meats, and enriched cereals. There is considerable controversy over the physiological availability of much dietary iron, however, and until the controversy is resolved many people would benefit from the regular ingestion of a well-utilized iron supplement, such as ferric ammonium citrate, ferrous sulfate, ferrous gluconate, ferrous fumarate, ferrous tartrate, or ferrous ammonium sulfate.

Vitamin E deficiency anemia has been reported in diets very high in polyunsaturated fatty acids. Although vegetable oils are the richest sources of vitamin E, their polyunsaturated fatty acid content is sufficiently high to negate this dietary source. Therefore, whole grain products, fruits, and vegetables are the recommended dietary sources (Horwitt 1960).

Megaloblastic anemia has been reported from both folic acid and vitamin B_{12} deficiency, but vitamin B_{12} supplementation alone is rarely an effective treatment, except in strict vegetarians. Folic acid supplementation more often will correct the condition. This is particularly important during pregnancy, when many women exhibit a moderate folic acid deficiency. Current knowledge is limited concerning the availability for absorption of the various forms of folic acid in foods. Therefore, routine administration of folic acid supplements during pregnancy make good sense.

Copper is involved in iron utilization in the body. Some anemias will respond to copper supplementation of the diet; however, such cases are extremely rare, and a diet of even mediocre quality will provide the body's need for copper.

Obesity

Conservative estimates have pointed out that at least 20 million Americans need to lose weight to improve their life expectancy. In addition to its deleterious effect on health, obesity decreases physical attractiveness, causes mental depression, and dramatically restricts one's ability to get about. The arguments against being obese are overwhelming and are recognized by almost every obese person, yet 90% of the obese never achieve a long-range solution of their problem. The reason is that too few consider it more than a problem of counting calories and the use of "will power."

The stereotype of obesity as a result of gluttony is an oversimplification. The obese person does eat more than his or her body requires, but in actual fact he or she may eat less than those of normal weight. The major factor limiting the caloric needs of the obese is a very low level of physical activity. Unfortunately, a very sedentary level of existence seems to stimulate appetite over that found in the moderately active. As a result, the physically inactive person needs the fewest calories, but desires more. Will power in such a situation is tested rather severely. Additionally, some obese people have a poorly functioning appetite control mechanism and must consciously decide when they have had enough to eat—a decision that is often hard to make.

Obesity due to gluttony, when it does occur, is often the result of more basic psychological problems. Another factor can be dilution of the diet with foods such as sugar, fats, and alcohol, which provide little more to the body than calories. Overeating due to psychological depression can be temporarily corrected by appetite-depressing drugs of the benzedrine and dexedrine family (speed). Habitual control of obesity with stimulants is not only ineffective but also dangerous.

The long-term treatment of obesity requires a nutritionally adequate low calorie diet, an increase of moderate proportions in daily physical activity, and psychological reinforcement from persons with similar problems who are dealing with them successfully. Since sugar (sucrose) contributes about 450 kcal a day to the average American diet, and since it is free from all other nutrients, it is clearly the first choice for curtailment or elimination in a diet that is to be rich in nutrients but reduced in calories, As a matter of fact, of the three energy-contributing nutrients (protein, fat, carbohydrates), carbohydrates are the most easily restricted with the least effect on the palatability and nutritional quality of the diet. Yudkin has made a detailed nutritional comparison of normal and low carbohydrate diets. Table 2.6 indicates that in actual practice a low carbohydrate diet did not result in greatly increased intakes of protein or fat, even though no effort was made to restrict the intake of these nutrients. All nutrients considered, the low carbohydrate diet either provided more or not significantly less than the normal diet.

TABLE 2.6. COMPARISON OF NORMAL AND LOW-CARBOHYDRATE DIETS

	Normal	Low Carbohydrate	Difference
Calories	2340[1]	1390	−950
	2330[2]	1560	−770
Protein (g)	77	80	+3
	84	83	−1
Fat (g)	122	99	−23
	124	105	−19
Carbohydrate (g)	206	65	−141
	216	67	−149

Source: Yudkin and Carey (1960); Stock and Yudkin (1970).
[1] The upper figure is the mean of 6 subjects (Yudkin and Carey 1960).
[2] The lower figure is the mean of 11 subjects (Stock and Yudkin 1970).

A low carbohydrate diet has great social acceptability, since one can drastically reduce the intake of sugar, candy, cakes, cookies, soft drinks, potatoes, and pasta without being conspicuous. Dieting is easier on such a diet, since one can eat to satiety provided only that carbohydrate intake is held to 100 g. At least two cautionary points should be made. Severe carbohydrate restriction can cause ketosis and acidosis and is to be avoided. Carbohydrate restriction to the level indicated may cause electrolyte and water losses which appear as a rapid initial reduction in weight. This is psychologically exhilarating, but it should be remembered that later resumption of a more normal carbohydrate intake will cause this weight to be regained rapidly.

It is important to note that on a low carbohydrate diet one may eat as much as one likes of all these foods: meat, fish, eggs, cheese, butter, margarine, oils, cream, leafy vegetables. In addition, a pint of milk a day is recommended. Only the carbohydrate-rich foods need to be restricted, and then only in moderation. In practice, a low carbohydrate diet has been found to be the most effective and, nutritionally, the most desirable for the management of obese patients. In addition to the diet, a change in daily habits which moderately increases physical activity, such as an hour's walk each day (why not walk to work or, at least, part way?) will not only burn up more calories but also reduce appetite. Finally, joining a group such as TOPS (Take Off Pounds Sensibly) or Weight Watchers will help give the psychological reinforcement that has helped many. Under such a three-pronged approach—(1) low carbohydrate diet, (2) moderate physical activity, (3) psychological reinforcement—the excess pounds are likely to melt away.

Dental Caries

The characterization of dental caries as a nutritional disease is a viewpoint with an increasing number of adherents. The incidence of dental caries is much higher when the dietary carbohydrate is sugar (sucrose) rather than starch. Sucrose is much more cariogenic than other carbohydrates, since it can readily be converted to dextran in the mouth and the cariogenic bacteria, *Streptococcus acidophilus*, thrive on dextran (Yudkin 1972).

The avoidance of "empty calories" from sugar, then, helps control not only body weight but tooth decay as well. Additionally, dental hygiene and regular dental examinations are important, and the addition of 1 ppm fluoride to the drinking water of children will cut their incidence of dental caries in half. The high incedence of decayed, missing, and filled teeth was one of the more striking findings of the 1968–1970 ten-state nutrition survey (U.S. Dep. Health Educ. Welfare 1972).

Atherosclerosis and Heart Disease

Those who regard heart disease as primarily nutritional are split into at least two camps, divided by a great middle group of investigators who see diet as a very minor factor in this condition. The dietary theory of greatest longevity originated with Dr. Ancel Keys (1957) following his work with high fat diets during World War II. He observed that populations with the highest intakes of saturated fat from animal sources had the highest incidence of death from heart disease and the highest levels of circulating cholesterol in their blood. Based on this circumstantial evidence, he postulated that restricting saturated fat intake could help prevent heart disease. His theory was promptly adopted by the American Heart Association, which had been making dietary recommendations for years while searching for evidence that there really is a cause-and-effect relationship between saturated fat intake and heart disease. A second theory of more recent origin came from Dr. John Yudkin (1960) who reevaluated the dietary data from some of the same populations considered by Dr. Keys. In actual fact, Yudkin found a closer correlation between sucrose intake and heart disease than between saturated fat intake and heart disease. This caused the American Heart Association to include sugar restriction in its dietary recommendations.

Most investigators have recognized that atherosclerotic heart disease is a multifaceted problem: genetic background, lack of exercise, stress, high blood pressure, sex, age, obesity, cigarette smoking, and maturity-onset diabetes all play a role, in addition to diet. The importance of diet is controversial and is probably influenced by most of the other factors involved in the development of the disease. Fredrickson and coworkers (Anon. 1970) identified five different types of hyperlipoproteinemia, and recommended distinctly different diets to deal with each one. The most common type (Type IV) is associated with obesity and responds well to the restriction of dietary carbohydrate. The second most common type (Type II) is improved by a diet low in saturated fat and cholesterol. Mismatching a Type IV diet to a Type II person, or vice versa, not only doesn't help, but aggravates the disease. Therefore, in a joint statement of the Food and Nutrition Board—National Acadamy of Sciences, National Research Council and the American Medical Association's Council on Foods and Nutrition, it has been recommended that: "Measurement of the plasma lipid profile . . . become a routine part of all health maintenance physical examinations . . . . Persons falling into 'risk categories' on the basis of their plasma lipid levels be made aware of this and receive appropriate dietary advice" (Anon. 1972C).

Diabetes Mellitus

There are two main types of diabetes mellitus. The juvenile-onset type usually develops during the first 40 years of life in persons of normal or less than normal weight. Insulin therapy is usually mandatory in these cases. The adult or maturity-onset type usually appears in middle-aged or elderly patients who are often obese and in whom the disease can usually be controlled by dietary means alone. People in this category rarely develop ketosis and the disease is less severe than in the juvenile-onset type.

Hereditary factors are important in the development of the disease, particularly in diabetics who develop the disease at an early age. Obesity is definitely associated with the development of the maturity-onset type. Additionally, age (80% of cases appear after the age of 50); sex (males predominate in juvenile-onset cases, females account for most maturity-onset cases); infections (may unmask latent diabetes); and stress (either physical injury or emotional disturbance may change a latent form of the disease into clinical diabetes) all seem to play a role. The diet factor in the development of diabetes mellitus is, again, controversial. Cohen (1971) has shown that high sucrose diets produce pathological changes which result in diabetes in the rat and he has associated an increased incidence of diabetes in Yemenite Jews in Israel with their increasing sucrose intake. Historically, discussions of diabetes mellitus have not listed high sucrose intake as one of its root causes.

Whether or not high sucrose intakes cause diabetes, the best diets for management have involved the restriction of both carbohydrate and calorie intake. The best way to do this without sacrificing nutritional quality of the diet is to restrict sucrose intake to a minimum.

Osteoporosis

This is a bone disease, largely of the elderly, which is common in all countries. The bones become decalcified, brittle, and are easily fractured. Many hospital beds are occupied by elderly people with fractures who require much attention from both nursing and medical personnel. Albright and Reifenstein (1948) suggested that senile osteoporosis was an endocrine disorder arising from failure of the sex hormones to maintain the protein matrix of the skeleton. The fact that osteoporosis is both more common and more severe in elderly women than in older men could be explained by the earlier and more abrupt cessation of gonadal function at the menopause in women. Lack of dietary calcium was not considered to be a major factor.

It has been demonstrated repeatedly that patients with senile osteoporosis given large doses of calcium retain a significant portion of it. Healthy controls, when given such high calcium diets, retain little or none of the extra mineral. In reviewing the problem Garn et al. (1967) were not as enthusiastic about calcium supplements in the elderly, but they saw some value to high calcium intakes before age 25 so that maximum skeletal mass is achieved (Fig. 2.3). The sex difference in incidence and

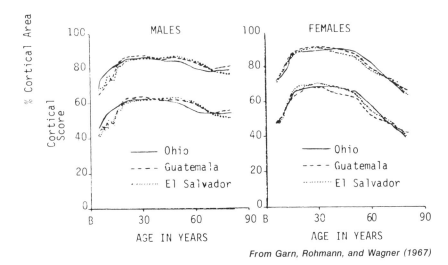

From Garn, Rohmann, and Wagner (1967)

FIG. 2.3. SEX DIFFERENCES AND POPULATION SIMILARITIES IN

severity of osteoporosis may be due to the fact that within a given family the father and sons are much more likely to have adequate calcium intakes than the mother and daughters. The senile osteoperosis of many elderly women may well be the end result of a lifetime of calcium-poor diets devoid of milk and dairy products.

Almost all investigators agree that physical inactivity is a predisposing factor to osteoporosis. An active life and a well-balanced diet containing a pint of milk daily make good sense from a number of health aspects and they appear to be the best ways to prevent this bone fragility in old age. Additionally, fluoridation of the water supply in some communities seems to have reduced the incidence of osteoporosis in its elderly population. The role of fluoride in strengthening bones and teeth is not well understood.

Vitamin A Deficiency

Although biochemical and dietary data indicate that many Americans, particularly Spanish-Americans, have dangerously low vitamin A status, clinical evidence of vitamin A deficiency diseases is minimal. It should be remembered, however, that on a world basis 20,000 children a year go blind from vitamin A deficiency. Parrish (1971) has pointed out that the availability of vitamin A in the American dietary has been declining due to a number of socioeconomic factors. The potential for clinical vitamin A deficiency symptoms to increase in the American population is certainly present, and care should be taken to consume the dark green and deep yellow vegetables which are the best sources of this vitamin.

Vitamin C Deficiency

Although USDA surveys indicate that many Americans do not consume their recommended daily allowance of vitamin C, biochemical or clinical evidence of scurvy is minimal. This is because the American concept that vitamin C tissue saturation promotes the best health has caused recommendation of vitamin C intake well above that known to prevent scurvy. It is not known if those individuals whose tissues are not saturated with vitamin C are actually less healthy than those whose tissues are saturated with the substance.

Pauling (1970) has written a controversial book in which he recommends supersaturation of the tissues with huge daily doses of vitamin C (2 to 9 g) to prevent the common cold. Although his book was initially attacked by a number of nutritionists, most were speaking or writing well out of their area of expertise. Most nutritionists have never encouraged the level of vitamin C intake recommended by Pauling, and it is certainly not available in a well-balanced diet. Such levels are called "pharmacological" doses and could, more appropriately, be discussed in a textbook on pharmacology, as would massive doses of other nutrients, particularly vitamins E and K, which are alleged to cure all ills.

Iodine Deficiency

Although most convenience foods are seasoned with noniodized salt and convenience foods are accounting for more and more of the food dollar, dietary, clinical, or biochemical evidence of iodine deficiency as evidenced by simple goiter was minimal in all segments of the U.S. population surveyed in 1968—1970.

Riboflavin Deficiency

Much of the nonwhite population of the U.S. suffers from an inability to digest lactose (milk sugar). Ingestion of milk causes them to develop diarrhea and other digestive upsets. Since milk and dairy products contribute about 50% of the riboflavin in the American diet, many Blacks and Spanish-Americans show evidence of riboflavin deficiency. Such a deficiency may result in cheilosis (lesions of the lips and fissures at the angles of the mouth). People who suffer from a lactose deficiency (inability to digest lactose) can still get good amounts of riboflavin from cheese, organ meats, eggs, green leafy vegetables, and enriched cereals.

Although vitamin deficiencies have been mentioned by various investigators as dietary problems in the U.S., the evidence for these as major threats to health is not decisive. These and other nutrient deficiencies are common elsewhere, particularly in the developing countries.

NUTRIENTS, DRUGS AND ALLERGIES

Before we leave this chapter devoted to what we need to eat, we should repeat that we do not intend to cover the vast field of drugs designed to alleviate illness caused by anything other than nutrient deficiencies. We have, however, referred briefly to some situations where massive doses of some nutrients are presumed to help cure anything from the common cold to cancer. While we cannot dismiss all such claims, we should certainly view them with caution and adopt the attitude that there is a limit to the consumption of all nutrients. In fact, toxicity from overdoses of vitamins A and D are well-documented (N.A.S.-N.R.C. 1980).

Practically all of the mineral micronutrients are toxic if consumed above recommended levels. To prevent such problems, nutrient labeling guidelines may include a directive that any food which provides more than 150% RDA of a nutrient in one serving should be classified as a drug, not as a food.

Perhaps the major reason that we cannot dismiss nutrient overdosing out-of-hand is the very substantial variability among individuals in their tolerance as well as requirement for specific nutrients. This variation in response frequently becomes obvious as an allergy. This is discussed in Chapter 4 on consumer protection.

3

We Live To Eat

*Sensory Quality versus Nutritive Value
as the basis for food acceptability*

We have seen in Chapter 2 that food is the sole source of nutrients that are essential for normal growth and development of man. Although almost any raw food source may contain trace levels of practically all the essential macro- and micronutrients, there are few if any plant or animal foods that provide a sufficient level of all the nutrients. Thus the more varied the food intake, the greater the likelihood that the individual will obtain a satisfactory diet from the nutritional standpoint.

Many raw food materials contain naturally occurring toxins, or they can be infected with pathogenic or toxin-forming materials. It would seem, therefore, that man, as well as other animals, would have an innate sense that would guide him to select and ingest foods that provide the necessary nutrients, and prevent him from eating foods that are not nourishing or that might be poisonous. Such a selective capability is present in most animals and also in man at a very early age. Experiments conducted with infants and toddlers have demonstrated that when presented with a broad spectrum of foods, children up to age 2 will eventually settle on a choice of foods that provide them with all their nutrient requirements. Beyond the age of 2, perhaps 3, the natural instinctive selection is no longer evident, since the child has already become "sophisticated" to the point where he will select those foods to which he had become accustomed or that he had observed were being selected by his elders.

As various civilizations evolved and the individual became less dependent on the flora and fauna within his immediate grasp, and as he was able to preserve food materials, there arose a class—usually a small minority until very recent times—who had access to more food than was required. These people were able to consume much more than they needed, which led to obesity and other problems related to overeating. They could also eat exotic, expensive foods rather than the more broadly nutritive foods of the masses, thereby inducing some nutrient deficiencies, excesses, and intoxications.

A more frequent basis for the selection of preference of a diet that is not completely nutritious was, and still is, the tendency to select and eat just one type of food as, for example, rice in Southeast Asia or corn in South America. Thus, even where food resources are sufficiently abundant to provide all the necessary nutrients, many people choose for themselves foods that they do not necessarily like instinctively, but that they acquire a liking for, on the basis of the customs and traditions of their society.

Paddy-rice farmers who subsist largely on rice and therefore suffer from less than optimal, if not obviously deficient, protein levels will frequently sell whatever fish they find in their paddies rather than use this protein-rich food for themselves and their families. Similarly, in protein-deficient areas of South America infants will not be fed beans— just corn, because custom decrees that infants cannot digest beans. The result of this unfortunate practice is that too many infants die of avoidable protein deficiency.

Although man instinctively prefers foods that are sweet, sweet and sour, odorless, or fragrant, and will not accept food that is more than just slightly bitter or salty or putrid, he has learned to consume and select huge quantities of "bitters," or putrid fermented fish sauce, simply because such foods were originally a necessity. Later he became accustomed to these strange flavors and found that they did not appear to harm him. With familiarity he grew to like these "unnatural" foods. It may therefore be generalized that people like and eat what they are accustomed to and not necessarily to satisfy their nutritional requirements. They will accept and consume foods that they do not like instinctively, because they are educated to select these foods, because it is necessary to eat them, or because educational-propagandizing efforts by leaders of their society have influenced their choice.

SENSORY QUALITY—PHYSIOLOGICAL OR PSYCHOLOGICAL?

A substantial portion of the world population, including the vast majority of the developed world, selects its food not on the basis of its contribution to a balanced diet that provides all the essential nutrients in adequate quantities, but to satisfy the senses of sight, feel, taste, smell, and hearing. Most important is the sense of sight. We first decide whether to purchase and consume some material on the basis of its appearance. Then the tactile (feel) sense comes into play when the item is tested with the fingers (or fork). Odor is next in those situations when the item may be sniffed. It is only after the food undergoes all these tests and is placed in the mouth that the senses of taste and sound receive consideration.

Let us observe a housewife who is about to decide whether she is going to buy some peaches that are on display. She first inspects them visually to see that they are not too green, that they are of the right size, and that they are not wormy, moldy, or misshapen. After the product passes such an "eyeball test" she will visually select individual peaches, and probably squeeze each one gently and retain for purchase only those units that not only "look" good but also "feel" good; that is, upon squeezing, the flesh yields just a bit, not very much, so that the peach is neither too mushy nor too unyielding—not too soft but not too hard. She may in some instances sniff the peaches to make sure that they don't smell moldy or overripe, or perhaps to see if they have a pleasant peach aroma. She is not likely to continue with the rest of the sensory evaluation before purchase. It is only after the transaction has been made that she and other members of the household will place one of the purchased peaches in the mouth and during the process of chewing the peaches will be tested further for their taste. At the same time as the chewing and swallowing is performed, the senses of feel (mouthfeel) and odor again come into play. The sound sense is generally ignored, but may be important for some special commodities, such as "crisp" breakfast foods, or the "fizz" of a carbonated beverage.

Contrast to this sensory evaluation of a natural product, an evaluation that may be performed by the housewife on a manufactured product such as wine. Is the housewife in a position to do any kind of sensory testing, beyond looking at the shape and size of the bottle and the label? Even if she or any other purchaser of a bottle of wine had the opportunity of examining the wine further, would the purchaser be honest with himself and purchase that wine that he or she prefers on the basis of sensory evaluation? Very likely not. In such instances the purchaser would be guided by the opinion of an expert "master" taster, who decides for the consumer what he or she should buy, and the price to be paid, based primarily on the availability of the particular "brand." The amazing thing is that with very few exceptions, consumers purchase such manufactured items and pay premium prices on the basis of someone else's sensory evaluation, even when it conflicts violently with their own sensory preferences.

A distillery produces a blended whiskey which consists 70% of distilled grain alcohol to which is added a blend of whiskies distilled from different grains and aged in barrels. The aged ingredient is carefully blended so that each new batch is not distinguishable from the previous batch.

The distilled alcohol provides no flavor—just the sting. The same distillery produces a bonded whiskey, produced entirely from grain-distilled liquor which is aged in barrels for at least 5 years. The bonded whiskey is substantially more expensive, and supposedly better than the blend. When consumers were asked which whiskey they preferred at least 80% responded that they preferred the more expensive bonded whiskey. However, time and again when consumer panels are asked to 'blind' taste the two whiskies and indicate which they prefer, about 80% invariably indicate they prefer the taste of the less expensive blend. Obviously, such products are purchased by the consumer not on the basis of his sensory preference, but on the basis of someone else's, in this case the distillery's master taster's decision.

There still remains the question as to why on a blindfold test the consumer prefers the cheaper product. The answer is that it has the appearance, taste, odor, and mouthfeel to which he is most accustomed. An endless number of examples can be cited to prove this point. Let us consider a few, to demonstrate that such preferences are not limited to manufactured foods.

A study was made in one of the agricultural universities to determine consumer preference for vine-ripened versus mature-green harvested fresh tomatoes. The study was made to determine whether there was any advantage from the consumer acceptability standpoint of permitting tomatoes to ripen on the vine and ship them to the market in that condition, although price would be higher since there would be more damaged and unusable tomatoes at the retail end if harvested at that point. If, however, the consumer really preferred the vine-ripened tomatoes, then they could be sold at a higher price to balance the loss that would be sustained from the greater proportion of damaged fruit that would have to be discarded. The results obtained from this study were most unusual in that they seemed to be sex-linked. Practically all the female members of the consumer panel preferred the greenwrap, storage-ripened tomatoes, whereas practically all the males on the consumer panel preferred the vine-ripened tomatoes. Upon further investigation, it was found that practically all the males on the consumer panel were faculty members and research assistants in the college of agriculture who were familiar with the flavor and appearance of vine-ripened tomatoes; on the other hand, practically all the female members of this consumer panel were administrative-clerical personnel who had at no time had access to vine-ripened tomatoes, particularly while the test was performed in the spring. When they did use tomatoes, they purchased what was usually available, namely, the greenwrap tomato. Thus the sex-linked results were strictly coincidental, and the real explanation for these conclusions was that each member of this panel indicated a preference for a product to which he or she was accustomed. Even such the obviously superior flavor in fully vine-ripened tomatoes is not favored unless the individual had previous experience with the flavor differences.

In another study with canned peas, a large number of consumers were requested to taste-test one sample of fancy grade A canned peas, and to compare it to a second sample of standard grade C canned peas. They were first asked to indicate which sample they preferred, then to state whether they would pay a higher price for the product they preferred. The consumer panel included all levels of income and was limited to an equal number of male and female adults. The results showed that there was a practically even division among the consumers who indicated a preference for the grade A peas, and those who preferred the grade C peas. This was not surprising when it was noted that the comments made by those who preferred the grade A peas were to the effect that they liked them because of their smaller size and sweeter and juicier taste, while those who indicated a preference for the grade C peas indicated that the grade A peas were too watery and had no pea flavor, in other words, de gustibus non disputandum.

What was surprising about these results was the highly significant negative correlation between income level and willingness to pay a higher price for the preferred peas. Taken literally, these results would be interpreted as indicating that the lower the income level, the more likely is the consumer to pay a higher price for a quality that he desires. A more realistic interpretation, however, is that the lower the income level the more likely such a response in a questionnaire, yet the response would not necessarily be an indication of the action that would be taken in reality.

This latter interpretation of consumer attitudes and behavior is substantiated by many experiences of consumer-oriented organizations. For example, the vast majority of people who subscribe to such organizations as the Consumers Union and who get information on the relative value of items of different brands, thereby obtaining a good basis for savings, are highly educated higher-income people who do not need such information and services as much as do the lower-income groups who constitute a very small proportion of membership in consumer organizations.

In 1964 the Florida Citrus Commission was faced with exceptionally heavy yields which resulted in a very large quantity of orange juice available for distribution for the following year. One method considered for increasing consumption of citrus juice was to increase the concentration of frozen orange juice from a minimum of 40% fruit solids to a minimum of 44%. This would automatically give the consumer 10% more orange juice. Before following this procedure the commission conducted a survey to see whether the consumer would appreciate the fact that he is getting about 10% more juice in the same size container. To test this, a large number of consumers were given samples of concentrated orange juice reconstituted to levels that would be equivalent to 36, 38, 40, 42, 44, 46 and 48% solids. The results showed an increasing preference for increasing juice concentrations up to 40% solids, then a very abrupt leveling off to 44%, at which point there was a further increase in preference with increasing solids. This plateau between 40 and 44% could be explained only by the fact that citrus juice concentrate was marketed at the range of 40-44% solids, to assure the presence of the minimum requirement of 40% solids. The consumers were so completely familiar with this level that they were not able to distinguish a difference in this range. However, when they were presented with samples having a concentration of solids lower than 40% or higher than 44%, they very promptly noticed the difference, again demonstrating that they liked what they had become accustomed to.

NATURAL IS BEST?

Another overriding principle controlling consumer behavior, not necessarily limited to housewives, but applicable even to highly trained institutional buyers, dieticians, nutritionists, and physicians, is that the product which is most like the fresh natural product is the best. (See Davis [1970] for numerous examples of this bias). This is frequently maintained despite the fact that if the consumers had made their selections strictly on the basis of sensory quality, they would not necessarily so choose. In 1967 three universities conducted consumer surveys in three different states on preferences for the retail purchase by housewives of fresh, cleaned eviscerated chickens as against frozen. Results of all three studies were practically identical showing that about 85% of all housewives indicated that they would not buy frozen poultry if they could buy the fresh refrigerated product. When asked what they do with the fresh product when they bring it home, about 85% of the consumer respondents stated that they placed the fresh poultry into the freezer compartment in their home refrigerator or freezer chest as soon as possible. Obviously, this response was not due to the fact that poultry purchase frozen from the slaughtering plant was inferior to poultry purchased from the same slaughtering plant and handled in the same manner, but only refrigerated at the plant and later frozen in the home freezer—undoubtedly the poorest method of freezing that could be used. The real reason behind the consumer's response in this manner was the suspicion that the frozen item may have been frozen to mask something unwholesome. In any event, this demonstrates the reluctance on the part of the consumer to purchase a product which is certainly not inferior and probably superior, but is different in some manner from the product to which he or she is accustomed.

WHAT IS FRESH?

There is much discussion now about informing the consumer regarding the *freshness* of packaged foods, on the assumption that "fresh is best." Yet the term itself is not readily understood. To some, *fresh* means just harvested or slaughtered. To others it means raw food that has not been preserved, except perhaps by refrigeration. Still others consider fresh as an adjective, as for example *fresh-baked*, although the flour may be several years old, or *fresh-frozen*, although the produce may be in the freezer for a year or longer. It should be recognized that such fresh-baked, or fresh-frozens are frequently of much better-quality than raw-fresh. Nevertheless "Open-dating" is now a popular issue which is now largely limited to short-life products, especially milk, but may soon expand to all packaged foods, although the value to the consumer is dubious. The most likely form of open-dating which will soon be required is the "pack-date" which will state the date the unit was processed and/or packaged. A more useful form is the "pull-date" which prints the date before which the unit may be sold, or a "use by" date. Perhaps the most useful form of open-dating is: "Best if used by. . . ".

ACCEPTABILITY OF NEW PRODUCTS

With such a strong tendency toward preference for customary familiar foods, how do new foods become established in the market place? After all, we do know that the rate of introduction of new food items on the food market shelves is going on at such a rapid rate that it is estimated that 80% of the products now appearing on food shelves were not in existence 20 years ago. This explosion of new products is to some extent misleading, since many products are called new that are merely slight modifications or combinations of old products and were developed simply for greater convenience. An example is the very large number of frozen vegetables with sauce or with another vegetable or other products added. Canned whole-kernel corn had been on the market for several generations; then a "new product" called vacuum-packed whole kernel corn made its appearance. The only difference between these two products is that in the vacuum pack there is less liquor than in standard whole-kernel canned corn. A few years later a new product named Mexicorn made its appearance. This is still essentially whole-kernel corn, but with a small quantity of peppers added. Frozen whole-kernel corn was still another "new" product, although the only difference between it and the canned product is that one is canned and the other frozen. Some years later still another new corn product made its appearance: it was the same whole-kernel corn in a boil-in-bag to which butter sauce had been added.

Thus, many new successful products are simply slight modifications of a generally acceptable product with some additional material or process used, providing a more completely prepared item. Frequently such a modification is based on commonly existing processes, except that one additional step in preparation of the item for consumption is performed in the processing plant instead of by the cook.

From the consumer's standpoint therefore, the pressure toward such new products has come about primarily to reduce labor costs or time in the final preparation. Most new products are successful only if they meet the sensory tests of the consumer, and it is estimated that only one of ten new products developed and introduced to the market survives.

Even slight variations in methods of processing or packaging are not successful unless dictated by economic necessity, and then they are not completely successful until a new generation of buyers with a new life style makes its appearance.

Packaging of produce, now a common phenomenon, took a generation and more to become generally acceptable. Many years passed before the housewife would accept a prepackaged bag of potatoes or a cylinder of tomatoes. It may well be asked why the consumer took so long to accept a 5- or 10-lb bag of potatoes in preference to doing his own bagging when in the packaged product he was guaranteed a cleaner, less mishandled end-product. The reason was, of course, the same—suspicion by the consumer (not always unjustified, particularly in the past) that somewhere in the bag are buried some rotten potatoes that he cannot see. I distinctly recall watching a consumer at a produce counter slit open half a dozen or so tubes of tomatoes to select those four tomatoes that he (this time it was not a she) wanted to purchase. In addition to the suspicion that some unwholesome material is being sold to the consumer sight unseen, there is the common desire for freedom of choice, in this case having the option of selecting superior (?) units from a lot on display.

Tremendous efforts are made by manufacturers of food products to develop new products that are similar in every detail to standard products, but are more nutritious, tastier, and/or less expensive then the old reliables. The reason for this huge and expensive research effort to simulate the old foods is none other than the reluctance of the consumer to buy something entirely new.

Economic necessity is undoubtedly the driving force behind the introduction of new and modified products. It is far more economical to clean, eviscerate, package in consumer-size units, and freeze many items that are now still marketed in the fresh state. Because of the tremendous peaks in sale of turkeys during the Thanksgiving-Christmas season, it became absolutely essential to freeze and package turkey if prices were to be maintained at reasonable levels. Prices of beef, as the consumer well knows, have been rising rapidly as a result of increasing demand and general inflationary trends in recent years. The only way to rationalize beef and poultry operations, thereby reducing rising costs, is by portion control at the processors' level and distribution of packaged portion-controlled cuts to the retail and institutional markets. This will come within the next few years, despite reluctance of the consumer, simply because the very substantial saving in price will overcome much consumer reluctance.

It required more than a generation for consumers to give up their efforts to purchase peas in the pod instead of canned. The reason for the success of canned peas was the tremendous price differential and the kitchen-labor saving. The new generation brought up on canned peas, however, actually preferred them to fresh peas to the point that when fresh peas were served they thought there was something wrong with them.

A cannery situated on a mountainside introduced a new, efficient, and very rapid process for canning peas. This consisted of trucking freshly harvested pea plants to the mountain top, where they were promptly vined (shelled), flumed in cold spring water to a continuous blancher, quality-graded, filled into cans, and processed within one hour of the time they left the field. The quality of this canned product was so much like the fresh that it was downgraded by both government inspectors and consumers because of off-flavor. To upgrade the product, the shelled peas had to be held at elevated temperatures for several hours before blanching until they developed a less fresh canned-pea flavor to which consumers had by then become accustomed.

Similarly, when frozen peas made their appearance, purchases were first made reluctantly, although it was indicated and demonstrated that frozen peas were more like fresh peas than were the canned. After another generation, however, purchases of frozen peas exceeded those of canned.

With the increasingly cosmopolitan nature of the world's population, new products, which were old products in other areas, have been introduced and quickly adopted. Thus, in the heterogeneous population of the United States, many new products have appeared because they were old standbys of specific ethnic groups. Very rapidly these foods became popular with the population at large. A manufactured item such as a pizza is now purchased in huge quantities by Americans from all ethnic origins, with the possible exception of some Italians who may still make their own at home.

Often we find new and old foods or combinations of foods enjoying great popularity with a certain population group. Such food fads are discussed in considerable detail in Chapter 5. Generally, a new food which is introduced and becomes a "fad" goes through a typical growth curve, reaching its zenith over a 4−5 year period, where it may remain at the same level for many years, or may just as suddenly drop in sales, and practically disappear from the market. It was estimated in 1970 that some 12,000 new food items appeared on the shelves annually, and some 7000 faded away (Ullensvang 1970). With a net increase of 5000 items annually, it stands to reason that the old standbys must be reduced in terms of per capita consumption, although they may maintain, or even increase slightly, in total sales because of the continuously increasing population base.

MEASURING FOOD ACCEPTABILITY

Sensory Properties

Since the probability of a food being acceptable depends on its sensory qualities, the only true method of determining its degree of acceptability is to have it tested by a consumer taste panel.

To be effective, these panels must be representative of the target population. A product intended for use by the entire family should include all members of the family, young and old. A fermented, alcoholic beverage such as beer, consumed primarily by adult males, should be tested by adult males and no others. If a product is intended for use by Southeast Asians, the panel should consist of Southeast Asians—not Americans. There are some exceptions to this rule. For example, although it would be preferable to have baby food judged for acceptability by babies, since the mother usually determines the choice of baby food on the basis of acceptability to her, test results based on preferences shown by the babies may not be realistic in terms of developing a successful product.

The representativeness of the panel is more important than its size. To determine whether a particular product is acceptable or unacceptable, or whether one product is grossly better than another, a panel of as few as 40 usually suffices. To obtain a more accurate quantitative evaluation, panels as large as 200 may be needed, but not larger (Anon. 1968). Any differences in acceptability that would require more than 200 panelists may be of interest to the researcher, but are not likely to be distinguishable by the average consumer.

It is essential that each panelist see the product as he would receive it for consumption and that he actually taste it before rendering his opinion. In the process of examination, each panelist is first asked to state his or her opinion of the appearance of the product. Then, after the usual manipulation by hand or utensil such as a fork or spoon, the food is placed in the mouth, and after chewing and swallowing, the consumer may be asked to evaluate it for texture and flavor, and finally for overall acceptability. There is usually also some place left on the scoring sheet for any comments, which in some instances prove very helpful.

Each of these items—appearance, texture, flavor, and general acceptability—is usually scored on a "hedonic" scale, that is, degree of like or dislike. The most common and simplest of these is a 3-point scale: 1—like, 2—neither like nor dislike, and 3—dislike. At times more elaborate scales containing 5, 7, or 9 points are used.

Ordinarily the results are reported in terms of percent of panelists who "like" the product undergoing the test, and if 50% or more indicate "like," the product is considered acceptable. This frequently is an oversimplification, and some standards for different types of food need to be established. For example, if a new frozen dessert is being tested on a panel representing a target population of children and young adults, most of whom like frozen desserts of any kind, a "like" percentage of 75 or 80 may be required before it may be concluded that this new dessert is as good as or superior to existing frozen desserts. Similarly, a new vegetable product may require a "like" percentage response of only 40% for it to be considered as acceptable or more acceptable than similar products.

Another way of overcoming this problem of interpreting panel results is to present a panel with two or more samples at the same time, asking the panelists to rank the most desirable sample as first, second-best, and so on, the least acceptable sample being ranked last. This method is particularly effective when a food processor wishes to test the acceptability of a new product or formulation he is thinking of offering to the market in comparison with similar products manufactured by him or his competitors.

In the case of products already on the market and new products for which sensory taste panel evaluations indicate high acceptability, specifications may be prepared to assure continued manufacture of the product in the same manner, so that the end product maintains a uniform quality level. Specifications in terms of a formulation (how much of each of a number of ingredients is to be used in the recipe) and the method of preparation and processing are not sufficient. There are so many differences in the quality of the ingredients and in methods of processing that a final test to ensure the sensory quality of the finished product is still needed. This can and frequently is done by the use of the human instrument, i.e., the taste panel. This method, however, is too expensive, since a substantial number of people are needed to obtain sufficiently precise results. If a single "master" taster or inspector is used, results may be unreliable because of drift, fatigue, or simply personal bias.

For continuous maintenance of uniform quality, therefore, it is desirable to use objective (instrumental) physical-chemical tests to measure

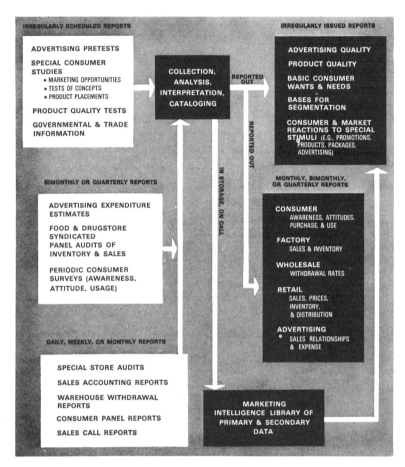

THE FOOD MARKETING CHAIN

the quality attributes interest. Generally there is little problem in determining the appearance quality of any product objectively. There are colorimeters, gloss meters, turbidity testers, consistometers, sizers, etc. that, alone or in combination, will predict consumer response with a high degree of accuracy. The same is true of texture (sense of feel). Objective evaluation of flavor is more difficult.

The English word flavor covers both senses of taste and smell and is not present in many other languages. Although a consumer can be asked, and respond directly to, a question about flavor as such, an objective evaluation of flavor must be performed separately for taste and for aroma. There is general agreement that taste consists of the four attributes of sweet, sour, salty, and bitter. These reactions are sensed by taste receptors located on about 400 papillae of the tongue. Although some of the receptors respond better to sugars, while others respond better to acids, etc., the combined effect of all the receptors is an impression of all four types of taste. It is only possible to determine taste objectively, therefore, if the kind of sugar, acid, salt, and bitter substances are known. This limits the opportunity for accurate evaluation of taste to a very few natural foods and a few simple processed foods, such as syrup. Milk and tomato juice, for example, contain approximately the same amount of sugar. Milk sugar (lactose) however, is only about $\frac{1}{10}$ as sweet as tomato sugars (fructose and glucose). Thus a simple measurement for soluble solids is useful for measuring sweetness only when the soluble solids are known to consist mostly of sugars of known sweetness value.

The aroma (or odor) problem is even more difficult, since it is not known how many dimensions there are to odor. A complete analysis of the volatile substances that contribute to the odor of a product must be made. Such an objective evaluation, although now technically feasible, is much more involved than a subjective sensory evaluation. In practice, therefore, the typical, desired flavor is not controlled too carefully, and more attention is paid to objectionable off-flavors. Since such off-flavors can be anticipated, they can be readily detected by a chemical test, but rarely as effectively as by the human nose.

In practice, therefore, most foods are tested for their sensory quality by a combination of sensory and objective methods. In some instances a total evaluation of a food product can be made quite satisfactorily by testing only for the "worst offender." For example, nuts or foods containing nuts can be tested for rancid off-flavor, while beef or peas may be tested for tenderness, and tomato juice just for color, on the assumption that if the most probable worst offender is acceptable, all other attributes of sensory quality will also be acceptable. While this is possible in some instances, and is generally practiced in more than just some instances, sensory quality of a fresh or processed food usually requires the evaluation of at least three different attributes and the integration of such test results into a single grade value.

Hidden Attributes of Quality

It is true that the consumer selects his food purchases on the basis of sensory quality. Yet the food, to be marketable, must also meet certain hidden quality requirements, most of which are negative (such as freedom from harmful or harmless adulterants) but in rare cases are positive (such as meeting minimal nutrient levels).

Although numerous methods of analysis have been developed for the determination of every known nutritional component occurring in foods naturally or added intentionally, their use in labeling for consumer information, was used rarely until very recently when nutrition labeling was introduced. Nutritive value was not of economic importance, because consumers either took it for granted or simply did not care.

The nutritional analyses that were performed routinely were usually not to determine whether the nutrient was present in the amount claimed, but to indicate adulteration. Thus, determination of butterfat content in milk was and is still being made, not so much to assure the presence of the minimal required quantity of this high-energy nutrient as to indicate that the milk has not been adulterated by dilution with water. Although it is now generally agreed that protein content of milk is of greater value nutritionally than its fat content, fat determination still remains the major nutrient to be controlled rather than protein or total solids. Control of soluble solids, largely sugars, in fruit-juice concentrates is another example of a nutritional analysis performed not so much to determine nutritive value (in this instance caloric content), as to provide an objective method for measuring the sensory characteristic of taste. Control of vitamin C content of fruit juices, on the other hand, is one of the few examples where nutritional quality is supported by the presence of a nutrient in substantial quantity.

One reason suggested for very limited nutritional labeling was that analyses are expensive and time-consuming, and their results for a particular lot become available only after that lot has been packed and shipped. That this is a significant factor in limiting use of nutritional labeling is substantiated by the fact that most common nutritional methods used routinely were for total solids, fat, and vitamin C—all relatively simple and rapid procedures. Research is in process for the development of rapid, automated procedures for determining nutritional components.

The major reason for the lack of nutritional information on food labels was undoubtedly lack of consumer interest. The consumer normally took it for granted that he automatically ingested a nutritionally adequate diet if he paid enough for the food. Certainly not enough education has been provided to consumers at large to make them aware of the importance of nutritional quality (in addition to sensory quality) to their welfare. The most effective methods for eliminating not only hunger as such, but "hunger on a full stomach" is by education beginning at the elementary school level (Anon. 1972D). It has already been established that to solve the problems of malnutrition, certain nutrients need to be added to foods that are now acceptable and within the economic reach of all (Clausi 1971).

Nutrient information on food labels can be a big first step in nutritional education. Such labeling now in progress on a voluntary basis can provide the consumer with readily available information that will enable him to decide to what extent the product fits into his daily meal plan in terms of nutritional adequacy. The question that must be decided within the next few years is to what extent such information is utilized by the consumer. Unfortunately, the responses from surveys currently indicate that the average consumer does not pay much attention to labels in general, or to nutritional information on the labels in particular. He does, however, like to see the nutrition label, and will select a unit so labeled over one that is not nutritionally labeled, even if the nutrition information indicates a lack of nutrients. Thus the nutrient label is frequently just another sales promotion stunt. It may be anticipated, therefore, that even with general usage of nutritional labeling, the majority of consumers will not purchase food primarily on the basis of its nutritional contribution, but largely on the basis of its contribution to sensory satisfaction. It appears that in the foreseeable future, as well as in the past, institutional residents will continue to be fed more nutritionally adequate food and continue to complain more, justifiably or not, about its sensory quality than the independent consumer who is free to select the food he wishes.

As a result of the rapid proliferation of new prepared, fabricated, and synthetic foods which simulate natural products but may differ from them substantially in nutritive value, as well as of new information indicating that nutritional insufficiency is prevalent in the developed world, government is taking positive steps to regulate the nutritive value of the food supply. Guidelines for nutritional labeling were established by the FDA (Edwards 1973) which require that any new food product must be at least as nutritious as the natural product it simulates. An essential requirement of any nutritional label is that every container must declare at least the quantity, by weight, of each nutrient present, not only at the time of manufacture but for its entire sojourn in the market place. Moreover, the ingredients must be listed in order of predominance by weight—the main ingredient first, the next most plentiful second, etc.

One reason given for the disappointing performance of nutrient labeling is the method of reporting the macronutrients, 5 vitamins and 2 minerals in terms of RDAs which are confusing to the consumer. Alternate methods have been suggested recently. Hansen et al. (1979), in their *Nutritional Quality Index of Foods*, express nutrient levels in terms of energy contributions.

CONTROLLING QUALITY

The food manufacturer, like any supplier, must satisfy the buyer if he expects to develop and retain a market for his product. Because food is a prime necessity, the food manufacturer must not only satisfy the sensory requirements of the buyer (the product must look, feel, smell, and taste good), but also meet other requirements which the consumer cannot evaluate with his senses. As will be discussed in greater detail in Chapter 4, label declarations of sensory or nutritive value are "permissive," that is, claims of the presence of these attributes at certain levels may or may not be stated on the label. Once such a claim is made, the food manufacturer is responsible for maintaining that quality level in each unit of the product.

In addition to these permissive attributes of quality, there are many mandatory quality standards which the food manufacturer must meet; these are subject to continuous policing by government agencies. Many, if not all, of these mandatory attributes have to do with safety and wholesomeness, which means protection of the health and welfare of the consumer. Thus, every food supplier must maintain a thorough quality control system, to assure not only consumer acceptance of his product because it "looks and tastes good," but also to have the greatest possible degree of assurance that he is "within the law" and that his product will be in no way harmful.

For this reason a quality control system operated by a food manufacturer begins and ends with the buyer's specifications, which the vendor must meet. Even in the case of perishable—and most foods are perishables—there is not only one vendor and buyer, but a number of buyers who in turn become vendors before the ultimate buyer, the consumer, is reached. At each stage there exists a complete quality control cycle, beginning and ending with the respective buyer's specifications. This is recognized by standardization branches of government and trade agencies who may have separate grades and standards (specifications) for the same product depending on whether it is to be offered for manufacturing purposes or for direct consumption. This is necessary because the same commodity enters the trade in every conceivable form, from freshly harvested or slaughtered to further-processed products of every kind. Special tests or modifications of test procedures must be employed for different end products of the same commodity.

For example, the attribute of firmness is of major importance in the quality evaluation of tomatoes intended for the fresh market, but much less important for tomatoes intended for processing. Wholeness and drained weight are of greater importance than firmness for whole, canned tomatoes. Color quality is of major importance to both the fresh and processed tomato industry. For the fresh market, surface color is of major importance, while internal color, specifically the red to yellow ratio, is the color standard by which processed tomatoes are evaluated. Total solids is of practically no interest to the fresh tomato industry, whereas it is perhaps the most important factor of quality from the economic standpoint for comminuted, concentrated tomato products such as ketchup and paste.

The stages in the market channel are not linearly sequential, but cyclic. We cannot say that the farmer at one end of the line is only a vendor, while the consumer is at the other end of the line and is only a buyer (see Fig. 3.1). It might be assumed that the farmer is the initial vendor who sells to a buyer, who is not the ultimate consumer, except at road-side stands. But the farmer is also a buyer who has a vendor or vendors who supply him not only with farm machinery and chemicals for plant nutrition and pest control, but also agricultural products such as organic feeds and fertilizers, seed, and livestock. In fact a farmer who purchases chicks or calves for resale as broilers or steers is no less a further processor than a processor who buys frozen poultry or beef from which he manufactures frozen precooked entrées. Although suppliers are required to provide the farmer with materials that are satisfactory for his purposes, to assure his obtaining supplies of proper quality, each farmer as well as buyer should perform an acceptance inspection of every material he buys. Since however, most farmers cannot afford extensive testing, much of this control is provided by federal government, state, and local regulatory agencies. The buyer of the farmer's product, on the other hand, has little government assistance in determining whether the supplies he purchases conform to his requirements, whether they are permissive or mandatory, and he must therefore maintain an elaborate acceptance inspection station to test the quality of the farm products which he will further package and/or process. In many instances, the food processor or distributor who purchases the farmer's products either does the quality control for the farmer, or at least assists the farmer in maintaining appropriate control of quality.

When the raw farm produce arrives at the processing or packaging plant, the processor tests all ingredients not so much for their quality at the time of purchase, as for an indication of the quality of the finished product which must conform to his buyer's specifications. Thus, not only for the food processor, but for every buyer in the food-marketing chain as well, acceptance inspection is the most important and rewarding part of the quality control system. This is the only point at which the processor can reject a product that does not meet specifications. It is also the only point in the operation where, if he chooses to accept, he can negotiate price on the basis of quality. Furthermore, on the basis of the tests performed at this point, he can determine the operational procedures necessary to yield a product that will meet his buyer's specifications.

After the supplies pass inspection, they must be checked again and again during the various manufacturing operations, which may involve washing, sorting, trimming, blending, comminuting, heating, and cooling, etc., and usually ending by filling into a container and packaging. At every stage in such operations, which may be at times quite complex, it is necessary to control the product primarily to ensure compliance with the buyer's specifications, thereby minimizing the opportunity for rejection. Where such acceptance and in-plant inspection is performed adequately, final inspection of the finished product before it is shipped out may be reduced to a minimum. In fact, inspection of the end product provides the least opportunity for quality control, since it is a "post mortem" operation which can only identify units already produced that are not acceptable. The only action that can be taken at that point is to remove it from the shipment and sustain the loss, which is, of course, less costly than distributing the units and later recalling them.

Seasonal and preserved foods that may be in the channels of trade for months, a year, and longer, may require further inspection while they are in storage and in the market.

At every inspection station, quality control personnel are responsible not only for continuous sampling and testing of the product, but also for recording and reporting the results of their tests in such a way that appropriate action can be taken immediately when an out-of-control situation develops. This opportunity for prompt action is a major asset of a good quality control system, since most food-manufacturing operations today consist of high-speed assembly lines; a delay of only a few minutes in correcting an out-of-control situation may result in a loss of hundreds or even thousands of dollars.

For illustration, let us follow a quality control operation that must be performed in the production of canned tomatoes from the time the seeds are planted until purchase of the canned tomatoes by the consumer. Even before the farmer plants the tomato seed, he must prepare the field for planting. His own knowledge and experience is generously supported by advice and laboratory tests that can be made for him at his request through his county agent or directly from his state agricultural extension service, who will perform soil analyses to determine the plant nutrient levels available and suggest the kind of fertilizers he should use. He can also obtain advice and information on whether to apply preemergence or post-emergence sprays which would prevent growth of weeds, but not affect the yield or quality of the tomato crop. He may also receive advice from the same sources on selection of a variety that is likely to give him the best yield of the best quality tomatoes that will be free of any harmful pesticidal residues. Other state agricultural agencies provide the farmer with the actual control of quality of these ingredients, such as the presence in the declared amounts of the plant nutrients in the fertilizer, and the active ingredient in the pesticides, or the assurance that the seeds have a satisfactory percentage of germination and are in fact the variety he had ordered.

In the case of exceptionally large-scale tomato growers, these functions may be performed by the grower himself. More frequently, when the grower is also the processor, or where there is a contractual agreement between grower and processor, the processor would not only perform these control and inspection services for the farmer, but may even supply the farmer with such ingredients and services. The processor may also direct the farmer not only how but when to plant the tomatoes, so that the fruit will be ripe and ready for harvest at a time when the processor can handle them.

The grower (or the processor's field man) would then continue to inspect the tomato field to ensure that there is an adequacy of plant nutrients, including water, and that the plants are protected from weeds, disease, and insect infestation. As the crop approaches maturity, it must be watched carefully, to determine the optimal time of harvest. With the increasing use of mechanical tomato harvesters, the decision of exactly when to harvest has become more important than ever before, since the entire crop is harvested at one time; this time must be selected so that there is a minimal amount of overripe and underripe fruit and a maximum yield of good quality, usable fruit.

Acceptance Inspection

The specific tests performed before harvest are usually similar to the tests made by the processor when he receives the tomatoes. Thus, the pre-test can be considered as the farmer's inspection of the finished product, which is not too different from the acceptance inspection of every lot of tomatoes offered to the processor would normally be as follows: 100-200 tomatoes are selected at random and weighed. Average tomato weight is an indication of size. If small tomatoes cannot be used, the tomatoes may be sorted for size, and the percent by weight of small tomatoes also obtained. Each tomato is then inspected for any visible defects, including cracks, cores, rot and green or yellow portions. These trimmings, plus those fruits that are completely unusable, are then weighed, and the weight of the trimmed tomatoes divided by total weight of the sample is the percent of usable fruit.

The remaining usable tomato material is then passed through a laboratory-size chopper-strainer. The strained juice weight may be used as an indication of percent yield of juice. This juice is then used to fill the cell of a colorimeter which determines the color quality. This is probably the most important sensory attribute of tomatoes. The redder and less yellow the color, the more valuable is the product. Acidity and total solids are also determined at this point, not only to indicate the sensory flavor quality of the product, but in the case of acidity to determine whether the tomatoes can be processed safely as a high-acid product without risking development of botulism.

The above inspection procedure provides information on the quantity and quality of the raw material. On the basis of such a test, the processor may reject the material outright, if he finds the quality to be so poor that reworking it into an acceptable, salable product is simply not possible. Outright rejection on such a sensory quality basis is rare. The usual basis for outright rejection of a lot is a finding (by means of tests not yet mentioned) which discloses the presence of pathogenic or toxin-producing microorganisms, or excessive amounts of pesticide or other chemical residues. Since many of these test procedures involve the use of relatively difficult, time-consuming laboratory techniques, testing for such un-wholesome hidden attributes is not done rigidly at this point by the processor. Like the farmer, the processor is inclined to depend to a considerable extent on government control agencies or consulting labora-tories for assurance that the material he is purchasing and processing is free of toxic agents. At the acceptance inspection station, therefore, the processor is likely to limit his efforts in this direction to rapid screening techniques. These relatively rapid and inexpensive methods will inform him whether the material is free of toxic agents, or whether there is a possibility that they may be present. He would then send samples of only the suspect material to a government or consulting laboratory to confirm their presence or clear the material.

If the product is not rejected, then the results of the above test provide a basis for paying on a "sliding-scale" basis. If the lot is totally usable, and the test indicates that the end product will be of high quality, a top price will be paid. If, on the other hand, it is found that a certain fraction of the material is not usuable, then a deduction is usually made not only for the weight of the unusable product, but something more to compen-sate for the work required to remove the defects. Thus, for example, if it is found that $\frac{1}{5}$ of half the tomatoes need to be trimmed to emove de-fective material, the deduction will be not by 10% (0.20 × 0.50), but perhaps by as much as 20% to compensete for the work required to re-move the defective material, and also to encourage the grower to provide sound, defect-free material.

Such testing for percent usable material or frequency of occurrence of defective material provides the processor with information on how to handle the product during manufacture. It is at this time, therefore, that he determines whether hand-sorting is required, and to what extent, as well as the number of sorters he needs to employ.

Other measurements of sensory quality, in this case color particularly, also provide the processor with a basis for payment, as well as the method of processing. Thus if he finds the lot of fruit to be deep red-orange, no deduction in price would be called for, since the material will provide a top-quality end product. If, on the other hand, he finds that the sample of the lot indicates that the color is more orange than red, he could very well reduce the price paid to the grower substantially, since the end product would not be top quality and if sold, would command a lower price. Such information could also be used to determine whether the particular lot should be processed as such, or whether it should be blended with other lots of tomatoes, in order to upgrade the lot if blended with higher-quality material, or upgrade other lots if blended with poorer-quality material.

Tests for acidity and solids are also made for two reasons. The first, and by far the more important from the consumer protection standpoint, is that the acidity test can be used to determine how much if any acid should be added to prevent the possibility of botulism. The test is also important to control flavor quality, since the amount of acid that can be added depends on the amount of solids, mostly sugars, that are present. The higher the solids content therefore, the more acid can be added, at the same time retaining an acceptably flavored end product that is not too acid for consumers' tastes.

The solids analysis is also useful as an indication of the wholeness and firmness of the tomatoes. High-solids fruit is likely to be firm, and will retain its wholeness even after heat-processing. If, on the other hand, solids are low, addition of a calcium salt is indicated to firm up and retain wholeness in the end product.

It should be noted that nothing as yet has been stated regarding nutritive value. In fact until very recently, practically no analyses of nutritional values were made either at the point of acceptance of the raw material or at any other time. This is not because tomatoes contain an exceptionally high amount of water (92–96%), since they are considered to be good sources of vitamins A and C, and if consumed in sufficient quantities, of protein also. On the average, canned tomatoes or tomato juice contain enough vitamin C so that one serving provides about ⅓ of the total recommended daily requirement. The labeling problem, however, is that the vitamin C contribution of a serving of tomatoes may vary from practically zero to more than half the recommended daily requirement. Thus, if the label on an end-product can of tomatoes states that it contains a certain amount of vitamin C, every lot of raw fruit must be tested for vitamin C content to assure the presence of this vitamin in at least the declared amount in every container of canned tomatoes so labeled.

If such a test were made, it would be useful for two purposes. The first, and again the more important, would be to assure the presence of the vitamin. The second would provide the processor with information as to whether the tomatoes can be processed and labeled as such, or whether they should be blended with other lots that may not meet the required level. Unlike the addition of acid, the processor, at least at this time, may not add ascorbic acid (vitamin C) to a batch of tomatoes that are deficient in the vitamin, because canned tomatoes are among the "standardized" items in which the end product must contain only tomatoes and tomato juice, and not more than 1% salt. The only other item that may be added, and if it is added, must be declared on the label, is a calcium salt up to 30 ppm to make the tomatoes firmer and maintain their wholeness. In fact this standardization is so rigidly maintained that, unlike other "unstandardized" products, tomatoes cannot be heat-processed by steam injection, since some of the steam may condense, thereby "adulterating" the end product with usually an infinitesimal, but nevertheless with a certain amount of water.

On-the-line Inspection

Once the lot of fruit has been accepted, it is dumped into wash tanks alone, or if lot-blending is indicated, with other lots. The tomatoes are then automatically conveyed to sorting belts where each fruit is carefully examined. If it is found to be defective, either because it is too yellow-green, or obviously rotten and moldy, it is considered a cull and discarded entirely. Less serious defects, such as green or yellow shoulders and other discolored or overripe-soft portions and cores, are trimmed. The second inspection station, and the first in-plant station, is usually just after the tomatoes leave the sorting belt. At this point a sample of the washed, sorted, and trimmed tomatoes is tested primarily to evaluate the effectiveness of the sorting belt operation. Another important test performed at this point is for the presence of mold and fly eggs; there is a very low tolerance for mold, and no tolerance for fly eggs. (For a more detailed discussion of zero tolerance, see Chapter 4.) If mold or fly eggs or too many other defects are found, the product going through the line is either discarded or returned to pass over the inspection belts a second time. If satisfactory, it proceeds through a scalder and is peeled, either mechanically or by hand. Regardless of how the peeling is done, there is need at this point for another in-plant inspection, if for no other reason than to ensure the practically total removal of peel. Strange as it may seem to the consumer, the presence of a bit of peel on canned tomatoes appears to be so important, that a combined surface area of more than 1 sq in. of peel per lb of canned tomatoes requires that they be labeled substandard. It should be pointed out that this specification is not a voluntary one which a processor may or may not adhere to. It is mandatory. If a manufacturer should market whole canned tomatoes that contain more than the permitted amount of peel without declaring them to be substandard, he is breaking the law of the land, and subjecting himself to serious penalties. But more about this in the next chapter.

The peeled tomatoes are then conveyed to a filler. At the same time, a portion of the same tomatoes are comminuted into juice. The filling of whole tomatoes is a somewhat awkward operation, since not only a net weight, but a drained weight must be maintained. If the tomatoes are filled first and then topped with juice, it is possible that the whole tomatoes will "bridge" and cause an empty airspace, which will result in a low net weight. On the other hand, if more than enough juice is filled first, and then the whole tomatoes, the juice may splash out of the can, or the tomatoes may even float and the drained weight will be deficient. To overcome these problems, a part of the juice is filled first, the whole tomatoes then added, and the cans are topped with additional juice. To ensure proper net and drained weights, it is essential to maintain an in-plant control station at the filler. At this point, the filled cans of tomatoes are weighed, the juice screened out, and the weight of the whole tomatoes is an indication of drained weight. Fortunately these tests are quick and simple, since they must be performed at frequent intervals, and conformity to such requirements can also be determined very easily by regulatory agencies.

After filling, the filled cans are usually exhausted—that is, they are heated to allow the trapped gases to escape, and upon closing and cooling there will be a vacuum rather than pressure within the container. After exhaustion about all that is needed for quality assurance is to check the temperature of the can contents. The exhausted cans are then closed, heat-processed, and cooled. Inspection of the filling-closing operation is at all times a very important examination, not quite as critical for acid foods such as tomatoes as for non-acid foods. This test is so critical for non-acid foods which include vegetables, meats, and other animal products, that the food industry, in cooperation with the Food and Drug Administration, has developed a special course for processors of these products to instruct them very specifically on how to identify such critical control points, and how to test to assure the safety of these products. These courses have some to be known as HACCP (Hazard Analysis of Critical Control Points).

The efficacy of the closure of a supposedly hermetically sealed container was considered so critical, that until about twenty-five years ago, manufacturers of can-closing machines insisted on leasing rather than selling them to food processors. In this manner they provided continuous control of the closure operation for the processor and incidentally protected themselves against unwarranted claims that spoilage was caused by faulty equipment of their manufacture. Because of interpretations of regulations intended to prevent monopolistic practices, closing machine manufacturers, who are usually also container manufacturers, were required to sell their equipment outright to the processors, so that each processor is now fully responsible for the quality of the closure. Of course, the reason for the importance of closing every can in such a way that it remains hermetically sealed is the ever-present possibility of botulism, should a hermetically sealed container containing nonacid foods spring a leak. Fortunately for the consuming public, other organisms than *Clostridium botulinum* are likely to grow before this dread organism does. The other organisms frequently form gases which cause the cans to swell and eventually "blow," so that an imperfectly sealed container usually gives evidence of not being adequately closed or processed before any appreciable growth of the organism causing botulism. Nevertheless, this in-plant station checking the efficacy of the closure is extremely important, and is essential in all commercial food-processing plants. This is undoubtedly the reason for the very rare cases of botulism poisoning from commercially processed food, as compared to the much more frequent cases resulting from home-canned foods.

Products such as canned food, unless they are canned aseptically, must be sterilized, usually by heat, to prevent spoilage. For this reason alone, the retorting (pressure-cooking) operation is also a HACCP point, and must be carefully controlled. Much of the heat-processing of tomatoes and other vegetables is now done in continuous retorts, with automatic continuous recording of both temperature and pressure. Some commercial operations, however, still employ stationary retorts controlled primarily by pressure and only indirectly by temperature. In these instances it is especially important to ensure the complete evacuation of air with steam. Only under these conditions is the pressure in the retort an accurate indicator of the temperature.

Following heat processing the cans are cooled rapidly, but not to the extent that the outside of the can surface will not dry. Each can is then labeled and cased. All these operations require quality control to assure conformity to buyers' specifications for condition of container, such as presence of rust spots, dents, imperfect labels, etc.

Finished-product Inspection

After the product is packed and processed, it is still necessary to make a final inspection of the finished product before it is shipped. As stated previously, the quality control system should be so organized that this last inspection should be minimized to consist of little more than spot-checking to provide final assurance that nothing but acceptable product leaves the plant. If, however, inadequate control is maintained during acceptance inspection and processing and packaging, then this "post-mortem" operation becomes more important and must be performed with much greater thoroughness. This is an improper procedure, which is not practiced by the vast majority of processors, since the only information obtainable at this point is whether the product should be shipped or discarded. Any manufacturer who relies primarily on end-product inspection does not stay in business very long.

The buyer of canned whole peeled tomatoes may be a broker, another processor who may use them for further processing, or a large institutional marketer or distributor-retailer (Fig. 3.1). Whoever the buyer may be, he should perform an acceptance inspection on the material he is buying, in much the same way as a processor is required to perform acceptance inspection of the raw tomatoes he buys from the grower. A very poor technique for this buyer to use is to test the acceptability of the lot offered for sale on the basis of presubmitted samples. It is natural for the vendor to submit specially selected samples to the buyer so that the

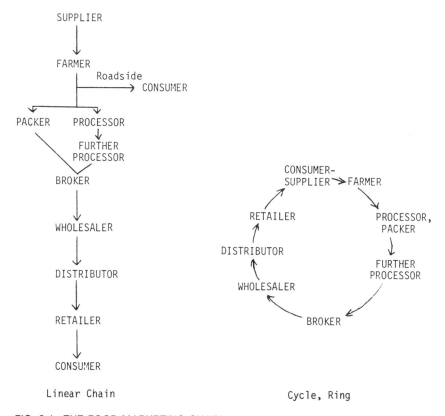

FIG. 3.1. THE FOOD MARKETING CHAIN

sample is not necessarily truly representative of the quality of the entire lot. Although this method of inspection is obviously fallacious, it is surprising how frequently it is used, particularly by institutional buyers.

The buyer of such finished products has two good alternatives. He may participate in the testing of the finished product on samples which he selects. In this way the vendors' finished product inspection is the same as the buyers' acceptance inspection, thereby omitting the necessity for duplicating this operation and providing an opportunity for some cost reduction for the benefit of the processor, distributor, and consumer. Some buyers at this point in the marketing chain, particularly those who will use the processed material for further processing, may in fact have their quality inspection teams in the processing plant observing and assisting in the in-plant testing, so that they can utilize all the processor's quality control data to assure themselves that they are buying a product that meets their specifications.

The other and more expensive procedure is to carry out a complete acceptance inspection of each lot received, not only for the sensory attributes of quality, but also for the hidden attributes. The buyer would then have to repeat practically all the tests that had been performed at least once by the processor. In addition, where there is no assurance that the processor may not have adulterated the product in some manner, the buyer may need to perform many additional rather complex tests to make sure, for example, that some natural or even artificial coloring had not been used to make the product appear more attractive than it actually is, or that water, sugar, or other adulterants had not been added. That these adulterants are harmless is in this case immaterial, because canned tomatoes are a standardized product.

Every time the lot changes hands, the same procedure must be followed. One method frequently used to avoid repeating quality testing time and again is for the product to be officially graded during processing, or later, but before a lot is shipped. Most of such official inspection is provided by federal agencies, particularly the USDA, which provides two types of services. One is continuous inspection, that is, an entire lot having a given code number is inspected continuously during its manufacture, and an official USDA grade may be placed on the label of each container. To obtain such official grades on the label, the processor must employ an official government grader who is present at all times while the product is being manufactured and is therefore in a position to supervise not only the conformity of the product to the buyer's sensory quality specifications, but also to guarantee that the product had been manufactured under good sanitary practice, and that no harmful or harmless adulterants had been added.

If the processor wishes to have such a guarantee but does not wish to employ an official inspector full time, he may request a "warehouse" inspection. This is usually the equivalent of a finished-product inspection that would be performed by the processor or an acceptance inspection that would be performed by the buyer. Sampling and testing procedures follow rigid techniques promulgated by the USDA. When a lot of a product passes such inspection, the processor pays for the inspection costs and receives a certificate of inspection, certifying that the lot of his product is of the certified quality grade.

The official grade on the label, or certificate, is most useful in the channels of trade. Thus, a lot of a product may change hands any number of times without need for repeat inspection. Since this inspection is made by official, disinterested third parties, it carries more weight than the processor's own grading or other indication of quality.

This, of course, does not mean that once a lot of a product has received a given grade, it remains in that grade for an indefinite period of time, regardless of conditions under which it is stored. With the aid of a code and other information required by law, however, a grade once given to a product such as canned tomatoes should hold up satisfactorily for a reasonable time. The code and other information on the label indicate the date and location of manufacture. Since tomatoes are generally processed throughout the northern hemisphere during August-September, a buyer who purchases the canned product during this season can determine readily whether he is purchasing freshly processed tomatoes, or those that have been carried over from the previous season. Normally, freshly processed tomatoes should be better, although they carry the same grade (See discussion on What is Fresh, p. 51).

Even with an official grade on the label or certificate, the buyer may still need to inspect a lot of materials for defects that may have developed in the lot during its transportation or storage. For instance, if the lot had been exposed to water and some of the cans began to rust, they would not be acceptable, even with the official grade indicating that they were the top-grade A quality. Changes in hidden quality are even more insidious. If the tomatoes had been held at very high temperatures for more than just a few days, their quality, wholeness, drained weight, and nutritive value could be seriously reduced, and they may go "out of grade" as a result of such storage conditions.

This problem of maintaining a product in grade during its entire time in the market place is much more serious for more perishable products. For instance, a carload of potatoes could be graded A by an official USDA grader in California, and then shipped across the country. By the time it reaches the Eastern buyer, the amount of rot, internal browning, and other defects may have increased to such an extent that it would no longer meet grade A standards. In such instances, the buyer may ask for a regrading of the carlot of potatoes. If the reinspection indicates that the potatoes are not in the certified grade, then the buyer may reject the lot, or pay a lower price in accordance with the reduced quality of the product. The loss in this case is sustained by the vendor, unless he can prove that proper care was not taken in transit or storage of the product from the time it left his hands until it reached the buyer. More control and inspection is needed even after the product has been purchased from the processor, while the material was handled, transported, and stored under conditions less than optimal. Open-dating may be of some value.

Ultimately the consumer purchases the product. Following the same reasoning we have been using throughout this example, the consumer should also perform a complete acceptance inspection of each lot he purchases. This obviously is impractical if for no other reason than the fact that the lot size purchased by the consumer is so small that after thorough inspection there would be nothing left to accept or reject. The ultimate consumer (with the exception of the institutional buyer) must, therefore, rely on the information provided on the label, the proficiency and honesty of the manufacturer, and the policing activities of regulatory government agencies. The latter are discussed in the next chapter, while various methods of consumer information follow.

Describing Quality to the Buyer

Practically no foods, and certainly no processed and packaged foods, can be evaluated by the consumer at time of purchase. It is, therefore, required by law that all packaged food products carry a label identifying the product and guaranteeing its wholesomeness, that is, freedom from any toxic materials or other substances that may be injurious to health. Sensory quality, however, is usually stated on the label only on a voluntary basis. A major exception to this general rule is the mandatory grade-labeling of meats. It should also be noted that any statement made on the label, whether mandatory (required by law), or voluntary, is subject to conformity. For example, if a carcass or cut of beef is labeled "prime," its sensory attributes of quality must conform to specifications meeting this grade. Similarly, if a can of tomato juice is labeled grade A, or Fancy, it must meet the sensory specifications for that grade, although in this instance the grade declaration was made voluntarily.

A very common method for indicating product quality in one term is by grade-labeling (Table 3.1). Federal government grades and standards frequently use numbers or letters: U.S. No. 1, or grade A, indicates the best quality; No. 2, or grade B, the intermediate quality level; and No. 3, or grade C, the lowest acceptable quality level. If a product does not

TABLE 3.1. SOME TERMS USED BY USDA TO INDICATE QUALITY GRADE LEVELS

	Eggs	Fruits		Meats	Poultry	Vegetables	
Top grade	AA	U.S. 1 A	Fancy	Prime	U.S. 1 A	U.S. 1 A	Fancy
2nd grade	A	U.S. 2 B	Choice	Choice	U.S. 2 B	U.S. 2 B	Extra standard
3rd grade	B		C Standard	Good	U.S. 3 C		C Standard
Other	C	Culls	Substandard	Commercial Utility Cutter Canner		Culls	Substandard

conform to U.S. No. 3, or grade C, it is usually considered to be unacceptable, or substandard. In each case, every grade is specified for each of a number of sensory quality attributes, wherever possible by the use of objective tests. Grade A peas, for example, are the smallest size, tenderest, and are practically free of defects or foreign matter. Grade C canned peas, on the other hand, may be considerably larger, are starchier and mealier, and may contain a limited amount of harmless extraneous matter. By this system, therefore, the consumer is told that best quality canned peas are the smallest and tenderest peas.

Although this sytem provides the consumer with a certain amount of information regarding the sensory quality of the product, it has a number of limitations. The first is that grade limits are usually determined by agreement between industry and government, and although usually they may begin by reflecting majority consumer preferences, may gradually drift away from these to other aspects of quality that are not of interest to the consumer. For example, because of competitive pressures, the wholesale buyer may insist on some quality characteristic, such as total absence of such harmless extraneous matter as loose skins, not because the consumer cares whether that can of peas is completely free of loose skins or not, but because it is very difficult for the processor to meet this requirement so that the buyer can purchase this particular lot at a lower price.

A more serious limitation of this procedure is that the individual consumer is told what is best quality, when in fact he as an individual has his own, perhaps different idea of what he likes best. In the case of our can of peas, an individual consumer may actually prefer peas that he can "sink his teeth into" in preference to the tiny undeveloped watery peas that are graded A.

Brand-labeling avoids these problems to some extent. The pea manufacturer can call his top grade by some brand name and a lower grade by another name. The consumer, after experiencing the various brand names, will then be able to purchase the brand he likes best.

A still better method of overcoming these problems is by means of "descriptive labeling." In this system, the consumer is not told by a numbering or lettering system what product he is supposed to like, but the product is described. The descriptive label contains information on the size, hardness, sweetness, of the peas without prejudicing the consumer in the direction of smaller less mature and more watery peas. Consumers may therefore read the description on the label and decide to purchase the product that they know they prefer. All these methods of furnishing the consumer with information regarding sensory quality of packaged foods are voluntary, that is, the manufacturer and/or distributor is free to provide any such information he wishes, or none at all. However, once any information on sensory quality is given, it becomes mandatory for the manufacturer to conform to such declarations.

Providing information on nutritive value, that is, nutritional labeling, is also voluntary, at least as of this writing. But in this instance, also, as soon as nutritive value is claimed by means of label declaration, it becomes subject to regulation just as are mandatory declarations for fill, identity, and wholesomeness.

Open-dating (as opposed to code dating) is already practiced for short-life products, particularly milk products, in many states, and mandatory Federal legislation for open-dating for all packaged foods is imminent. The remaining question is whether so-called non-perishable stabilized food purported to maintain high-quality shelf life for more than a year, will be included, or permitted to continue using coded dates (U.S. Congress, O.T.A., 1979).

Quality control is an indispensable part of food processing devoted to providing the consumer with food that is not only safe, wholesome and nutritious, but satisfies his sensory-aesthetic requirements. It is no wonder, therefore, that more food scientists and engineers are involved in quality control than in any other area of the food industry.

4

Consumer Protection

"When you get right down to it, the consumer is really our only constit- uency."

Charles C. Edwards, M.D.
Commissioner, FDA (1972)

Anthropologists, archeologists, and nutritionists seem to agree that man's "ideal" diet is the one to which he adapted during the long period between his emergence as a distintive species and the domestication of plants and animals which led him to produce his food instead of hunting and gathering it. In prehistoric times, therefore, man had developed an instinctive liking for meat and fruit which incidentally provided him all the protein, vitamins, mineral elements, and calories he required. When he ate what he liked, he ate what he needed. Modern science and technology made it possible to separate the two associated, but distinct factors of palatability (sensory quality) and nutrition. It is no longer true that when you eat what you like, you eat what you need (Ucko and Dimbleby 1968).

It would appear that protecting man from himself by ensuring nutritive value of his food supply would be the first priority in any program of consumer protection. Obviously this is not the case. The wonders accomplished in modern times in improving rates of growth and development, health, and life spans of animals and pets by improving the nutrient value of their feed not only did not promote similar efforts for the improvement of human nutrition, but produced a negative response. The consumer does not want to be fed like an animal, but prefers to select his food on the basis of its sensory value as we have seen in preceding chapters.

The nutritive value of various raw and processed foods has been investigated extensively. For over half a century the USDA has released information on nutritive value of various food commodities, as well as suggestions for balanced meals to provide adequate nutrition. A number of responsible, public welfare-minded food manufacturers invested substantial sums in nutritional analyses of their own products and other foods for the benefit of dieticians and the general public. A notable example is the Heinz Company, which published *Nutritional Charts* in 1934, and *Nutritional Data* in 1949, containing nutritional values not only for its "57 Varieties" but for all types of foods. In the forties and fifties a number of food trade associations, notably the National Canners' Association and the National Association of Frozen Food Packers, undertook extensive investigations of the nutritive value of canned and frozen foods. These data, together with additional data obtained from analysis of military rations, civilian defense rations, and other studies, culminated in the development of the *USDA Handbook No. 8* (U.S. Dep. Agric. 1963) which is a very comprehensive, continuously updated tabulation of nutritive values for most of the fresh and processed foods on the market today. *Handbook No. 8* is the basis for menu planning by most dieticians, but is known by few consumers who prepare their meals at home, and is used for menu planning by even fewer consumers.

Even if *Handbook No. 8* were in the hands of every consumer, it might not provide adequate information on the nutritive value of the specific unit purchased. For example, a serving of fresh green asparagus, cooled immediately upon harvesting and refrigerated until consumed a week later, should provide half the daily requirement of vitamin C. If not cooled and refrigerated, the same asparagus serving would provide only 1/10 of the daily vitamin C requirement. A serving of canned peas that has been on the shelf for just a few weeks should provide about 1/2 the daily requirement of vitamin B_1. A year or two later, unless held in cold storage, the contribution of vitamin B_1 by this can of peas would be reduced to 1/4 or less. Two containers of tomato juice may vary in their contribution to vitamin C needs from more than 1/2 the daily requirements to practically nothing.

Certain new trends in food-product development and consumer eating habits, however, have caused a marked increase in consumer interest in the nutritive value of foods. Among these are:

(1) The rapid proliferation of new prepared, fabricated, and/or synthetic foods which may simulate natural products, but may differ from them substantially in nutritive value.

(2) Rapid increase in institutional feeding, where more careful and intelligent control is used to assure nutritional sufficiency.

(3) New information indicating that nutritional insufficiency is prevalent not only in distant primitive societies, but in large pockets and segments of populations (not necessarily limited to the poor) in the Western world.

(4) Increased interest and attention to special diet requirements and in general, differences in nutritional requirements among individuals.

NUTRITION LABELING

This consumer interest was greatly stimulated by the White House Conference on Food Nutrition and Health (Dec. 1969) in which representatives of the food industry, consumers, government, and science participated. Although the headlines were on matters such as a guaranteed family income and payments in food stamps or cash to the needy, the lasting effect of the conference was to put into motion a number of experiments in nutrition labeling. These in turn led to the enactment of regulations for the enforcement of nutrition labeling (Edwards 1973).

Only a minority of the consumers and consumer groups and none of the others involved in the development of these regulations advocated that nutrition labeling should be mandatory. The regulations therefore state that:

"Except for some standardized foods, the decision to add a vitamin or mineral to, or make a nutritional claim for, a food *is entirely voluntary.* . . . where a nutrient is added to a food, e.g., the addition of vitamin C to a breakfast drink, or a claim or information with respect to nutritional properties of a food is included in labeling or advertising, e.g., the amount of vitamin C in orange juice. . . , or a general or specific reference to the caloric or fat content of a food, or any other representation that a food is useful in the daily diet because of any of the nutrient qualities covered in this regulation, *the full nutrition labeling established in this regulation must be utilized.* Only by having available this full nutrition labeling for a food to which such a nutrient is added or for which such claim or information is provided can such claim or information be evaluated and understood, and the food properly used in the diet. Without full nutritional labeling such claims or information would be confusing and misleading for lack of completeness, and could deceive consumers about the true nutritional value of the food, its overall nutritional contributon to the daily diet, and its nutritional weaknesses as well as strengths."

Thus, if any nutrition claim is made, the label must state not only the level of that nutrient, but also levels of vitamins A, C, B_1, B_2, niacin, calcium, and iron (if 4 or more of these nutrients are present at levels of less than 2% of the recommended daily allowance, only those having more than 2% need be listed), together with the content of calories, protein, carbohydrates, and fat. Other vitamin and mineral nutrients may also be listed. Sodium and cholesterol may be declared for special dietary foods without listing all the nutrients. On the other hand, fabricated food made to simulate natural foods must contain at least the average amount of nutrients present in the natural food.

Although nutrition labeling is now optional (that is, the food manufacturer is not forced to use it), it is generally believed that most food manufacturers will be required to do so because of competitive pressures. Del Monte, which has already come out in favor of nutritional labeling, did so because its market research indicated that customers want this information. If several food industry giants are already committed, will the rest be far behind?

The advent of nutrition labeling is a good example of the protection the consumer can get if he wants it, and makes his wishes known. It seems doubtful, however, that the mere presentation of nutrition information on the labels of packaged foods will guide the consumer back to a nutritionally ideal diet where he would buy and eat "what he needs," if it does not coincide with what he likes. Present regulations may be adequate to assure the presence of nutrients in the declared amounts, but they provide no assurance that the consumer will not continue to purchase "empty calories," such as soft drinks, in preference to more nutritious fruit juices, or totally nutrition-free (if not harmful) coffee in preference to milk.

There are some instances, and undoubtedly there will be more, where the consumer will be actively discouraged from purchasing food having low nutritive value. Some states and municipalities, in addition to taxing alcohol and tobacco, also tax soft drinks. Even this measure appears to have little effect on consumer purchasing habits, but it is beneficial in those cases where such tax funds are appropriated for health research and education. The difficulty in providing such consumer protection is that the protection is imposed on the consumer, presumably "for his own good." In a democratic society this is very difficult to do, as demonstrated by the rise and fall of the Eighteenth Amendment prohibiting alcoholic beverages.

QUANTITY—A FULL MEASURE

Net Weight

The first and sometimes the only protection provided the consumer is the assurance that he gets what he pays for in terms of quantity. Thus the weights and measures inspection services at local, state and federal levels are the most effective and complete line of consumer protection. If consumers are protected against nothing else, they are practically always assured of getting a full measure of the food they purchase. For example, two 1 pound loaves of bread, or TV dinners, or cans of juice, or chocolate bars, may vary substantially in their sensory and nutritional qualities. But customers may rest assured that any item labeled and sold as having a net weight of 1 pound will in fact contain at least 1 full pound of the product.

Drained Weight

Conformance to declared weights in packaged goods is not always adequate protection to assure customers that they get all they pay for. Many processed food containers are filled with units of food, after which a liquor is added that consists mostly of water, plus some sugar, salt, or other ingredients. In such packaged foods, the indicated net weight (total weight minus container weight) does not provide sufficient indication to the consumer as to how much solid food and how much of the less expensive liquor he is getting. In such instances, there is usually a mandatory requirement of "drained weight" that must be met. At times the requirement to meet a given drained weight imposes a hardship on the packer, so that he may have to pretreat the product and in the process cause it to be less acceptable and less nutritious. Spinach, for instance, must be wilted, usually by means of precooking (blanching) to enable enough weight of leaves to be stuffed into the container to meet the drained weight requirement. During this precooking some nutrients are leached out.

Although such drained weight requirements may occasionally impose additional costs on the processor and result in a poorer-quality product for the consumer, usually they do provide the consumer with much-needed protection. Otherwise, there would be nothing to prevent the consumer, for instance, from getting 2 or 3 apricot halves floating in a quart of syrup. Of course, even without rigid regulations an apricot packer could not consistently grossly slack-fill, and expect the consumer to keep him in business. But suppose he underfills by 10-20%? Most consumers would not notice the difference, and to meet the competition, all packers would reduce the fill-in weights of fruit to that of the packer who put in the least amount.

Not only canned foods require minimum limits for drained weights. Prepared food such as fresh or frozen pies, for instance, may be processed in such a way that there is little evidence of the presence of the named ingredient. Chicken pot pie, for example, was so abused from the standpoint of presence of recognizable pieces of chicken meat that a regulation was promulgated requiring that a 6-ounce pie contain not less than 1 ounce of recognizable chicken meat.

Overrun

Consumer protection becomes more difficult when size or volume becomes the criterion of acceptability instead of weight. Any foods in which air is incorporated will appear to occupy more space, that is they will have a greater volume. The same quart of liquid ice-cream mix can be whipped into little more than a quart, or to more than 2 quarts. As with drained weights, it was found necessary to set limits to such "overruns" of volume, to protect not only the consumer but also the ice-cream manufacturer against unfair competition.

At this time, chilled and frozen "whips" are occupying much space on retail shelves. On the basis of weight or nutritive value these whips are very expensive. But consumers continue to buy such items undoubtedly because they like them, and they either do not wish or are unable to produce the whips themselves. The overrun on these whips is several hundred percent. Probably some limits on the amount of overrun permissible for these products will eventually be legislated, perhaps as a result of consumer complaints, but more likely because of competitive pressures among manufacturers of the ready-made whips.

IDENTITY—THE REAL THING

Just as weight and volume standards provide consumers with the assurance that they get the amount they pay for, so do identity standards provide the assurance that consumers get the quality they pay for. Apparently it is of major importance to the consumer (why else would it be so strictly regulated?) that a product he purchases conform strictly to its natural composition, and in some instances, to a specific location where the product has been grown.

Standards of identity protect the buyer from getting something other than what he is led to believe he is purchasing, not only quantitatively, but qualitatively as well. Protection of identity is jealously guarded to assure that natural products remain just as they are. It may surprise some consumers to realize to what extent this protection is carried out to ensure the customer's purchase of an "unadulterated" natural product, although the additive (adulterant) may be a wholesome, desirable nutrient. For example, provitamin A (carotene B), a naturally occurring plant pigment, is not permitted to be added to some citrus products because it might improve the color of such *imitation* juice over the natural product. Some of us may remember when this same pigment was not permitted to be added to margarine to avoid the consumer's mistaking the less expensive vegetable fat for *real* butter.

Conformation to the Natural or Standard

Protection of the identity of a product with little or no benefit to the consumer can be demonstrated strikingly by the regulations governing the identity of shucked oysters. Here, a compromise had to be made with the general rule that the consumer who buys shucked oysters should receive nothing but oyster meats. For sanitary reasons, and to dispose of sand and other harmless matter that may accumulate on oyster meat, it is necessary to wash the oysters, during which operation the meats invariably pick up some water. By law, therefore, oysters may pick up as much as 20% of their weight of water, but no more. If they gain more than 20% water, then they can no longer be sold as shucked oysters. Some rather poor, lean oysters are naturally composed of 90% water, whereas high-quality "fat" oysters may have as little as 80% water. Thus, the 80% moisture oysters have twice as much meat solids as the lean 90% oysters. Neither of these, however, can be watered during the washing operation by more than 20% of their weight, so that the lean oysters may be reduced in solids to 8%, and the fat oysters may be reduced in solids to no less than 16%. It would seem more reasonable to have quality standards indicating that oysters having 8-12% solids are low-quality, those having 12-16% solids are Choice, and those having more than 16% solids are Select. But this is not the case. Select oysters are large oysters, while standard oysters are small oysters, and no one pays any attention to the solids content except to ascertain the extent to which the oysters had been watered.

An even more trivial form of identity protection is insistence of remaining true to location of the product. Although oysters from the Gulf of Mexico are identical in every respect with those in Chesapeake Bay, it is illegal to sell Gulf oysters as Bay oysters, or vice versa.

Certainly these last examples of identity protection are of little practical value to the consumer; yet the regulations remain on the books and are enforced largely for economic reasons. This may be readily understood if one thinks of foods such as cheese or wine, both products of microorganic fermentation. (Most foods that undergo fermentation are considered to be spoiled. See Chapter 6). These fermentation products develop very distinctive flavor and other quality attributes as a result of the activity of certain microorganisms present in a particular location; hence the association of a locality name with a particular cheese or wine. If milk or grape juice were to be pasteurized, and inoculated with these same organisms, a similar product would develop as a result of such fermentation. In fact, this is now the usual process by which many wines and cheeses are manufactured. It is for this reason that perfectly satisfactory Swiss or Roquefort cheese can be manufactured in Wisconsin, and a Champagne or Moselle wine in New York state. With time, however, economic value is attached to the location, so that champagne from Champagne, France, commands a high price than *imitation* champagne from anywhere else.

The above "location-identity" examples of cheese and wine may have some merit for consumer protection, since there may yet remain subtle sensory-quality differences between those produced in their original locale and elsewhere. And of course there is always the snob-appeal of purchasing authentic originals. But even such subtle benefits are difficult to discern in other food materials, such as spices. Saigon cinnamon and Jamaican ginger, for instance, are considered to be of substantially higher quality and therefore command a much higher price than the same spices obtained from other localities. With the possible exception of some areas in Southeast Asia, ginger is used sparingly, and only as an additive to provide a degree of ginger flavor. It might be assumed, therefore, that Jamaican ginger has a more intense ginger flavor, so that the same amount of it will go further than, say, ginger obtained from Africa or Australia. In fact, this assumption was the basis for establishing the high price of Jamaican ginger. Extensive recent work, however, has demonstrated that there is no significant difference in intensity of ginger flavor from any source. Furthermore, the less expensive Australian ginger is more likely to be free of harmless (and possibly harmful) foreign matter than Jamaican ginger (Bednarczyk and Kramer 1971).

Conformance to the Product

A better case for identity protection can be made for product identification. It may be assumed that natural pure unrefined olive oil is in fact different from some oil-seed vegetable oil, such as soybean or cottonseed, adulterated by the addition of coloring and flavoring to make it look and taste like natural pressed olive oil. Certainly imitation olive oil is much less expensive to produce than the pure product; but if the consumer actually is willing to pay the higher price for the *real* product, he is entitled to receive what he has paid for, although the imitation oil may be indistinguishable from and probably more stable than the true oil.

WHOLESOMENESS—FOOD SAFETY

Zero Tolerance

The area which undoubtedly deserves the major attention in terms of consumer protection is that of wholesomeness and safety. No one can dispute the importance of protection of the consumer against injury; in fact, so rigid are the regulations (if not the enforcement) governing matters of wholesomeness that the usual tolerance for the presence of unwholesome materials in foods is zero. This is a statistical fiction in two respects. Theoretically at least, if sufficient sampling is done, or if a sample size is large enough, some quantity—it may be no more than trace—of the offending materials will be found.

Microorganic count, for instance, is made in terms of number per gram or milliliter. Usually dilutions are made so that eventual counts are made in terms of discrete digits per g. Thus, for example, 5×10^3 indicates a count of 5×1000, or 5000 microorganisms, while 5×10^6 indicates a count of 5,000,000 per g or ml. However, if no microorganisms are found, even in the undiluted sample, the analyst cannot really state that the count of the specific microorganism is zero, but only less than 10 ($<1 \times 10^1$). A similar problem is encountered with chemical analyses. Practically all official testing procedures for detecting substances that may be injurious to health are so precise that the presence of the unwholesome material can be detected at levels of from 1 part per million to 1 part per billion. Still, the sensitivity of the method itself provides some tolerance above zero.

Heptachlor, a chlorinated hydrocarbon spray material used as an insecticide to protect certain crops from insect damage, was found, upon extensive investigation, to be injurious to the health of test animals. Federal regulations were therefore enacted, providing a zero tolerance for presence of heptachlor in milk, as well as in other products. Dairy farmers were advised not to use it on pastures or other crops for at least 2 weeks before feeding their dairy cows. No heptachlor was found in the milk as long as the test was used; at that time the test was sensitive to as little as 1 ppm of heptachlor. Then an improved and more precise technique for measuring heptachlor was developed, capable of detecting 1 part per billion. This led to the rejection of substantial quantities of milk, in which heptachlor was found at levels of approximately 0.1 ppm. Presumably, this level was also present in the milk previously tested, but it was not detected by the less precise test then used.

It would appear, therefore, that "zero tolerance," which is never real, should be replaced with some measurable limit. True, this limit may be lower than present practical limits of up to 10 microorganisms per g or 1 ppm of some substance, whether it is present naturally in the food or added intentionally or unintentionally. This problem has been recognized by some international standardization agencies who are recommending standards indicating values with a negative subscript. For example, tolerance for the presence of pathogenic *Staphlococcus* (staph) may be stated as 1×10^{-2}, which means not more than 1 organism per sample of 100 g instead of the usual 1 g. In the case of *Salmonella* which does not cause discomfort unless present at levels of over 20,000 per g, a tolerance of 1×10^{-1} g may be satisfactory or even too rigid. On the other hand, the *Clostridium botulinum* limit should be perhaps 1×10^{-3}, which indicates that a sample of 1 kg rather than 1 g should be tested. Similarly, copper, an essential mineral micronutrient, may be tolerated up to several hundred ppm, whereas heptachlor should have a tolerance level of less than 1.0, perhaps 0.1 ppm.

Such defined tolerances would protect the consumer against unwholesome foods at known levels, rather than depend on the vagaries of administrators' interpretations of results obtained by methods of analysis which may change in their precision with the nature of the test itself, or with the method and size of sampling. Logical as some defined tolerance may be, it is forbidden by law for any substance even remotely suspected of being carcinogenic (causing cancer). The law in question is the highly controversial Delaney Amendment to the Food, Drug & Cosmetic Act which legislates zero tolerance for any substance suspected of being carcinogenic although the indicated carcinogenicity relates to a test animal and then only in quantities equivalent to total daily food intake of the substance for the greater part of its life span. This obviously impractical legislation has caused many materials that are practically harmless to be banned. FDA is in a position that it cannot exercise judgment. If any study demonstrates the least possibility of a substance being carcinogenic, FDA must act to remove the substance from the market. This has led to the recent phased withdrawal of the long established sweeteners, cyclamate and saccharine, and the imminent withdrawal of nitrite (which has been on the GRAS list for generations) from use in the curing of meat products. It is suspected that during curing or in frying of cured meat such as bacon, the added nitrite may form nitrosamines which were demonstrated to be carcinogenic to some animals. Although a tolerance of up to 10 parts per million has been demonstrated, no tolerance is permitted according to the provisions of the Delaney Amendment because at some higher level nitrite may cause cancer.

Substances which may increase mutation rates are called mutagens, and are in fact closely related to carcinogens. While most medical researchers consider carcinogenicity and mutagenicity to be the same, FDA distinguishes among them, perhaps because any substance that is shown to be mutagenic would also be automatically withdrawn from human consumption. Yet, it is possible for a product to show an increased mutagenic rate at a high level, and be permitted for use at a low level which would not increase the mutagenic rate.

A Story About Worms

Although uncompromising zero tolerance for dreaded carcinogens may be understandable, it takes some explaining to appreciate the need for zero tolerances for substances that are considered unwholesome not because they are injurious to health, but because they offend our cultural patterns. How often do we find large and small insects (or do we call them worms?) in freshly harvested ears of corn? We do not discard the ears; we trim the ears or wash away the worms, then proceed to prepare the corn for eating, assuming we got rid of the offenders. When we buy canned or frozen corn, however, we are guaranteed that there is not one fragment of a worm in the package, since, by law, there is a zero tolerance for insect fragments in processed corn. Everyone knows that there must be some, perhaps very few, fragments of insects in these processed foods. Yet the zero tolerance remains, presumably because the consumer would object to some regulation that might read "not more than one worm fragment per 10 oz."

That this is no idle concern is attested by the lavish abuse heaped on sincere and dedicated government regulatory agents by some consumer advocates for permitting a tolerance for insect fragments in wheat flour. Thus, the consumer pays more for a worm-free product that cannot be totally free of some minute quantity of insect fragments; the processor is perpetually in a situation where some inspector may condemn his otherwise high-quality product because he did by chance find a single piece of worm in the sample he inspected; and the inspector is in a dilemma as to whether to condemn a lot of perhaps thousands of cases of perfectly good food just because he happened to find a worm fragment. The end result is that some processors who don't like the odds go out of business, while the gamblers remain. As for the government inspectors, they set up their own confidential tolerances. It is rumored, for instance, that most inspectors will not condemn a lot of canned cream-style corn if they find only one very small insect fragment per ounce of sample; nor will they condemn tomato juice if it contains less than 6 fly eggs per ounce. One fly egg, however, is sufficient for condemnation—but then those are only rumors. Would it not be to everyone's advantage to have clearly stated tolerances for such harmless adulterants as insect fragments or fly eggs? Obviously, yes; but who in his right mind is going to tell the consumer that he is devouring several insect fragments or a few fly eggs plus thousands of microorganisms with every bite of food he puts in his mouth? The fact that he is inhaling as much or more filth than this with every breath he takes is little consolation.

Are we being picayune when we consider this problem from the worm's standpoint? Behold a vigorous corn ear worm in the prime of life chewing away on the kernels near the tip of the ear. Fortunately for him, he escaped the deadly spray because it could not be applied later than 2 weeks before harvest, so as not to leave a residue on the harvested ears. Then the ear, which is his home and his sustenance, is picked while he is busy chewing with one end of his body and depositing the digested waste from the other end. By the time the ear is picked and tossed into a crate, he is crushed into many pieces. So the one worm has turned into any number of insect fragments. During the ride to the processing plant some of the fragments may fall off, others break up into more pieces, some of which become deeply imbedded in and among the kernels. As the ear goes through the husker, some of the fragments are removed with the husk, but the total fragment count remains about the same because of additional fragmentation.

The husked ears now go through a series of washers and scrubbers that do a far more thorough cleaning job than any one can possibly do in the home kitchen. This should remove practically all the pieces that are not imbedded in or among the kernels. But the remaining fragments have not escaped detection yet, since they must now pass over a sorting belt, where each ear is inspected and any defect noticed is trimmed out. By now practically all parts of our worm have been removed—that is, practically all—but perhaps a fragment was so tighly lodged among the kernels that it escaped the washing, cleaning, and trimming. Does this mean that this one worm contributed just one fragment to the lot being processed? No indeed. Now as the kernels are cut and scraped the one fragment is further disintegrated, and is comminuted still more when the corn slurry is blended. During blending and precooking, the fragments distribute themselves nicely throughout the tank so that eventually any number of consumer-size containers, not just one, receive one or more fragments from the single embedded fragment of the original worm, who survived because the corn could not be sprayed too soon before harvest. The moral of this story is that one worm is one worm but many fragments, and every fragment may be many fragments.

If safety, i.e., potential injury to the health of consumer is involved there is no argument about the need for strict regulation and enforcement. Even if zero tolerance for the presence of such injurious substances is a theoretical impossibility, a tolerance approaching zero can be established by reducing acceptable levels of harmful substances to substantially less than 1 ppm. In the case of counts of pathogenic microorganisms, some level above zero can be stipulated, but sample size may be increased beyond 1 gram or milliliter to 10 (1×10^{-1}), 100 (1×10^{-2}), or even 1000 (1×10^{-3}).

For other substances that are considered unwholesome but are not actually injurious to health (as, for instance, harmless insect fragments, and particularly those organisms that grow in a symbiotic relationship with food materials), there is no excuse for insisting on zero tolerances. For such items the consumer is well advised to accept a reasonable tolerance of such defects in processed foods. The actual level of the tolerance can be safely placed in the hands of regulatory agencies who may put these levels at a point that they find can be met by food manufacturers and distributors who practice rigid sanitary controls in accordance with required codes of sanitation and safety. The actual level that may be permitted by regulations may appear to the uninitiated consumer to be excessively high, and he may in fact be able to prove that 95 or 99% of the processed food commodity contains far lower levels of the offending materials. It should be noted, however, as in the case of the worm fragments described, that such apparently lenient tolerances are applied only to materials that are proved not to be injurious to health and occur rarely.

Before leaving the subject of wholesomeness we should consider the fact that practically all foods and food ingredients, including required nutrients, have not one, but two levels of tolerance. The kinds of substances we considered in connection with zero tolerances naturally have only a maximum tolerance, if any, because they are not required nutrients, but are, or may be harmful. The vast majority of foods, even if entirely free of harmful ingredients, are not likely to be "complete" foods—that is, one or more of the required nutrients may not be present at all, or in sufficient quantities for normal health. Even cows' milk, generally considered as the most complete food, would result in severe malnutrition if consumed exclusively for several months, and in gastric disturbances and constipation in less time. It follows, therefore, that even for such a highly nutritious food as cows' milk, there is a maximum tolerance, although this tolerance is closer to 100% than to 0%.

Practically all foods and food ingredients that are not only beneficial, but essential for normal human growth and development, are injurious and even deadly if consumed in excess. The ubiquitous sodium chloride (common table salt) when consumed regularly at levels of more than 1 or 2% is injurious to the health, not only of sufferers from cardiac insufficiency and others who tend to retain excessive amounts of fluid, but to normal, healthy people. At the same time, it is recognized that a minimal amount of salt is an essential requirement for the normal diet. Many other nutrients, including vitamins, minerals, and amino acids, such as vitamin D, iodine, and methionine (one of the 8 essential amino acids that must be present in protein for the protein to be nutritionally useful), which are absolutely essential in very small quantities, are injurious to health when consumed excessively. In these instances, excessive may be much less than 1% of the diet.

Natural Toxicants and Allergens

In recent years new areas of concern have been revealed that stagger the imagination. They indicate that many matters now of prime concern to regulatory agencies, such as the amount of peel left on a processed fruit, insect fragments in wheat flour, weevils in beans, propionates in bread, benzoates in fruit juice, or total bacterial counts in red meats, fish, or fowl are of relatively trivial consequence.

Of course man has known for millenia that certain plant and animal substances are poisonous, not because of microbial infections or insect or rodent infestations, but by their very nature. We now call these naturally occurring toxicants. In 1966 the National Academy of Sciences published a volume prepared by the Food Protection Committee entitled *Toxicants Occurring Naturally in Foods* (N.A.S.N.R.C. 1966) summarizing much of what was known about such toxicants which occur in foods that were considered perfectly harmless. Since then the list of naturally occurring toxicants has increased, and additional evidence has developed that new genetic varieties produced by plant and animal breeders for purposes of sensory quality enhancement, increased yields or disease resistance, may have inadvertently programmed the cytoplasm of the new varieties to include toxicants that may not have been in the same commodity previously.

The arts, if not the sciences, of pharmacy and toxicology developed primarily by studying plant and animal products that contained substances that were injurious if consumed beyond a certain level. Up to a given level, however, these same toxicants, or poisons, were found to have healing properties. The toxic properties of certain fungi (e.g., Mushrooms) and reptile venom (e.g., Rauwolfia) were well known to the ancients. It is only in recent decades that the antibiotic fungal extracts have been used medicinally, although many fascinating old wives tales are told of physicians and others with less scientific claim to medical knowledge who developed reputations for allaying fever by the use of bread molds (*Penicillium* sp.?). Similarly, it is only in recent years that cobra venom was used successfully and became the basis for other more effective antihypertension remedies.

Some people appear to be allergic to certain natural foods, and a few are allergic to practically all natural foods. The fava or horsebean *(Viscia faba)*, has been known as a serious allergen for millenia. There is good evidence that allergic response to this food is inherited and occurs with high frequency among some families, tribes, and entire ethnic groups, but is practically unknown in others. It is interesting to note that in spite of the rather extensive studies made on the clinical manifestations of favism, the causative substance of this disease has not been identified with any degree of certainty to this date. One of the difficulties is that it as been impossible to reproduce the disease in experimental animals (N.A.S.N.R.C. 1966).

Numerous seemingly selective benefits from abstention from consuming specific foods may be due to allergens, which are present in certain foods, but whose specific chemical composition is not, as yet, known. Childress (1976), for example, now has thousands of well documented cases of reprieve from severe arthritic pain solely by total avoidance of consumption of all *Solanacea* (potato-tomato family of plants). Yet because more people did not respond to this treatment, there is a tendency to dismiss this treatment entirely.

Chocolate and cows' milk cause mild to severe ill effects on some individuals. It is only in recent times that the specific naturally occurring substances causing these ill effects have been isolated and identified for some, but certainly not for all, the allergenic foods. It is now known, for instance, that individuals incapable of utilizing milk suffer from a low level of the enzyme lactase which hydrolyzes lactose, the milk sugar, making it available for metabolic processes of the human body.

From the consumer protection standpoint we may well ask two serious questions:

(1) What percentage of the population must suffer an allergic response to a substance before its presence should be declared on packaged food labels? How much higher should the percentage of sufferers be, and/or how much more intense the effects, before the substance or food containing it is forbidden entirely?

(2) If severe allergic reactions are suffered by a few, are less severe, subclinical effects suffered by many? Might they be chronic or accumulative, so that clinical manifestations are apparent only after long and continuous usage, or the manifestation is demonstrable only by a shorter life span?

The insidious and complex nature of some of the naturally occurring toxicants and their effects can be illustrated by "the great potato debate." Although a number of researchers demonstrated a high correlation between consumption of potatoes infected with a fungus disease called Late Blight *(Phytophthora infestans)* and the incidence of certain very serious (teratogenic) birth defects, there is not only disagreement as to whether the teratogenicity is caused by the invading fungus, or by certain antibodies created by the growing potato tuber to counteract the infection. If the latter theory proves to be correct, is it not possible that all potatoes that are resistant to attack by this particular fungus are resistant because they contain as part of their germ plasm the ability to produce the teratogenic substance? Obviously mothers, particularly in the first few months of child bearing, should avoid blighted potatoes; but if the second theory is correct, perhaps they should avoid all potatoes that show resistance to this fungus. At this time official advice in the U.S. is that "we see no need to alert consumers against eating damaged potatoes. . . because we have no solid evidence of the relationship between damaged potatoes and congenital malformations." The FDA adds that it has consistently warned consumers against eating damaged food products of any kind, and that this agency will step in "if it is determined that a hazardous substance is associated with blighted potatoes."

Perhaps the ultimate advice comes from none other than Dr. James H. Renwick of the London School of Hygiene and Tropical Medicine, who started the great potato debate, with a letter to *Lancet* addressed "to a husband. . . Before you pregnate her, get right on the ball, imperfect potater makes monsters *et al.*, then show her the data how risks are not small, to save regrets later in babes hospital, advise and berate her first month with the call, potater first rater or no spud at all."

If blighted potatoes are subjects of debate because "we have no solid evidence of the relationship between damaged potatoes and congenital malformations," there has been abundant evidence for over two centuries that the bean *Lathyrus sativus* (also known as black pea, or khesakidal in India), when consumed in quantity, causes a nervous disease, affecting especially young men between the ages of 15 and 45. The disease has been found wherever the plant grows, from India to Southern Russia and the Mediterranean area, and it has occurred time and again in epidemic proportions during years of drought when other crops failed. Even now there are areas in central India where the entire male population is crippled by this disease, which can be easily prevented either by not eating the bean or by peeling the skins, boiling for several hours, and discarding the water.

This procedure removes most of the toxic substance (or substances), one of which was identified in 1963. Even then, the use of the bean was not forbidden, but several state governments in India have imposed restrictions on interstate movement. Additional work now in progress should soon provide a rapid and simple method for the detection of this seed in seed mixtures. Geneticists in India are also attempting to "breed out" most if not all of the toxin, so that a low-toxin or toxin-free variety may be used for cultivation in areas where *Lathyrus* cultivation is already in vogue.

Such hazards are summarized by Kehr (1973) in the following statement: "Many plants and animals that man uses for food contain as natural constituents chemical substances known to have toxic properties. Others have produced toxic effects, but the substances responsible are unknown. . . . Man has learned to avoid dangerous exposure to natural chemical components of his foods, but under some conditions the food may be more toxic than anticipated, or man may through ignorance or carelessness misuse the food. Thus, though acute poisoning is usually avoided, it is not invariably so. The public health significance associated with the naturally occurring toxicants in the food supply is to be sought . . . . primarily in the realm of chronic toxicity."

It appears, therefore, that many foods that we have taken for granted as being perfectly safe and nutritious may under given circumstances be most hazardous. Since we know less about the chemical makeup and toxicology of our natural food sources than we know about additives and residues, should not more attention be given to these supposedly safe natural foods, instead of exhaustively testing and re-testing safety of additives, about which much more is known? The National Academy of Sciences Food Protection Committee does not recommend diversion of attention from safety of additives to safety of natural foods. It is suggested, however, that consideration should be given to the additional potential problems that might arise from the simultaneous presence and consequent chemical and toxicological interactions of these two groups of materials. "As far as man's food intake is concerned, our ultimate goal is to achieve a knowledge not only what, under various circumstances, constitutes the ultimate in nutritional content, but also of what involves the minimum of long-range toxicologic hazards in the diet" (N.A.S.N.R.C. 1966).

SENSORY QUALITY—DO YOU LIKE IT?

Voluntary Standards

The most important consumer protection is provided by the consumer himself by his selection of the items he purchases, and by means of regulations which either he or his representatives impose. In our democratic society, where the "customer is always right," the quality of all commodities, including food, is geared to the satisfaction of the customer. The consumer then protects himself by purchasing only those items which are most attractive at the lowest price obtainable. Every food supplier, therefore, attempts to provide the consumer with products that have greater appeal at a lower price than those of a competitive manufacturer. This appeal, of course, is based on sensory attributes of quality—namely, appearance of the product, and how it feels, tastes, and smells. It also includes any convenience or incidental services offered. A consumer may wish to purchase a ready-to-serve sliced bread or a carton of orange juice instead of the ingredients that would go into bread or into juice that he would produce himself, although he might prefer the quality of the latter. He would be even more inclined to buy a manufactured food instead of raw ingredients if it turned out to be less expensive. He might also be willing to sacrifice some degree of sensory quality and perhaps also pay more for the manufactured product, simply to gain the convenience in labor saving.

The consumer may sometimes elect to purchase a product he would not otherwise buy because in addition to the food item he may also receive a prize, or a chance for a prize. In such instances he is knowingly gambling that the prize is worth more than the difference in cost and quality of a similar item without the prize.

Thus, consumer protection against sensory or convenience inadequacies are primarily matters of direct concern between the food manufacturer and the consumer, and little, if any, regulation is required from government agencies. Whatever regulations of this kind are provided are usually voluntary—that is, they may or may not be used in the channels of trade. Whenever they are used, the food manufacturer obligates himself to meet the standards, and the consumer, theoretically, if not in fact, knows the sensory and convenience qualities of the food at time of purchase, in advance of actual consumption.

Mandatory Standards

In some countries, sensory quality is completely subject to the adage: "Let the buyer beware." In the U.S. and in other countries, there are some standards of sensory quality that are mandatory. These are usually applied to processed foods, particularly when the consumer has no opportunity of seeing what is in the container prior to purchase. For example, there is no restriction against purchasing fresh, wormy apples. However, there are very strict regulations against the presence of worm and insect fragments in processed apples or apple products.

Considering such greatly increased and stringently controlled regulations on processed foods, why should the food supplier bother to provide them? Traditionally, a commodity is grown, harvested, and marketed locally. As long as such a production and marketing operation remains profitable, production increases until the local market is saturated and profitability diminishes. Then, either production of the commodity dwindles, or new profitable markets are found to absorb the increased production. Expanded markets for seasonal commodities can be obtained by extending the season during which the commodity can be offered for sale and/or reach new and farther markets. To accomplish this goal by either of the above means, an extension of the shelf life by one form of processing or another is required. At this stage, it is often found that neither the particular variety used nor the methods of cultivation and harvesting, are satisfactory to provide a product which is acceptable in the new markets. Thus substantial genetic, cultural, technical-mechanical research is required to develop appropriate varieties and methods for their production as "processed" products. But even such a research program seldom yields a variety that is ideally suited for marketing as a processed product, which ripens into entirely uniform shape at a satisfactory level of quality in every sensory category.

It is for such reasons that some mandatory standards of quality need to be enacted and enforced for the benefit of the consumer. Products that are sealed and hidden in containers cannot be evaluated for their sensory attributes (that is, "taste-tested") by the buyer at the time of purchase.

With the few exceptions noted above, mandatory standards that are promulgated for the benefit of the consumer consist of quantity and identity, and especially wholesomeness, to assure the buyer that he is getting what he pays for, and that the foods will be safe.

WHO PROTECTS THE CONSUMER?

During the rise in "consumerism," there was the impression that the general buying public was at the mercy of profit-grabbing industrialists until Ralph Nader came along. For instance, the *Washington Post* stated that Nader was "responsible for the fact that there are now more than 1000 federal government consumer programs in operation. At the state and local level, 23 states currently offer consumer protection departments; 39 consumer fraud units, and more than 50 cities boast other agencies designed to protect the consumer. Nader came upon the scene at the time when big business, protected by big government, was foisting upon the buying public a variety of shoddy products and services. Working within the system, Nader proved wrongs could be righted, that the price of good government and honest capitalism is eternal vigilance. . . . Nader has remained untouched, . . . Mr. Clean. . . by recruiting American youth into his various programs, he is ensuring some continuity of his purpose, to keep U.S. business and government honest, no easy job in the highly competitive jungle of American society."[1]

The above highly exaggerated, though basically correct statement, points to the fact that the consumer gets what he wants, which is not necessarily what he needs, and he gets the protection he needs only when he demands it. For decades, dedicated food scientists in government and industry have been concerned about the lack of interest of consumers and their representatives in promulgating laws and regulations regarding food safety and quality. As a result of the ferment, consumers and consumer advocates are now actively participating in these activities, instead of leaving food regulations and their enforcement entirely in the hands of government and the food industry.

Our government, in 1978 supported (perhaps too violently) by Nader *et al.*, failed in a first attempt to form a federal department for consumer affairs by a narrow margin. While the tide of consumer activism appears to be ebbing at this moment, additional acts and regulations are continuously being promulgated in the name of consumer protection which

---

[1] *The Washington Post,* March 25, 1973.

may or may not improve the safety and quality of the food supply. They do, however, increase food costs, and occasionally result in conflicting requirements which cannot be met entirely by a food manufacturer, regardless of the seriousness of his intentions to conform to all requirements.

Long before Nader arrived on the scene—in fact, long before he was born—there was in this country a substantial network of government and consumer organizations looking out for the welfare of the consumer. The first federal food inspection act was passed by the Congress in 1890, providing for inspection of meat for export by the USDA. The Pure Food and Drug Law and the Meat Inspection Act came into being in 1906. These laws have been amended and revised continually. At least one act, the Filled Milk Act of 1923, which precludes the substitution of any fat or oil for milk fat in milk or cream, was found to be unconstitutional and was revoked in 1972. The Consumer Product Safety Act signed into law in 1972, hailed by Jensen and Folkes (1973) as heralding "a new era in consumer safety," has little effect on consumer protection of food, which remains with the FDA.

Consumer organizations which act entirely independently of government support have also existed for a long time. The most important of these, Consumers Union, has been quite effective in reporting to its one million subscribers, on best, good, poor, and unsafe, products of all kinds. Total income is from membership dues; no advertising is accepted. From the standpoint of food protection, the major limitations to the impact of consumer organizations are : (1) their influence is largely limited to their membership which consists mostly of professionals who are the last to require this service, and (2) even members are more likely to consult *Consumer Reports* and similar publications for large items such as major appliances, or automobiles, rather than for individual food items of relatively low cost per unit; therefore differences which are reported in prices and quality of food items tend to be ignored.

The Federal Food and Drug Law

The basic statute of the U.S. Food and Drug Law is the Federal Food, Drug and Cosmetic Act of 1938, as amended. The basic purpose of the act was to prohibit the movement in interstate commerce of adulterated and misbranded food, drugs, devices, and cosmetics. This act succeeded the original act of 1906, to which Dr. Harvey W. Wiley was chief contributor and first administrator. The act applies to all foods, beverages, drugs, and cosmetics intended for use by man or domestic animal, and to all components of such products.

Its regulations are mandatory, since they can be enforced by seizure and injunction proceedings in the federal courts. The act authorized its administrator to promulgate regulations for its efficient enforcement, to make enforcement inspections of food establishments and their records, to collect and examine enforcement samples, and to make enforcement publications. In subsequent amendments, such as Public Law 83-518, the Miller Pesticide Residue Amendment to the Act in 1954, the administrator was authorized to establish general safety controls on residues of pesticide chemicals used in the production of raw agricultural commodities. The food regulations under the act may be summarized as follows:

(1) Establishment of reasonable standards of identity, quality, and fill of container for any food (with a few exceptions); conformance to these standards of identity at all times; and label declaration of substandard quality or fill in the event that the food falls below these standards.

(2) Condemnation of any food (a) that has been manufactured or stored under unsanitary conditions whereby it may have been contaminated with filth or rendered injurious to health; (b) that is unfit for human consumption; (c) that contains a natural or added poisonous or deleterious substance which may render it dangerous to health; (d) that contains a coal-tar color which has not been certified as harmless; (e) that has a deceptive composition; and (f) condemnation of any food container that has a poisonous or deleterious composition which may render the contents injurious to health.

(3) Prohibition of any imitation food unless it is so labeled; and any food offered for sale under the name of another food.

(4) Requirement that any food label shall not be false or misleading in any particular; and prohibition of any food container that is so made or formed or filled as to be misleading.

(5) Requirement that any packaged food shall bear a label containing the name and business address of its manufacturer or distributor and a statement of its net weight or measure or numerical count; that a food without identity standard shall be labeled with its own name and if consisting of two or more ingredients, with the name of each ingredient (with certain exceptions). Except for a few specific cases, any food containing artificial flavoring, artificial coloring, or any chemical preservative is required to be labeled to show that fact. Foods represented as or purporting to have special dietary properties are required to be labeled in conformity with prevailing regulations.

There are some 200 commodities covered by standards of identity which specify in detail what can and what cannot be packaged under the name of the commodity. Products for which there are no standards of identity still fall under the general provisions of the act, but their manufacture leaves some room for variations. Lists of standards showing what substances may be added to standardized food without label declaration, as well as chemical pesticides with the tolerance levels, are available from the FDA, trade associations, and other interested groups.

Regulations under the act are constantly being revised and expanded, so that it is imperative for the food processor to know how old or new provisions apply to his business. Such detailed requirements may be obtained from the FDA, or from trade associations who usually keep close contact with FDA activities in order to inform their members. Analytical procedures used by FDA are included in the Association of Official Analytical Chemists' volume on Methods of Analysis, updated and revised every 5 years.

No new provisions are recommended by FDA unless there seems to be an urgent need for them. New provisions or modifications may be requested by any interested group or by the FDA itself. Following a thorough investigation, FDA may by order grant the request, or deny it. This order is published in the *Federal Register*, and if there are no objections, the order stands as a part of the regulations. If there is an objection, then all interested parties participate in a hearing conducted under judicial-like proceedings and the findings of fact in such hearings then determine the action taken. Individuals, firms, and trade associations are always in a position to contest any action of the FDA through the federal courts.

FDA standards are usually minimal requirements which may be substantially below buyer specifications. Standards of quality and fill of container, in fact, differentiate between the standard and sub-standard quality level only so that additional grades and standards are needed to determine high levels of quality.

In general, FDA supervision and regulation of the food industry has been and can be most helpful to the legitimate food processor. A visit from a Food and Drug inspector should be considered as an opportunity to review together the adequacy of the sanitary conditions and quality control methods employed. Any suggestions made by him on changes and improvements should be given serious consideration, since they come from one experienced with what is needed to operate under the act with confidence. Any questions that arise between inspections, or in connection with the initiation of a new line or the manufacture of a new product, may be directed to FDA, or to the respective trade association, which is probably in day-to-day contact with FDA. The federal Food and Drug law applies only to articles in interstate commerce; however, most states have either adopted the law *in toto*, or have similar regulations covering foods that do not cross state lines.

In recent years, FDA activities have changed and expanded, largely because of the new support gained from consumer groups. From 1970 to 1980 the FDA budget rose from under $100,000,000 to close to $325,000,000 and from less than 4000 employees to more than 7600. Although much of the recent effort has been devoted to "building up. . . the inspection staff," the agency today is stronger in terms of scientific knowledge. The decisions that must be made every day are based on the best available scientific and technological evidence. It is always possible that new evidence may develop that would make an earlier decision seem unwise or against the best interests of the consumer. More than ever before, FDA is listening to consumers and to consumer advocates. FDA now meets regularly on a monthly basis with leaders of consumer groups. Within the last few years, therefore, there has developed a situation where consumers are actively participating in decisions regarding food protection. At the same time they are becoming educated to the extremely complex nature of matters on which the decisions must be made.

FDA activities are also moving, we believe in the right direction, to a greater concentration on problems of food safety and nutritive value, without reducing concern for sensory quality or economic considerations. A major current activity is a review of all food additives now on the GRAS (generally recognized as safe) list. This is a very substantial and worthwhile undertaking, since many items are on the list only because of the "grandfather clause"—that is, certain substances that were used many years ago did not appear to be harmful, and thus were automatically put on the GRAS list. It is now recognized that, with the very extensive testing performed before a new additive is permitted for use in food some of these substances would never have been allowed in the first place. But to second-guess FDA, we question the review of the entire list. Certainly it would be of little value to study further materials that have been exhaustively evaluated within recent years. Also, there should be some epidemiological data before a particular food additive, or a food itself for that matter, should be re-investigated. The relationship between cigarette smoking and lung cancer is a case in point. Only after rather substantial and conclusive epidemiological evidence had been gathered was it possible to do something—not to prohibit the sale of cigarettes, but just to reduce opporunities for advertising.

Epidemiological evidence indicating a relationship between intake of saturated fats and build-up of cholesterol and heart disease was not considered sufficiently conclusive to forbid, or even discourage, the use of saturated fats. Thus FDA did not permit the advertising of foods for low saturated fat and high unsaturated fat content, or low cholesterol content, until very recent times, largely because of consumer pressures. As stated previously in this chapter, present FDA attitude toward the great potato controversy is that there are insufficient data to deny or even alert the public against eating potatoes that may have been infected with late blight, or have developed antibodies that caused the potatoes to be resistant to late blight.

It would seem to us that this is the major remaining weakness of FDA. FDA is now in a relatively stable period. It keeps on top of most scientific developments and reacts appropriately when the time comes.

FDA, perhaps because of absence of funds, is not investigating on its own, or supporting research by qualified scientists, on such problems as the potato controversy, or saturation of fats, or determining just what is the deleterious substance in coffee. Instead, it is embarking on a rerun of GRAS list items, most of which had been thoroughly investigated previously.

Enforcement

Laws, acts, and regulations are apparently necessary in "this age of the lawyer." But all such rules are worthless if they are not acted upon and enforced. Many countries have based regulations on the U.S. Food, Drug and Cosmetic Act, making local alterations which should have made the regulations more applicable and enforceable, but enforcement has been sporadic at best. The American consumer, however, is getting good value for his tax dollar from the Food and Drug Administration. There is practically no facet of the food industry that has not been substantially influenced by Food and Drug personnel in the direction of improving sanitation in the processing and transportation procedures. In some instances, improvements were so far-reaching that the original operation could not be recognized. Usually such changes were made without forcing the manufacturer out of business, but rather by working with him on a gradual basis to improve his operation so that it was far superior to the average, and equal to the best sanitary techniques used in the home.

The Food, Drug and Cosmetic Act may also be modified by Congress. At this time there is a modification to the act in the House of Representatives which is intended to clarify certain requirements, and also to enable mandatory or mandatory/voluntary guidelines for open-dating. Similar legislation which would require open-dating in the form of "pack date," or "use by date" is also under consideration in the Senate.

Other Mandatory Standards

Food and Drug activities are closely integrated with federal and local public health authorities who do much of the regulation of milk, dairy, and meat products.

Slaughter of meat for interstate distribution must be done under the continuous inspection of the Meat Inspection Division of the USDA. Veterinarians of this division inspect each carcass for wholesomeness, freedom from disease, and also for quality. This activity is being transferred to state agricultural or health authorities as state organizations demonstrate their competence to perform this service.

There are many specific mandatory standards issued by individual states or more local authorities covering the shipment of particular commodities. Examples of minimum state standards are the Arizona and California requirements governing the marketing of many principal fresh fruits and vegetables. The state of Florida does not permit the shipment of fresh oranges unless they meet minimum requirements. Similarly, the state of Maryland does not permit the shipment of cantaloupes unless they contain a minimum level of soluble solids of 8%. Information on such regulations, too, may be obtained from local authorities, or from trade or growers associations.

U.S. Department of Agriculture (A.M.S.) Standards

In contrast to Food and Drug standards, which are mandatory, grades and standards of quality established by the Agricultural Marketing Service of the USDA, are voluntary in nature. Any person in the food industry may use them only if he so wishes.

These voluntary standards have usually been set in cooperation with interested trade groups such as growers, processors, packers, handlers, wholesalers, and retailers. They cover practically all important fresh and processed fruits and vegetables. Some standards which have been developed for poultry products, dairy products, and meats, are now mandatory. The Marine Fisheries Service, of the National Oceanic & Atmospheric Administration (Dept. of Commerce) has established similar standards for a number of seafoods. Details of the procedures are available from the respective agencies.

Standards for grades are designed to aid processors in packing better and more uniform quality products. They also enable processors, distributors, and retailers to market their products in a more orderly and efficient manner; to aid loan agencies in arriving at equitable loan values; to assist in adjustment of damage claims; and to permit inspection and certification as to quality, condition, and grade by federal, federal-state, or state inspection services.

The Standardization and Inspection branches of the Agricultural Marketing Service, USDA, are actually service organizations. They are responsible for two main activities. One is development of grade-standards, and the other is making inspection service available to industry. The voluntary inspection-grading activities are essentially self-sustaining that is, fees are charged to cover cost of rendering the service.

The functions performed by these branches of USDA are authorized under the Agricultural Marketing Act of 1946, as amended. The inspection service activities are conducted under regulations issued pursuant to the act by the Secretary of Agriculture. These regulations describe the conditions under which inspection and certification may be made, including sampling procedures, sanitary requirements for processing plants that operate under USDA continuous inspection, and the fees charged for the service. They also describe the conditions under which official identification marks may be used.

The act also provides that any official certificate issued under it shall be received by all officials and all federal courts in the United States as *prima facie* evidence of the truth of the statements therein contained. Nearly all states have similar laws, which require state courts to receive these certificates as *prima facie* evidence.

Among other things, the act provides criminal penalties for intentionally altering inspection certificates or misusing offical marks. Any processor operating under USDA continuous inspection, or distributor of the products packed under this type of inspection, who wishes to use official identification marks—that is, the Department Shield, "U.S." grade statement, and continuous inspection legend—on their labels or to advertise with reference to continuous inspection should submit proofs of such labels or advertising material for approval before such materials are printed. This may be done through a local field inspection office in the area or direct to the main office in Washington, D.C.

Presently, there have been developed grade-standards for 146 different processed fruits and vegetables and related processed foods. These standards were developed with the cooperation of industry, and every effort was made to have them reflect good commercial practice and to have old standards revised when necessary. Standards are developed and revised by the following procedure: (1) Agricultural Marketing Service specialists first make a thorough study of the product. Samples are selected from a broad range of quality from products processed under varying conditions and from differing qualities of raw produce. (2) After studying the samples, as well as information provided by the industry, the specialists draw up a preliminary draft of the standard for discussion with interested groups. (3) A tentative standard is then published in the *Federal Register*, and a press release issued to interested trade papers. Except in rare instances where an emergency makes immediate action imperative, interested parties are invited to study the proposal and submit their views. (4) After all comments have been carefully considered, the standard, now in final form, is published once again in the *Federal Register*, along with the date on which it will become effective. A press release also goes to the trade journals. The detailed standard is then printed in a handy leaflet, and thousands of copies are distributed without charge to those who request them.

Scoring System for U.S. Grade-standards

These grade-standards are usually set up on a 100-score basis, a certain portion of the total score being assigned to each of a number of factors. For example, the U.S. grade for orange juice assigns 40 points to the defects factor, 20 points to color, and 40 points to flavor, for a possible total of 100. For tomato juice, on the other hand, the factor of defects is assigned only 15 points with 30 for color, 40 for flavor, and 15 for consistency. In general, a total score of 90 to 100 indicates top grade (A), 80 to 89 intermediate grade (B), and 70 to 79 the standard grade (C), although these may vary considerably for individual products. There is also a limiting rule for some of the important factors, which means that even though a sample scores 90 or better, if a single factor is sufficiently poor, the grade must still be reduced.

Under the continuous-inspection system, a Federal inspector (or inspectors) is stationed in the plant at all times when raw material preparation and processing are going on. He checks the plant and equipment for sanitation and keeps constant watch on the quality of the raw materials being used. Samples are collected and examined throughout the production period for quality and grade or specification requirements. The inspector prepares a daily report for the plant management, summarizing his observations and including a probable grade for each lot packed. When inspection of the finished product is completed and upon request of the processor, he issues certificates showing the final grade of each lot packed.

In the case of processed fruits and vegetables, more than half the inspection (volume-wise) is done on a continuous basis. Processors using this type of inspection service may, if they choose, label their product with its U.S. grade as well as the continuous-inspection statement, provided all requirements of the inspection agreement and Department Regulations are met. If they pack a product for which there is no U.S. grade, they may use the continuous-inspection statement provided the product is one of good quality as determined by the USDA.

Industry Standards

Mandatory government regulations must be complied with, and must therefore be part of a quality control system in any food operation. Voluntary government and trade grades and standards may also be indispensable at times, and useful at other times. Yet, although such "ready-made" standards and procedures may be applicable in that they reflect consumer desires, there are many situations where certain trade groups and individual food manufacturers have developed their own standards. This was found to be desirable in cases where government standards were inadequate or too dependent on the inspector's personal evaluation, or because of a difference in philosophy or emphasis.

A case in point is the descriptive labeling program of the National Canners Association[1] (1960). Under this program, the association has endeavored to develop designated terms based as much as possible on objective, physical-chemical measurements, the different grades being defined as specifications, without implying that one grade level is necessarily better or poorer than another. Thus, rather than grade by letter, with the implication that grade A is better than B, etc., or by number, the specifications speak for themselves, and the consumer may select the product he prefers. For example, peas that would be graded B by the U.S. grading procedure would simply be labeled young, medium-sized peas, "young" being further defined as consisting of not less than 10% and not more than 13% alcohol-insoluble solids, and "medium size" indicating peas of 11/32 to 12/32 in. diam. Grade A peas would probably be labeled very young, small size, "very young" being defined as containing less than 10% alcohol-insoluble solids, and small size as not more than 10/32 in. diam. There is no implication that the very young, small peas are necessarily better than the young, medium-sized peas.

The buyer's specific requirements are the key to the particular standards and grading procedures to be employed in any given situation. If the buyer demands a U.S. grade certificate, then obviously U.S. grades and standards should be used. On the other hand, if a buyer's specifications are different, the packer may or may not be able to use the U.S. standards to advantage. Superimposed on the peculiarities and idiosyncrasies of buyer's requirements are the endless variations of each plant operation, which lead to special and unique variations in grading and standards to fit the specific buyer's and processor's conditions.

CONSUMER PROTECTION—AT WHAT PRICE?

Sooner or later the consumer, consumer advocate, as well as the lawyer, judge, and jury, must recognize that consumer protection from foods that

---

[1] Now known as the National Food Processors Association.

may be injurious (economically or healthwise) is, like everything else, a game of chance. The greater the protection, the lower the risk. After all, we recognize this situation in everything else we do on this earth—why not in the food we eat? We accept thousands of fatalities from automobile accidents and hundreds of thousands of injuries annually, and do nothing to abolish the automobile. True, the automobile industry is only approximately half the size of the food industry. Still, if we should be satisifed with an injury or safety level existing in connection with the use of automobiles, we do not need nearly as much consumer protection for food as we now have.

With the total value of the foods and food services we purchase annually approaching $200 billion, we can assume that the protection the consumer now receives by way of government inspection and control costs approximately 1% of this amount. It may be estimated that the quality control efforts of the food industry itself amount to at least another 1%. This would mean, therefore, that the present costs of assuring safety, quality, quantity (and now nutritive value and freshness, i.e., open dating) of our food supply costs us about $4 billion per year. Since there are very few fatalities directly attributable to processed foods, it may be assumed that doubling this cost, which would raise food costs by another 2—3%, may, perhaps, save one life a year. It should be understood that it is practically impossible to make the food supply absolutely safe, regardless of how much is spent, because of consumers' negligence, if for no other reason. Does this mean that we should not do more to protect the safety of our foods? Not necessarily. Although little further benefit would accrue if we should increase the level of inspection by government and industry, we can certainly do much more in the research and education areas. Although we know (or think we know) all the nutritional requirements of man, and are well-informed about what substances cause immediate ill effects, we still know very little about many of our foods and food ingredients in relation to possible long-term chronic effects. Certainly this nation can afford to invest 0.1% of what is spends on food to investigate not only additives but also naturally occurring toxicants in foods we commonly eat. We now have definite knowledge of some foods which cripple and cause early death in entire populations. We suspect quite a few more, but have we done as much as we should do to come up with some definite answers about many questions regarding possible chronic illnesses and shortening of life due to natural foods? Without a substantial input of additional research funds, controversies such as the great potato argument can go on endlessly. If another few hundred million a year were to be provided we could have definite answers to such questions as to whether, or under what conditions, saturated or unsaturated fats shorten the life span, and why some people or groups of people are old before they reach 40, while others are vigorous and virile up to 90 or even 100. Funds for such research of immense value to the consumer would be readily provided as soon as consumers indicate their desire for such research. Thus far many consumer advocates have been strangely silent about such matters and are concerning themselves more about what the consumer wants, rather than what he needs.

5

Food Codes and Habits

From Cannibalism
to Vegetarianism

Man is a creature of habit, and it should come as no surprise to anyone to read that much of man's dietary regime is also a matter of habit. Anyone who has traveled to other countries has observed instances of how these dietary habits may affect man's daily life. Indeed, much of the fascination of travel comes from tasting strange foods and experiencing novel customs of dining. But these food habits or codes, or taboos, go deeper than the eating of odd sandwiches in Denmark, raw herring in Amsterdam, or strange fruits in Asia. They are in many ways related to the whole development of civilization.

Before departing on our brief journey through gustatory history, however, we should remember that there is really more similarity than difference in all food habits, no matter how bizarre. The cannibal and the vegetarian, though at opposite poles of the food world, both eat essentially protein, fat, and carbohydrate. It is their packages that differ, not the contents.

ORIGINS OF FOOD HABITS

Man has inhabited the earth for one, perhaps several million years but we have written records for only the last 5000, or less than 1% of this time. Man's greatest achievements, the domestication of plants and animals, were realized before there were literary types to record the events. Thus we do not know how cabbages and kings first became associated. By the time written history began, all the common domestic animals and most of the plants were already well known, except those which were found in the Western hemisphere after 1492. They include among others, maize (which Americans call corn), the white potato, sweet potato, tomato, and tobacco. Although the latter is hardly a food, it is ingested in a food-like manner. Another American contribution to our diet, the turkey, was domesticated by the Aztec Indians and taken to Spain by the early explorers. It was called turkey because in some way it was confused with the African guinea fowl which had been imported to Europe via Turkey.

Modern man evolved from an omnivorous ancestor who discovered the arts of fire making and cooking. Pekin man, the earliest known ancestor of the genus *Homo* (according to some paleontologists), cooked his meat and ate just about anything he could capture, including many insects, small amphibians, and reptiles, as well as more familiar plants and larger animals. In southern Europe, where man lived for thousands of years in neolithic caves, he left a record of his diet in the debris, often as much as 40 ft deep (how's that for a waste disposal problem?), and in drawings (the original graffiti) on cave walls. It included large mammals as well as rodents, amphibians, reptiles, and insects. L.B. Jensen (1953) collected data on the vitamin content of some of these foods of primitive man and showed that our cave-dwelling ancestors enjoyed an ample supply of nutrients. Other students, however, now believe that the peculiar bone structures of the skulls of early men like the Neanderthals were actually due to a vitamin D-calcium imbalance, and that these early men were really members of the genus *Homo* like ourselves. The anatomical differences which caused early zoologists to classify them differently were the result of long ages spent in the reduced sunlight caused by the heavy clouds of the receding glaciers. Deprived of sunlight, they failed to synthesize or consume enough vitamin D for normal bone growth.

One food habit which seems especially distasteful to us, but which was evidently practiced by early man, was cannibalism. There are many theories to account for the rise of cannibalism, but we should be concerned more with explaining its persistence than its origin. By the time civilization advanced to late Stone Age culture, cannibalism was practiced more for ceremonial than nutritional purposes. The many accounts of early European travelers to North America which referred to the natives as cannibals were exaggerated opinions strengthened by a few genuine instances. The many authentic records of vast hordes of game birds and animals, make it clear that the pre-Columbian Americans did not depend on hunting each other for food, and even brief thought should convince one that it would hardly be economical for humans to decimate their own numbers by cannibalism. It was, however, a tribute to a brave enemy to eat him, because in so doing the eater was thought to absorb some of the slain enemy's bravery. Among the American Indians there was a reluctant tolerance shown toward persons who had been forced to eat their dead or dying comrades in an emergency, but there was universal acceptance of the eating of slain enemies after battles. These ceremonies were generally abandoned after contacts with Europeans and hardly occurred after about 1600.

Vegetarianism, at the other extreme of our food habits, is not a practice of ancient origin, but arose after farming became well established and where population density made meat economically difficult to obtain. It was also given religious significance, perhaps at first to make the poor more content with their meatless lot. It has never persisted long in any culture among the well-to-do, because it is difficult to maintain an adequate protein intake, properly balanced in amino acids, from vegetable sources.

DOMINANT INFLUENCES AND CONSTRAINTS

Nutritional—Economic Needs

Most food habits can be traced to either nutritional or economic conditions or, in the case of many modern food fads, to supposed nutritional needs. An example of how these forces operate may be seen in the long history of wheat culture and utilization. Early man domesticated several strains of wheat which he first ate as parched whole grains. In such a form any grain is only poorly digestible, so it was a significant accomplishment when the early Egyptians learned to grind wheat between stones and make flour. This allowed them to separate the chaff from the starch and protein and thus made it possible to discard some antimetabolites along with the chaff. They next learned how to ferment the wheat starch with yeasts, thus allowing them to make both bread and beer. By 2000 B.C. the Egyptians had professional millers, bakers and brewers. This technology affected the kinds of wheat grown, and specialized varieties for baking, or porridge, or stock feed were developed. This industrial knowledge of wheat was passed from the Egyptians to the Greeks and Romans and then spread over Europe, although in the Mediterranean lands the fermentation of grapes to produce wine rivaled and surpassed the brewing of beer. It has been claimed that no country colonized by the Romans gave up the eating of white bread or the drinking of wine. The Scandinavians, by contrast, became bakers of rye biscuits rather than of wheat bread.

So long as men depended on bread for a major part of both their protein and food energy, it was almost essential that they use partially refined flour; otherwise, they would consume too much roughage in proportion to their diet. For this reason refined flour came to be regarded as superior to unrefined; the more refined or whiter the flour, the better it seemed. In the process of refining, however many valuable nutrients were lost, especially minerals and B vitamins—a fact not well understood until the modern science of nutrition was developed. Now that high-quality protein sources, like eggs, meat, and milk are generally available, many people with some knowledge of nutrition become overly concerned about eating white bread, advocating a return to whole-wheat bread and even recommending that the wheat be "stone ground." Some extremists even feel that the flour will be more nutritious if the grinding stones are propelled by water power. The ancient Egyptians, or even Europeans of 200 years ago, who had to eat enough bread to provide about 2000 calories of energy per day, would have rebelled most strenuously at having to eat whole-wheat bread; but the modern food faddist who needs only two or three slices a day can relish the delectable qualities of brown bread.

Traditional-religious Constraints

As we have already stated, primitive man ate what he could find or capture in his immediate environment. With time, he learned to eat only those substances that did not obviously do him harm. Those substances which were harmful, or he thought were harmful, became taboo. New untried foods were also taboo unless there were no alternatives. In time the taboos hardened into codes of conduct and frequently sanctified as religious dogma.

In these enlightened days, we are inclined to attempt to rationalize these codes on the basis of our newly found knowledge of sanitation, nutrition, and toxicology. When we do this, we find certain practices appear to have a sound basis. Thus we can readily justify orthodox Jews banning pork now that we know about trichinosis, or some Mongol tribes' revulsion to the idea of drinking milk now that we know that as many as half of the Central and East Asiatic people suffer from lactase deficiency and therefore do not digest milk sugar.

However, when these taboos are studied objectively, one finds that usually they came about as a result of economic necessity rather than some intuitive knowledge of food values (Simoons 1961). The Jewish taboo against the use of pigs' flesh is readily explained on the basis of the fact that the ancient Jews who established the dogma were a nomadic people, and pigs are not a nomadic animal. Similarly, some Mongol tribes, relying heavily on the horse, consider mares' milk as a form of excretion suitable only for foals. When the Mongol became desperate he would drink mares' blood rather than milk.

Religious taboos may have been inspired also by a wish to differentiate among followers of different religions. Thus the Jews originally forbade the use not only of the pig, but also the camel for meat. Those Jews who became the first Christians removed this taboo, perhaps for no other reason than to convert the heathen. Centuries later, Mohammed, apparently in an attempt to distinguish his followers from Jews, did not forbid the eating of camel flesh, but did prohibit pork and alcoholic beverages to distinguish Moslem from Christian. The Jews in turn added substantially to their codes of behavior, including food usage, after the destruction of the second Temple purposely "to make a fence around the Torah" in a desperate effort to maintain their identity as a people even without the existence of a secular state. The many admirable sanitary regulations were added gradually and were not codified until the 13th century by Maimonides, one of the great physician-scholars of the enlightened Arab-Mediterranean period while Europe was in the grip of the dark Medieval Age.

Religious prohibition of all animal food, that is, vegetarianism, is very difficult to explain on a rational basis, and it must be explained on the basis of belief in the sanctity of animal life (Simoons 1961). This ancient belief, generally prevailing in India, has had adherents from time to time elsewhere, and is one of the basic practices of one of the most recent religions—that of the Seventh Day Adventists. The relationship between this religious sect and the founding of the two breakfast cereal giants of the food industry is described in a very readable fashion by Deutsch (1961). It is therefore most interesting to observe that the foods developed by Post and Kellogg, both dedicated, profoundly religious men, are now under severe attack by consumer advocates. Of course the science of food nutrition was just beginning when these men made their contributions, and the claims made then regarding the contribution to health and nutrition of these vegetarian foods simply would not hold up now.

Cultural-ethnic Constraints

Cultural-ethnic constraints differ from the religious constraints in that they involve few dogmatic prohibitions, so that ethnic foods spread from one geographic area to another more readily. In fact, there are more similarities than differences within types of food in different regions. Thus the Far Eastern chapati, the Middle Eastern pitta, and the European pizza are not only similar in kind, but even in name. The Mexican tortilla is similar, though the name is different. The Chinese eggroll, the European blintz and the Mexican enchilada are essentially the same. There are many more essential similarities. The differences are in the seasoning and other additives which depend on their availability in various locales.

With no dogmatic prohibitions against their use, ethnic foods tend to become widely adopted rapidly, particularly in melting-pot populations such as exist in the United States. In fact, the major sources of new prepared food items are the ethnic foods, many of which are quickly adopted by the population as a whole.

Neo-environmental Constraints

Neo-environmental constraints operate in two ways. By exploiting the highly conservative tendency of reverting to "the good old days," they give rise to movements such as organic foods. When coupled with partial information and misinformation on nutrition, the result is natural health foods. Such movements are likely to diminish simply because we can't afford such luxuries.

The other side of the neo-environmental coin is the use of wastes as foods, and in general the short cutting and improvement in the efficiency of the natural recycling system. But more about these foods of the future in Chapter 10. At this time we will simply point to the strange fact that some of these synthetic foods, such as soy and other protein derivatives, are highly favored by food faddists, while other synthetic foods such as vitamins are not acceptable.

Habit-forming Beverages

The most persistent food habits are those which have some physiological basis. Coffee and tea are good examples. Evidently tea was first used for its ability to add flavor to water and even to disguise or hide some naturally occurring unpleasant flavors. But the physiological effects of the caffeine it contains soon made it more a necessity than a luxury. Tea was known about 2700 B.C. in China and had become the favorite drink of Japan, India, China, and most of Eastern Asia by the beginning of our era. It was brought to Europe by Dutch traders in 1610 and spread rapidly through the rest of the world, even playing a celebrated role in the American revolution. Coffee is of more recent origin, but since it provides more caffeine in solution, its spread was more rapid. Coffee was developed as a beverage by Moslems in the 16th century as a substitute for wine, which they were forbidden to drink. This substitution was reasonably successful, and today there is an effort in some countries to get people to drink coffee or cola drinks (which contain caffeine) in preference to alcohol as a means of countering alcoholism.

Alcoholic beverages are of great antiquity, and universally known for their tenacious hold on men's appetites. Beer was brewed by the prehistoric wheat growers and must have been one of their early discoveries. Wine was produced in Asia Minor, and viticulture spread all around the Mediterranean basin before the beginning of recorded history. Mead (fermented honey) may be of even greater antiquity than wine, according to the ancient Greeks who wrote that it was used before the discovery of wine. Other primitive peoples prepared fermented beverages from various carbohydrate sources. The only people not known to use alcoholic beverages were the American Indians. Wine early enjoyed the official sanction of organized religion and thus it occupies a very special place in the history of ritual. All the great poets from Homer to modern times have celebrated its glories, and wine stands supreme as a special symbol to be employed on all formal or festive occasions. Sometime around 1400 the practice of distilling wine to produce brandy and a beer-like mash to produce whiskey was begun. The higher alcoholic content of these beverages and their counterparts like aquavit, gin, and vodka (as well as others) gives them a much stronger physiological hold over their users. Indeed, the application of distillation to the production of alcoholic beverages might be compared to a lethal mutation in genetics, as a sort of self-destroying development of technology. Nevertheless, they are not without redeeming features.

Cocoa, another popular beverage, and its homologue chocolate, were developed in the Western Hemisphere by the Aztecs, and the Spaniards took them back to Europe. Like tea and coffee they are sources of caffeine and owe their popularity, at least in part, to their physiological activity. Unlike tea and coffee, both cocoa and chocolate have some food value—chocolate quite a bit—because of the cocoa butter they contain.

A large number of beverages are based on extracts of the kola nut and also owe their habituating qualities to the presence of caffeine. Finally there is the large group of "soft drinks," which have no physiological action other than their supply of quickly available energy in the form of dissolved sugar. Thus nearly all the beverages to which man is habituated contain either alcohol, caffeine, or sugar, and, of course, in many instances, both sugar and caffeine.

OTHER INFLUENCES

Fads

While the general evolutionary influences described above affected man's habits with respect to his meat and drink, smaller but nonetheless powerful forces also influenced his adoption of food fads and preferences. We have reviewed some of the religious codes which govern diets, and indicated that any label declarations claiming conformance to any such codes are enforceable by law. Such religious constraints often remain as well-ingrained food habits, even after the original theological reasoning has changed, such as eating fish rather than red meat on Friday. Many foods are avoided because they are supposed to be poisonous, even though that may not be the case. Tomatoes were regarded as inedible until rather recent times, possibly because many other plants of the same botanic family, the Solanaceae, do produce harmful alkaloids. Since potatoes also belong to the Solanaceae, the logic was rather weak. Unlike the tomato, other salad greens like lettuce, endive, watercress, and celery were highly regarded by the ancients for their reputed medicinal properties, and their daily consumption by many Americans in the 20th century may well be the result of habits formed among the Greeks and Romans.

The belief that certain foods have a distinct beneficial effect is an important originator of food habits and of many food fads. In the 1920s many Americans were eating a cake of yeast each day because of its beneficial qualities. While this yeast was certainly an excellent source of B vitamins, the habit of eating it did not become well established, probably because of its unpleasant taste and the early availability of other, more palatable, sources of B vitamins.

In establishing a food habit it is not always important that the beneficial qualities actually exist, but only that they be thought to exist. This is well illustrated by the present-day cultists who advocate the eating of honey, blackstrap molasses, or raw sugar because of somewhat mystical qualities they are said to contain. While they do have a higher mineral content than ordinary granulated sugar, their lack of genuine physiological activity indicates that we are not likely to become habituated to their use.

Organic and Other Health(?) Foods

Another modern enthusiasm is the cult of "organic foods"—as if there were some kind of inorganic and inferior foods, which they can supplant. At the risk of belaboring the obvious, we will repeat the facts for the benefit of those who have never been exposed to the facts of chemistry.

All chemical compounds are arbitrarily divided into two classes, organic and inorganic. The organic compounds are compounds of carbon, and these make up most of the tissues of plants and animals. Organic compounds contain elements like nitrogen, oxygen, hydrogen, and many metals in combination with carbon. In the scheme of nature it is the function of plants to convert inorganic compounds (carbon dioxide and water) in the soil and air into organic compounds (sugars). Plants can metabolize inorganic food but animals (including humans) cannot, with the exception of water and very minute amounts of metals and salts.

All dead organic matter is broken down into its elements by soil bacteria and plants absorb the inorganic constituents. When organic fertilizers like manure and fish meal are used in gardening, they must be converted into inorganic consitutents in the soil before they can be utilized by plants. When the plant absorbs potassium and phosphorus from the soil it makes no difference whatsoever whether they were originally supplied as inorganic minerals or as bone meal, manure, and wood ashes; it is only important that they be available. Nitrogen is the element that is the essential constituent of amino acids and proteins, and hence is vital for all nutrition of both plants and animals. Though it is plentifully available in the air, it cannot be utilized by the plant until it has been transferred from the air to the soil and to plant roots by nitrogen-fixing bacteria; the plants then synthesize proteins. Man has learned how to convert nitrogen by chemical processes into ammonia for use as fertilizer.

When a grazing animal eats plants and when we eat the meat, milk, or eggs supplied by the animal, both we and the animal are eating organic food. It makes no difference to us if the plants on which the animal fed were fed by inorganic or organic fertilizers. Sooner or later all organic material will be returned to the inorganic form to be recycled by plants into organic material. The nitrogen and carbon cycles are nature's means of renewing our soil and plant resources, and when we extract nitrogen from the air or phosphate from rocks to use as fertilizers we are simply accelerating this natural process. Of course, every farmer knows that animal manures and compost are good soil conditioners and he uses them when it is economically feasible to do so. But the person who makes a fetish of using only "organically grown" food is either displaying his ignorance or distrust of natural processes, or is practicing the dogma of a new religion.

How has the food supplier, from farmer to retailer, reacted to this "neo-back-to-nature" phenomenon? There probably are a few believers who are attempting to provide organic foods in accordance with their understanding of the term. The skeptics, who are the vast majority, vary from "It's good business—Viva Suckers"—to a somewhat different attitude which may be expressed as: "The customer is always right, and if the customer wants an inferior product and pays more for it, I am ready to supply it provided I am left with as good or better margin of profit." Dr. Ruth Leverton, USDA, reported that in 1972 a market basket of organic food cost $21.90 at health food stores, $17.80 at natural foods stores, and $11.00 at supermarkets. A substantial part of the industry considers the organic food movement as nothing more than a fad at best and does not wish to be part of a hoax perpetrated on the consumer.

But now that sales of organic foods have passed well beyond the billion dollar level, it is no longer possible for the food industry to shrug off this phenomenon as an unimportant, hopefully harmless fad that will soon pass away. Hilda White (1972) of Northwestern University presents a reasoned discussion of this movement, what it is, and what the industry should do about it. From a number of sources, she defines organic foods as "foods grown without the use of any additives."[1] She says that true believers insist on organic foods as those being farmed by organic methods, implying the avoidance of what they call "toxic" chemicals. It is further suggested that modern agricultural methods are depleting the soil of essential minerals, that food grown with such chemicals cannot be used for composting, and would be a pollutant of fields and streams. Direct addition of any substances like food additives is totally condemned, since such additives are claimed to be "synthetic," although in fact they are identical with natural substances, whether they are extracted from plant materials or synthesized. The last, but not least, condemnation of non-organically grown processed foods is that they don't taste right and are less nutritious than true organic foods.

White considers these claims, first pointing out that the term "organic" is a misnomer, since plants are not capable of utilizing organic materials as nutrients, but derive their entire nutritional requirements from inorganic minerals, salts, and gases. In fact, a generation ago there was an attempt by some individuals and firms to produce and promote the use of "hydroponics," that is, foods grown in water to which the essential minerals have been added. At that time many claims were made that plants so grown were more nutritious and healthful than soil-grown equivalents. Such claims, as well as the reverse claims of the organic farmers, have been proven to be without basis in fact. White points out (as have so many others) that without the judicious use of chemical soil additives, not only could the "green revolution" not have come about, but the entire world would now be suffering from malnutrition and mass starvation.

On the other hand, injudicious use of agricultural chemicals has undoubtedly contributed to the pollution problem, but this can and is being controlled. For example, in recent years the DDT residue level in the average American breadbasket has been going down, although it has never been demonstrated that DDT as such and in amounts vastly greater than consumed by any human was at all harmful to humans. It has been demonstrated, however, that certain chemical plant additives have caused damage to some species of wildlife. Thus, the decision must be made whether to withhold all chemical additives and cause mass

---

[1] As of this writing FDA has not defined "organic" foods and consequently is not in a position to assure compliance whenever a food package is so labeled. The federal trade commission (FTC) is investigating the legality of using terms such as "organic," "natural," or "health" in advertising with the intention of forbidding their use if it can be shown that such terms are misleading to the consumer.

human starvation, or permit the controlled application of such chemicals to permit adequate nutrition for humanity and at the same time cause minimal damage to wildlife. It seems that a decision is not difficult to reach.

The distrust of food additives apparently also arose from consumers' ignorance of the fact that most food additives, such as cinnamon or mustard, are in fact natural products. It seems that the very words "chemical" and "synthetic" arouse fear. Even synthetic vitamins are condemned by promoters of natural and organic foods as being nutritionally inferior to naturally occurring vitamins, when, in fact, they are absolutely identical. This would be the same as stating that pure water collected in a clean rain barrel is inferior to the water in a tomato, which makes up more than 90% of its composition.

It is all too easy not only for the ordinary consumer, but even for scientists to be carried away by such a neonaturalist movement. For example, an outstanding professor of nutrition, writing a column for the Daily Press, described the ingredients in a coffee whitener as consisting of corn syrup solids, vegetable fat, sodium caseinate, dipotassium phosphate, monoglycerides, sodium silicoaluminate, calcium gluconate, beta-carotene, and riboflavin. Although he did not state that there was anything wrong with using such a product, it was implied that it is just too bad that such a synthetic product consisting of nothing but chemicals should be used instead of good old natural cows' milk or cream. What was left unstated was that the "chemicals" listed are essentially the same as those found in cream, but since the milk sugar and fat were replaced with vegetable sugar and fat, the product could not be called cream because of the rules and regulations we have to protect consumers against misbranding. From the nutritional standpoint, a case could be made in favor of the assortment of "chemicals." Certainly corn sugar causes problems to fewer people than does milk sugar, and some nutritionists believe that vegetable fat is preferable to butter fat. Other advantages of the coffee whitener are its greater convenience and stability.

As for differences in nutrition and taste, there is no evidence that organic foods are nutritionally superior or inferior to non-organic foods. From the taste standpoint, and in general from the aesthetic standpoint, there must be some differences, but these depend entirely on individual preference. To use a ridiculous example, some individuals may prefer apples decorated with worms (because the apples were organically grown) to apples not so decorated because they were sprayed with a pesticide (and therefore no longer organic). Since apples are not a good supply of protein, the wormy apples may also be more nutritious. At the same time, it must be recognized that from a health standpoint, it is the wormy rather than the worm-free apple that is hazardous.

It appears, therefore, that in many instances, particularly in the case of processed foods, regulations protecting consumers' health could automatically prevent the distribution of organic foods, such as those contaminated by various pests. Provided, however, organic foods conform to established regulations of wholesomeness, identity and quality, there is no valid reason for condemning their use. The user may be misled if he believes that such foods have any special virtue for maintaining health and providing better nutrition. There is some reason for concern if people of limited means are influenced by such beliefs to buy organic foods which often cost 2 or 3 times as much as their nonorganic counterparts. White then, makes the strong suggestion that food companies should have confidence in the quality and safety of their products and continue to provide these to the consumer, rather than jump on a bandwagon for organic foods.

White recommends that the food industry do even more than it has been doing in the direction of nutrition education in informing the public about the nature of food additives, the reasons for using them, and the regulations controlling their use. In this way industry could help allay the fears aroused by emotional environmentalists, so that in the long run such endeavors would be of benefit to the consumer as well as to the food industry.

TWO DIETS CONSIDERED

Vegetarian Diets

According to Labuza and Sloan (1977) a vegetarian who has sound nutritional education can benefit from a vegetarian diet. Surveys show that the incidence of heart disease among well-educated vegetarians is approximately 10 times less than for people who utilize meat in their diet. Weights of these people usually indicate that they are 20 lb under the standard for people of their average height and their cholesterol levels are usually 30% lower than that of normal meat eaters.

Labuza and Sloan reported that uneducated vegetarians are sometimes vegetarians because meat is unavailable; as a result of inadequately balanced protein in the diet, they will become malnourished. Vegetarians can be classified into three types: (1) vegans, those who eat fruits, nuts and vegetables exclusively; (2) ovo-vegetarians, those who consume the vegan diet plus eggs; and (3) lacto-vegetarians, those who supplement the vegan diet with milk and milk products and sometimes eggs. The ovo and lacto vegetarians can be very successful vegetarians because essential amino acids are consumed from the dairy products and eggs. The vegans have the greatest difficulty in eating a balanced diet because of the poor quality and low amounts of protein found in vegetables.

Vegetarians are often said to have anemia caused by a vitamin B_{12} deficiency since they don't eat meat, the main source of this vitamin. If one started out as a vegetarian at birth this would be a problem. Labuza and Sloan found that most vegetarians who consume milk and eggs are able to obtain their B_{12} requirement. If one ate only vegetables an anemic condition due to vitamin B_{12} deficiency would probably not become evident until 3 to 5 years after the commencement of the diet. The body is capable of storing the B_{12} vitamin for a period of time and using it only slowly. Doctors and nutritionists generally suggest that vegetarians obtain a vitamin B_{12} injection once a year or eat brewers' yeast as a source of B_{12}.

Zen Macrobiotic Diet

Zen macrobiotics is a term that is much maligned by people both for and against Zen macrobiotics, (Labuza 1977). It has caught on in the counterculture and has become quite popular. The diet was started by George Ohsawa who tried to initiate the diet in the United States but failed to do so. The goal of the Zen macrobiotic diet, as set down by Ohsawa, is the achievement of a calm soul through dietary practices. He professed that the diet, in conjunction with the inner calmness of the soul, can overcome any illness. His diet is based on the opposing forces of the Oriental philosophy of Taoism. The opposing forces are the Yin and the Yang. The diet has no connection to Zen Buddhism. Ohsawa felt that one had to have a certain ratio of yin to yang, and reclassified various foods on this basis.

Labuza's analysis shows that the Zen macrobiotic diet consists of 10 levels (−3 to 7). The beginning level, level −3, is a very well-balanced diet consisting of meats, vegetables, cereals, etc. Level 7 should only be used in specific circumstances and consists solely of cereal grains with very little water intake. The latter point is where brown rice has been given so much attention. Ohsawa ranked brown rice as having the best Yin-Yang ratio and therefore suggested that on level 7 only brown rice should be eaten. Brown rice lacks vitamin C, is low in protein and the protein quality is poor. There is no difference in protein content between brown and white rice. In order to acquire the recommended daily allowance of protein by eating rice, it would be necessary to eat at least 2 lb a day.

The Zen macrobiotic diet and philosophy is supposed to cure all diseases. If it fails to do so, Ohsawa stated that is because there is not enough faith among the practitioners or because the person has not practiced the diet long enough. There have been several cases of death resulting from the Zen macrobiotic diet because of lack of vitamin C and consequent loss of resistance to disease. (Labuza, 1977).

6

Food Preservation

"An army travels on its stomach."
Attributed to Napoleon Bonaparte

We have seen earlier in this book how civilization has evolved so that the work of the few who produce food can be enjoyed by the many who consume it. One of the central features of this development is the ability to preserve food as it is harvested from plants and animals so that it may be consumed at some later time. Primitive man was closely constrained by his day-to-day abilities to find food. His freedom to go on long journeys and even to exist when his usual food source was temporarily unproductive was severely limited by his ability to preserve his food. This was a far more serious limitation than man's ability to gather large quantities of food. Early accounts of the fish runs and bird migrations in North America give us an idea of the tremendous bounty of the earth when it was sparsely populated by humans. The great problem of primitive man was his inability to solve the technological problem of food preservation.

Early man was forced to set out on the road which led to our present state of technological advancement by the stress of life near the glaciers of the ice age and during the long winters when hunting was difficult and plant growth was largely dormant. Today in the United States, fewer than 8% of our population produces the food for all. This would be impossible without efficient means of preservation.

Food preservation is the application of some force, either chemical or physical, which will impede the processes of spoilage. Therefore, to understand how food is preserved, we must know something about how and why it spoils. Food spoilage can be considered in three categories, although, as is true of most natural processes, these categories are almost never independent of each other. They are microbial action, enzymic degradation, and chemical and physical changes. Because microbial action is often the source of other enzymatic and chemical changes and because it is itself responsible for most food spoilage, we will begin with this category.

MICROBIAL FOOD SPOILAGE AND ITS CONTROL

Three microscopic forms of plant life which grown readily on or in foodstuffs are yeasts, molds, and bacteria. Each of these represents a large group of species and genera. Many of the members of each group can produce beneficial changes. Many can have either beneficial or harmful effects, depending on circumstances, and many others always cause undesirable changes.

The molds are the most conspicuous of the food-spoilage organisms because they usually grow on the surface of the food where they are easily visible because they aggregate into large masses. Also most of the molds produce fruiting bodies called spores, which are often noticeably colored. Molds can grow in a relatively dry environment, and they require a plentiful supply of atmospheric oxygen or, as biologists express it, they are strongly aerobic. They are able to grow on a wide variety of materials and can use as food many chemicals which inhibit growth of other kinds of microorganisms. Molds have rather low heat resistance, and are easily killed by processes which involve mild heating. (Most molds and mold spores are killed by temperatures of 60°C [140°F] or higher.) They grow well at low pH (acid conditions), although some short-chain aliphatic acids (C_3 through C_7) are fairly good mold inhibitors. The propionates, for example, are widely used as mold inhibitors in baked goods and on food wrappers. Propionic and acetic acids are being considered as additives to stored feed to prevent growth of molds and their toxins (mycotoxins) (Berg 1972).

The molds are strong oxidizers and generally cause pronounced flavor changes. These may be desirable, as in blue mold cheese, or highly undesirable, as in bread or fruit. Molds often cause marked changes in texture, as well as in flavor.

Molds liberate spores which are very light in weight and remain suspended in the air for very long periods; hence they are found nearly everywhere, and excluding them from processed foods is difficult. Where foods susceptible to mold growth are packaged, special care must be taken to prevent molds from entering the packaging rooms, unless the food is heat-processed after packaging. For example, cured, sliced meats are packaged in rooms using filtered air at higher pressure than that of surrounding rooms; since the actual packages contain no air (vacuum- or gas-filled), the products are usually free of molds. Fresh fruit segments are packed in similar rooms and a preservative is added to the juice, mainly to prevent yeast growth. The tremendous increase in the use of food packaged in processing plants, together with techniques like vacuum packaging, gas packaging, and use of new packaging materials, has resulted in a marked decrease in the incidence of moldy food.

Yeasts are botanically somewhat similar to molds, but require more water for their growth; hence, they are more often a problem in liquid foods like fruit juices. The yeasts are also tolerant of acidic conditions and are active sugar fermenters. They are not so strongly aerobic as molds and some of them can grow with a limited oxygen supply. Like the molds, they are quite susceptible to destruction by heat. They may reproduce by spores, and although they generally lack the specialized structures of the molds for releasing their spores into the atmosphere, their spores are airborne. While yeasts are often a cause of spoilage in fruit and dairy products, they are, on the whole, very beneficial organisms and are essential in producing wine, beer, bread, some industrial solvents, and other products. Some yeasts are now being used to produce "synthetic" high-protein feed, and in the years to come we may see vast quantities of highly nutritious food ingredients and entire new foods that are yeasts, or are produced by yeasts (see Chapter 7).

The microorganisms of greatest concern in food preservation are the bacteria. These tiny single-celled plants are found almost everywhere and in all sorts of environments. Those that act as spoilage organisms are called saprophytes because they must have an external source of organic carbon for growth. Some, called anaerobes, can grow without free oxygen, relying for that element on the breakdown of oxygen-containing compounds. Some produce spores which are remarkably heat-resistant. All bacteria require relatively large amounts of water for growth, and they can be looked upon as living in the aqueous phase of any environment. Their tolerance of acids and alkalies is not as wide as that of the molds or yeasts; in the main, they grow best at neutral pH, that is neither acid nor alkaline.

Bacteria can grow over a wide temperature range, from a high of around 55° to 60°C (130 to 140°F), down to sub-freezing temperatures, if the water can be kept liquid (Fig. 6.1). In fact, the effectiveness of freezing in preventing bacterial growth is largely a matter of tying up water so that it is unavailable for their use. However, the growth of bacteria, like that of any organism, depends on a series of biochemical changes; and since chemical reactions proceed more rapidly as the temperature is raised, bacteria grow more rapidly at high temperatures than at low. Those kinds of bacteria which grow well at high temperature (40–60°C) are called thermophiles, those growing best at intermediate temperatures (25–39°C) are called mesophiles, and those growing well below 25°C are called psychrophiles. The three most important ways of preserving foods from spoilage by bacteria are: (1) the use of either heat

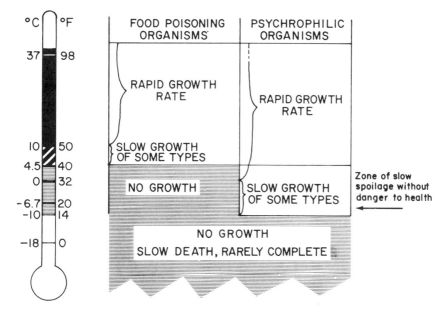

FIG. 6.1. THE TEMPERATURE RANGE OF GROWTH OF FOOD POISONING AND PSY-
CHROPHILIC ORGANISMS

or radiant energy to kill them; (2) the use of low temperatures to slow their growth; and (3) drying, freezing, or other means of limiting the availability of water. A less common method, the use of specific chemical inhibitors, should also be considered because it is sometimes useful. Food preservation is essentially a race against the growth of bacteria and the operations mentioned are man's way of "fixing" the race in his favor.

APPLICATIONS OF ENERGY

Microorganisms, like all other living things, depend for their life on chemical catalytic agents called enzymes. They produce these enzymes within their own bodies, and one bacterial cell, small as it is, contains thousands of them. Each enzyme is produced in response to information carried on the genetic material of the cell, the nucleic acid, DNA. When heat or some other form of energy is applied to the cell in sufficient amounts, it can damage one or more of the sites on the DNA molecule, and thus interfere with the production of one or more enzymes. If an essential enzyme, or a group of enzymes, is unavailable to the cell, it cannot grow and reproduce and, of course, cannot spoil the food. If excessive amounts of energy are applied, more extensive damage to the cell will result: the protein will be denatured, cell walls ruptured, and the organism completely destroyed.

Canning

These things happen when food is cooked, and cooked food would not spoil if microorganisms could be prevented from gaining access to it after it cooled. A Frenchman, Nicholas Appert, won a prize offered by Napoleon for a process for preserving food for the army, by sealing food in a metal container and then heating or cooking it. Thus, the process of canning was born.

Since all living tissue is rather similar, when enough heat is applied to destroy the bacteria, it is also enough to destroy, to some degree, the food itself. Therefore, it is important to heat the sealed cans only long enough to inactivate the bacteria present; otherwise, the food will be badly overcooked and of poor quality. The canner must calculate the minimal sterilization time and temperature for each food in each size and shape of can.

To do this he must know several things. First of all he needs to know what sort of bacteria he is dealing with. For example, an acid food like tomato juice will be spoiled by bacteria capable of living in an acid environment, whereas fish or lima beans will be subject to attack by quite different bacteria. Also, the scientist concerned with calculating process times must be sure that any process will ensure the destruction of the spores of the food-poisoning organism called *Clostridium botulinum*, since these spores are quite heat-resistant; should they survive the heat-processing, they might germinate and thus produce the toxin which causes the often fatal disease, botulism.

In calculating processing times, the food scientist makes use of mathematical models based on the "thermal death time curves" for *Clostridium botulinum* i.e., curves of the temperature and time required to kill a certain number of its spores, and the rate at which heat penetrates the can of food concerned. The details of the models used and the calculations are beyond the scope of this book, but it is useful to understand a few of the terms involved. In describing a process the term "F" or "F_0" is often used. This refers to the number of minutes at 250°F to which the process is actually equivalent. If the process is described in terms of some other temperature, the term F_T is used, in which T is the temperature referred to. Bacteria or their spores die at what is termed a logarithmic rate. This means that when the number of survivors is expressed as a logarithm and plotted against time, one gets a straight line. The time required for this line to descend one log cycle (in other words to reduce the number of survivors by 90%) is given the symbol D. When one hears of the "12 D concept" or a "12 D process," the reference is to process which is sufficiently intense to destroy 10^{12} spores of *C. botulinum*. In arriving at process times, spores of *C. botulinum* are seldom used. A more heat-resistant anaerobe, a variant of *Clostridium sporogenes* known by

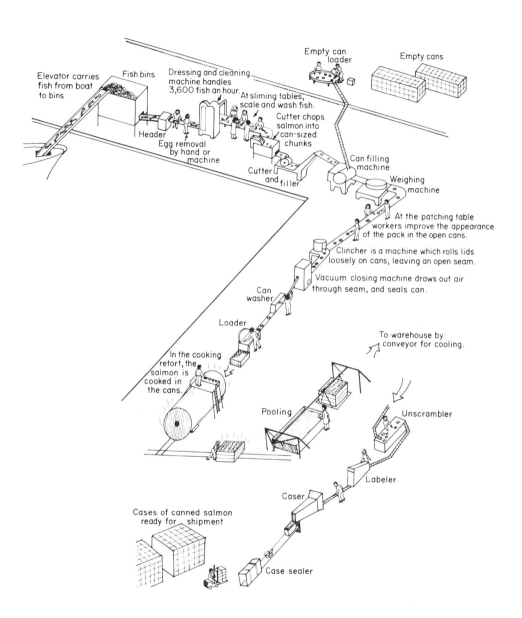

Elevator carries fish from boat to bins

Fish bins

Dressing and cleaning machine handles 3,600 fish an hour.

At sliming tables, scale and wash fish.

Header

Egg removal by hand or machine

Cutter chops salmon into can-sized chunks

Empty can loader

Empty cans

Can filling machine

Weighing machine

Cutter and filler

At the patching table workers improve the appearance of the pack in the open cans.

Clincher is a machine which rolls lids loosely on cans, leaving an open seam.

Vacuum closing machine draws out air through seam, and seals can.

Can washer

Loader

In the cooking retort, the salmon is cooked in the cans.

To warehouse by conveyor for cooling.

Pooling

Unscrambler

Labeler

Caser

Cases of canned salmon ready for shipment

Case sealer

SALMON CANNING

its culture designation, PA 3679, is commonly used in the United States for developing processes for nonacid foods. (For further details, see Stumbo 1965.)

Although canning started in France with the discoveries of Nicholas Appert about 160 years ago, it did not reach quantity production until the development of methods for the cheap and rapid production of the sanitary steel canister coated with tin, popularly known as the tin can, about the turn of the 20th century. This development occurred around the cities of Boston and Baltimore and very rapidly grew into a huge industry requiring not only large quantities of raw food materials, but thousands of tons of steel, tin, and rubber.

For several generations, the tin can has been commonplace in the American scene. The statement that all a newly married housewife needs is a can opener has a great deal of truth in it, since literally hundreds of kinds of food are available in canned form, ready to serve. The commercially prepared product has a nearly perfect record of safety. In spite of the enormous quantities consumed annually, years go by without a single case of food poisoning caused by commercially canned foods. Most cases of food poisoning usually result from home-canned foods.

Canning has come to cover all products which are placed in hermetically sealed containers and heat-sterilized; the containers are not necessarily tin-coated steel. Aluminum cans can be made without difficulty, but because of their pliability and for other reasons they have not gained broad acceptance. The use of aluminum foil in food packaging has made tremendous headway in the past few years. It is particularly useful in packaging butter, margarine, candies, and precooked frozen foods.

Glass containers such as jars and bottles have the obvious sales advantage of transparency, so that foods which are attractive in appearance are frequently processed in glass rather than in opaque cans. Glass containers are available in many shapes, sizes, and distinctive designs. Both glass and metal containers are relatively expensive, frequently costing as much as the food material itself. Recent developments with the steel can have made possible the use of less metal and a thinner tin coating, thus reducing the cost of the metal container.

When used once only, the glass container is more expensive than the metal; however, many glass containers, particularly bottles, are reused, so that their cost per use may be lower than that of the metal. Recently exceptionally strong light-weight "throw-away" glass containers have been made which are less expensive, and the consumer is not required to return the empty containers.

With all the advantages of the canned product, there exists one serious disadvantage. Most non-acid products are over-cooked if subjected to a 12 D process. Much research effort has gone into methods of overcoming the problem. One method is called "high-temperature short-time" process, or HTST, which is based on the observation that as the temperature of heat-processing is increased the time of processing may be reduced drastically, and sterilization may be accomplished with a lesser degree of overcooking. Thus, many products which in the past were processed at 212° to 240°F (100° to 115°C) are now being heated at 250° to 260°F and even higher, but for a much shorter time.

Another means of gaining the same end of reducing over-cooking is by means of agitating the containers during processing, so that the necessary heat for sterilization penetrates all parts of the container more rapidly. Still another development, limited largely to liquid and semi-liquid products, is aseptic canning, in which the food material and the container are sterilized separately and the container is then filled and sealed under aseptic conditions. This process is used commonly for baby foods, puddings, and similar products which have a poor rate of heat exchange.

Already in use in Europe and Japan, and about to explode on the American market, is the retortable pouch, an envelope-like container consisting of three layers, the middle layer is a very thin sheet of aluminum. The outer layer is a tough plastic film which protects the aluminum from damage, and an inner layer plastic which can be sealed easily and tightly. Because of its thinness, such pouches require shorter time and/or lower temperatures for sterilization and are therefore less likely to be overcooked. This "fallout" from the new combat (C) ration should become a new, better "can" as package and manufacturing costs are reduced.

Pasteurization

If other inhibitors are present, such as salt or acids, or if the canned food will be stored at low temperature, the less vigorous process of pasteurization is used. For example, large canned hams (over 3 lb net wt) are given a comparatively mild heat treatment and the cans then labeled "keep under refrigeration." This procedure has been successful because the salt content and mild acidity of the hams would not support the growth of *C. botulinum* in any event. However, the admonition to keep under refrigeration is frequently disregarded, resulting in hams of poor quality and some slight danger of food poisoning from staphylococci. Later in this chapter we will discuss the relationship between food preservation and some specific causes of food poisoning.

A more common use of sublethal heating, or pasteurization, is in the processing of milk, beer, and other liquids to prevent spoilage and also destroy some non-heat-resistant bacteria. To illustrate the dependence of pasteurization on temperature, practical storage life of pasteurized milk held at 38°–40°F (4°–5°C), the usual refrigerator temperature, is only 2–3 weeks. At a storage temperature of 32°F (0°C) the same milk will remain in good condition for as long as 20 weeks. This phenomenon has caused a new "super chilling" or "crust freezing" technique where high moisture foods are held in good condition for months by storage at 26°–30°F, where surface water may freeze, but the food itself is not frozen.

Ionizing Radiation

Heat is not the only form of energy that may be applied to the destruction of spoilage organisms in food preservation. Others are ionizing radiations, such as X-rays, gamma rays, electron beams, and even ultraviolet rays. Of these the gamma (γ) rays, which are given off by radioactive elements, have been the most widely advocated for food preservation by irradiation. The development of nuclear power has presented us with the problem of finding uses for the fuel from atomic power plants which, while still emitting a good deal of radiant energy, is not active enough for the needs of electric generators. Many enthusiastic supporters of the idea of food irradiation have strongly advocated using this spent fuel for food processing. Others have suggested building special atomic reactors for the purpose and still others have advocated the use of powerful electron-beam generators.

All these approaches are based on the same scientific principle. The radiant energy, as in the case of heat (thermal energy), must inactivate a sufficient number of sites on the nucleic acids of the microbes to render them incapable of growing and so spoiling the food. Also, as in the case of heat, when enough energy is applied to inactivate a large number of organisms, such as 10^{12} bacteria, rather significant chemical changes are induced in the food. Unfortunately, the chemical changes caused by irradiating the food are not the familiar ones resulting from heat (which we call cooking), but usually bring about the development of strange or unpleasant flavors. This is because ionizing radiations are potent generators of chemical forms called free radicals, which are highly reactive combining spontaneously with other free radicals and with oxygen. The resulting compounds, often peroxides, have unpleasant flavors. It is possible to irradiate foods under conditions which will minimize free radical formation, for example, under liquid nitrogen, but this is usually very expensive.

Another problem with radiation as a means of preservation is that it destroys some important nutrients, such as vitamins, but it is not very active in destroying enzymes which cause gradual loss of food quality.

Therefore, many foods must be heated to inactivate enzymes before they are irradiated. There is also some unresolved doubt about the safety of food irradiated at high dose levels. (Dosages of radiation are measured in units called "rads," and the amount of radiation needed to sterilize foods is at least 5,000,000 rads, or 5 Mrads.)

It now seems rather unlikely that completely shelf-stable foods comparable with sterile canned foods will be commercially produced by irradiation. However, it is quite likely that pasteurization by radiation, sometimes called "radurization," may become a very useful commercial process. The shelf-life of many foods can be materially increased by radiation with dosages in the neighborhood of 100,000 to 150,000 rads. This has been demonstrated with fish fillets, chilled poultry, packaged fresh meat, and many fruits and vegetables. Radiation pasteurization has the additional benefit of destroying many harmful organisms such as the bacteria of the genera *Salmonella* and *Shigella*.

The Use of Low Temperature

Microbial spoilage can be looked upon as a kind of chemical spoilage in which a living organism is the catalyst of a chemical reaction. All chemical reactions are temerature-dependent; i.e., they proceed more rapidly as the temperature is increased (up to a point), and more slowly as the temperature is decreased. This is the basis of preservation by refrigeration. As the temperature is reduced, the enzymatic processes which control the growth and reproduction of microorganisms proceed at a slower rate until they either do not grow at all or grow so slowly as to do little harm to food. While inhibiting microbial growth, low temperature also retards other chemical reactions, so that refrigeration comes very close to the ideal method of food preservation; i.e., it maintains the food in an unchanged state until it is used.

An example of how low temperature can preserve food is the familiar case of milk. Pasteurized milk has been heated (pasteurized) to a high enough temperature to kill a large percentage, but not all, of the bacteria contaminating it. If it is not refrigerated after pasteurization it will turn sour from the rapid growth of bacteria in a few hours. If the milk is cooled after pasteurization and held between 45° and 50°F (the temperature of ice boxes 50 years ago) it may keep for 1 to 3 days before becoming sour. If, however, milk is rapidly chilled immediately after pasteurization and held at 38°F, just a few degrees above its freezing point, it will keep quite satisfactorily for from 2 to 3 weeks. This familiar example should emphasize the fact that refrigeration works by slowing the rate of change (spoilage) rather than by exerting an absolute effect.

Freezing, which is a form of refrigeration, not only slows reaction rates, but also sequesters water by crystallizing it so that the bacteria which would grow slowly at low temperature (the psycrophites) do not have any water available for their life processes. We will refer in more detail to the function of water in the section on dehydration which follows.

Refrigeration is by no means a new method of food preservation. Early Europeans stored winter ice in insulated caves and cellars for use in cooling foods during the summer. Throughout the 19th century in this country, cutting ice from lakes and ponds during the winter and storing it in special ice houses for summer sale was a prominent commercial activity in all northern communities. In the 1870s the refrigerated rail car was developed, which made possible the shipment of perishable commodities for long distances. During the late 19th and early 20th century mechanical refrigeration was brought to a high state of development, and the ready availability of cheap electric power made the small domestic mechanical refrigerator a common household item by the early 1930s. This rapid development of refrigeration was not nearly so marked in the rest of the world as in the United States for many economic and geographic reasons. We owe much of the diversity and quality of our food supply to our widespread use of refrigeration. Modern systems for harvesting, preparing, distributing, and home storage of food could not function without it. Vegetables are harvested in California, cooled in the field by evaporative devices called hydrocoolers or vacuum coolers, shipped in refrigerated rail cars or trucks, displayed in refrigerated cases on the other side of the continent, and finally stored in household refrigerators until eaten. The system of slaughtering livestock in specific locations in the country is fundamentally based on refrigeration being readily and cheaply available from processing plant to the home kitchen.

It is not possible to understand the American food distribution system without having an idea of some of the complexities and variations of our refrigeration systems; all operate on less than 2% of our electric power supply, while air conditioning consumes 3%, and heating 8%. There is a general lack of awareness of the value of somewhat lower temperatures than are generally in use for keeping many foods. This is because we use one refrigerator for many purposes, and a refrigerator designed for the best protection of milk, meat, and poultry (that is one operating at 30°F) would seriously injure many fruits and vegetables by freezing them. How might this paradox be resolved? Should we compromise at some intermediate temperature? Should we build refrigerators with compartments which would maintain different temperatures?

LIMITING THE AVAILABILITY OF WATER

We referred above to the fact that spoilage organisms may be regarded as living in the aqueous phase of the food which supports them. This fact can be given quantitative expression by saying that any particular microorganism has a minimum "water availability" (A_W) below which it cannot grow (Fig. 6.2 and 6.3). The symbol A_W is derived from a physical-chemical law known as Raoult's law, which relates the vapor pressure of a solution to the concentration of dissolved substances which it contains.

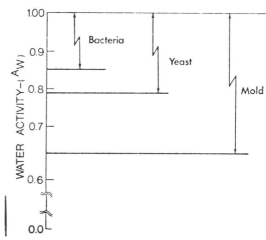

FIG. 6.2. EFFECT OF WATER ACTIVITY ON GROWTH OF MICROORGANISMS

After Kaplow (1970)

Since the water vapor pressure of a mixture like a food is also equal to the relative humidity of an atmosphere with which the food is in equilibrium (that is, the food neither gains nor loses weight due to evaporation or absorption of water), one can measure the A_W of a food by measuring the relative humidity, under carefully controlled conditions, of the atmosphere surrounding the food. The concept of water availability and its measurement has become recently of major importance in our understanding of food dehydration, pickling, salting, and other related means of food preservation on a quantitative basis and makes clear the reasons for many heretofore unexplainable phenomena.

The values of A_W are expressed as decimal fractions from 0 to 1.0. Most bacteria require high A_W values, betweeen 0.94 and 0.99. Only a very few species can grow at A_W values below 0.90. *Staphylococcus aureus*, which is mildly halophilic, or salt-tolerant, does not grow well below 0.94, but can grow slowly at values down to 0.86. Otherwise, only a few cocci and no rods are known to grow below 0.94. Yeasts generally have about the same requirements as bacteria except for the so-called osmophilic yeasts, which can grow in high sugar concentrations and are responsible for the spoilage of many fruits and fruit juices. These yeasts can grow at values as low as 0.62. Molds have the widest tolerance to restricted water

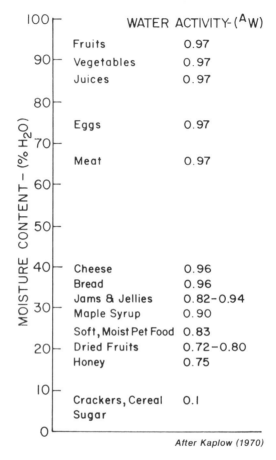

FIG. 6.3. MOISTURE CONTENT AND WATER
ACTIVITY OF SOME COMMON FOODS

availability and can grow at A_W values as low as 0.60. With this kind of knowledge, it is now possible to develop foods with just the right moisture level to withstand invasion by specific groups of microorganisms.

DEHYDRATION AND DRYING

Long before we understood the derivation of numerical values for water availability, man was taking advantage of the fact that dried foods resist spoilage. Biltong of Africa, xargue of South America, dried beef, pemican, jerky, dried dates and figs, and many other traditional and ancient foods owe their keeping quality to their low water availability. Nowadays, the drying or dehydrating of foods is an important part of the food processing industry. Dehydrated foods are particularly important as ingredients in convenience foods—such as the incorporation of dehydrated chicken and dehydrated vegetables in dry soup mixes. Dehydrated foods have been especially important in times of war and other emergencies. Their light weight and good keeping quality are especially advantageous. From 1940 to 1945 millions of pounds of dehydrated meat, milk, eggs, and vegetables were shipped from North and South America, Australia and New Zealand to Russia, Britain, and Europe as part of the war effort.

The old traditional products were and still are usually sun-dried, for example, fish and some fruits. Sun drying, however, is not practical in many parts of the world where time of harvest does not coincide with dry, sunny weather. Even where the weather is favorable, such methods frequently lead to very serious deterioration in quality. Thus, many artificial methods of drying were developed and are still in the process of development.

Kiln, tunnel, spray, roller, and vacuum drying have all been introduced within this century, and are all used on a variety of foods, often with relatively little loss of quality. By these methods, however, it was still practically impossible to eliminate some undesirable flavor changes, so that a search for new and better methods of drying is still going on. Since the major detrimental effects are caused by the presence of oxygen, which results in off-flavor or off-colored end products, some of the newer methods utilize various devices to eliminate this oxidation problem. Antioxidant chemicals are used, such as ascorbic acid (vitamin C), which counteract the effect of oxygen by serving as reducing agents. Inert gases may be used as a blanket, physically eliminating the presence of oxygen in the atmosphere. These gases are used to "puff up the product," so that it reconstitutes to its original form quickly and easily when water is added back.

The latest, and probably least damaging technique, called freeze drying, was borrowed from the biomedical procedure of lyophylization. By this process, fresh foods are first frozen, then heated to just below their eutectic point (temperature at which they would begin to thaw) and water vapor is removed by sublimation with the aid of vacuum. Freeze-dried products are usually of superior quality because they are not subjected to high temperatures. Also, because the water is expelled in gas form the frozen tissue does not collapse, and upon rehydration returns almost "instantly" to its original shape and texture.

Regardless of how they are prepared, dehydrated foods if properly dried and packaged, can be highly nutritious and quite palatable and offer many possibilities for relieving specific geographic food shortages.

For example, dried milk and dehydrated meat can be shipped to parts of the world where a protein shortage exists.

In general, the term "dehydrated" is used to designate a food dried by modern technological processes, while the term "dried" is used for older, more traditional, foods such as figs, dates, beans, or grains that are sun dried, or simply permitted to dry in the field.

INTERMEDIATE—MOISTURE FOODS

Commercially dehydrated foods have low A_W values, generally below 0.50. As we have seen, this is considerably lower than needed to obviate microbial spoilage and a new class of foods, called foods of intermediate moisture content, is now arriving. These will have an A_W value of from 0.75 to 0.85 and may rely on some specific mold inhibitors to aid in their preservation. Traditional foods which fall in this class are fermented sausages, partially dried fruits and bakery products and jams and jellies, which have a low pH (around 4.8—5.5) and A_W values of 0.80 to 0.85. The new foods are likely to achieve their moisture limitation by the addition of salt, sugar, glycerine or other glycols, and other additives. The moist dog foods already on the market are prepared in this way.

FREEZING

Freezing, one of the most popular methods of food preservation in the United States, is a technique for reducing A_W. In a frozen food water is "tied up" by freezing so that it is unavailable to the microorganisms which might use it. Freezing has the distinct advantage of coming closer than any other known method of food preservation to maintaining food in its fresh, unprocessed, form for a relatively long time.

Although freezing arrests microbiological activity, it only slows down, but does not completely inactivate other biochemical processes, particularly those catalyzed by the enzymes present in fresh foods. Since these enzymes are heat-labile, many fresh foods, particularly vegetables, are "blanched" by steaming or scalding before freezing.

The major undesirable effect of freezing plant and animal tissues is loss of firmness or turgidity, caused in part by rupturing of cell walls by ice crystals, and in part by movement of soluble solids ahead of the freezing front. It was found that both of these undesirable effects could be minimized if the rate of freezing is accelerated. If, for example, ripe but firm strawberries are placed in a still-air room at $+20°F$ ($-7°C$), they will eventually freeze. Upon thawing, however, they will sustain considerable "drip loss," and become soft and flabby because of the mechanical damage sustained by the cell walls. When eaten they will appear to be tasteless because the soluble sugars and acids moved to the center of the berries ahead of the freezing front. If, however, the same strawberries are frozen "cryogenically" by immersion in liquid nitrogen (−196°C) they will be frozen in a few seconds, and upon thawing will be almost as turgid and sweet as the fresh.

Rate of freezing is a function of temperature difference at the interface of the freezing agent and the frozen material. Thus, the rate of freezing of the strawberries held in a 20°F room could be accelerated simply by circulating the air in the room. If in addition the temperature of the room were reduced to −10 to −40°F we would have a conventional "blast freezer." A more rapid freezing rate can be accomplished by circulating the cold air vertically, partially suspending the individual berries in the column of air, thereby increasing the interface area. This type of freezer is called a "fluidized-bed freezer." The most rapid rate is achieved by suspending the berries in a liquid which boils at a very low temperature. Liquid nitrogen (LN), liquid carbon dioxide (LCO$_2$), and the refrigerant R-12 (Freon) are used for this purpose. In general, the more rapid the rate of freezing, the more expensive is the process, and the frozen food processor must decide whether the consumer will pay for the improved quality.

Freezing has the great disadvantage of requiring a continual expenditure of energy. Once the product is frozen, it must remain frozen until prepared for consumption. Unless stored in a moisture-saturated atmosphere (relative humidity = 100%) or tightly "shrink"-wrapped in a vapor-tight package, most foods (which contain 60−95% water) will desiccate. Even a small amount of desiccation causes unsightly but totally harmless "freezer-burn," which usually disappears when the product is prepared for consumption. However, freezer burn is carefully guarded against, not only because the consumer does not like the appearance of the freezer-burned product, but the water-loss reduces the weight of product the manufacturer has to sell, probably at reduced prices. For both these reasons a mildly freezer-burned product should be a bargain for the consumer.

Standard temperature of storage is just below 0°F. In practice, commercial freezer storages are maintained at about −5°F. At this temperature, raw and precooked lean meat can retain high quality for about 21 months, but fat meat for just about 1 year; lean fish for 6 months, and fat fish for only 2 months. Most precooked foods without gravy will maintain good quality for ½ year, vegetables for more than 1 year, and fruits for as long as 4 years. Thus, little damage is done to frozen foods during the freezing process and while it is in bulk storage. More damage is done when it is placed in an open display case where the temperature in certain spots may rise above 0°F, or when packages are left in the case too long. Undoubtedly however most of the damage in terms of loss of sensory and nutritional quality occurs in the home.

Neither freezing nor dehydration kill the spoilage (or even the pathogenic) organisms which might be present in the food. In fact both dehydration and freezing are commonly used in the laboratory to preserve living bacteria, and other microorganisms, for long periods of time. In food substrates, there will be a gradual reduction in the numbers of viable microorganisms with time, but a decreasing number remain ready to grow as soon as they are supplied with water and a favorable temperature. Otherwise, much that was said above about refrigeration applies to freezing.

CHEMICAL INHIBITORS

Another method of preventing food spoilage by microorganisms is the addition to the food of some chemical which has a specific inhibitory action on the principal spoilage organism concerned. In former years substances such as formaldehyde, sodium carbonate, and borax were so used, but these are now excluded by both federal and state regulations. Most of the common spices first came into use in ancient times because they had some preservative properties. Today, the only antibacterial substance used in the United States is sodium benzoate which is permitted in some foods in a maximum concentration of 0.1%. Sodium benzoate is only effective where the food is sufficiently acid to release benzoic acid, which is the active antibacterial part of the sodium benzoate molecule. It is therefore used in fresh fruit compotes, and a few meat products which are pickled in vinegar. It is also used in Northern Europe in certain "semipreserved" fish products.

In Great Britain, sodium sulfite is a permitted additive in fresh sausage and sodium sulfite or sulfur dioxide is used in nearly all the wine-making countries of the world to inhibit undesirable organisms, leaving a clear field to the desired yeasts.

Since any substance which can inhibit the growth of bacterial cells would also be likely to interfere with the cells of humans who eat the food containing it, there is a general feeling today that chemical inhibitors are not wholesome. This stricture does not, of course, apply to salt and sugar which are not specific inhibitors but do reduce A_w and are for this reason common preservatives. Some other traditional curing agents, notably the nitrates and nitrites, which are also non-specific, are now being subjected to minute examination. The fear is that nitrates are reduced to nitrites by bacteria and other natural reducing substances in living tissues. Nitrites may under proper conditions combine with secondary amines (protein break-down products present in most foods and in the digestive tract) to form compounds called nitrosamines. Some nitrosamines are powerful carcinogens. Thus, a very careful review is now under way to determine whether or not this could happen in, or as a result of eating, food (usually meat products) cured with nitrates or nitrites. Of course, many vegetables and much water contain as much or more nitrite than cured meats, and most human saliva naturally contains some nitrite.

Several antibiotics have been advanced as possible food preservatives. Some, like tylosin or subtilin, might be added to food prior to canning. They would reduce the amount of heat needed to kill microbial spores, improving the final quality. As attractive as this sounds, they have not proved as effective as claimed, and there is a general objection to the use of antibiotics on the grounds that they might sensitize consumers, resulting in allergies when antibiotics were later used in medical treatment. Since the antibiotics proposed for use in canned foods have no great future in medicine, it is possible that these, or others, might eventually be useful.

Although very few substances with antibacterial activity are permitted, several compounds are useful inhibitors of yeasts and molds. Short-chain fatty acids and their salts, such as propionates, are used to inhibit molds in baked goods and are often incorporated in paper used to wrap butter, cheese, and bacon to inhibit mold growth on the product. Sorbic acid and its salt are used to inhibit molds growing in fruit juices, jellies, and similar products. Some newer proprietory fungistats are available, and there are some compounds produced by microorganisms like antibiotics which have antifungal activity. On the whole, however, the selection of chemical inhibitors available to the food processor is seriously limited.

PUTTING MICROORGANISMS TO WORK

Although food preservation is primarily a race against bacterial growth, some harmless microorganisms can preserve food by fermenting it. The difference between fermentation and spoilage is that fermentation involves beneficial microorganisms which preserve food by changing its biochemical characteristics, so that the food does not support harmful microorganisms. Spoilage microorganisms, while not necessarily injurious to health, are nevertheless harmful because they render the food unfit for human consumption by the development of unacceptable sensory quality, usually off-flavor.

Processing by fermentation is an ancient art which is maintaining its position among processed foods, as evidenced by the present-day importance of pickled, fermented, or alcoholic foods or beverages. Though such foods may not have been reduced in volume, they are proportionately dwindling in relation to the newer processed foods that are appearing on the market daily. The important development in processing be fermentation is the use of pure cultures and controlled development of microorganisms which provide more uniformly acceptable products, as compared to similar products which in the past contained a wide assortment of organisms that were present by chance.

A fascinating new approach to food preservation is to prevent development of pathogenic bacteria by inoculating the foods with the harmless, highly competitive bacteria *Streptococcus diacetilactis*. The unique advantage of this organism is that it produces only small amounts of acid even when present in large numbers. Thus, the food in which these organisms grow does not become sour, and at the same time development of other bacteria is halted. Apparently *S. diacetilactis* competes successfully, particularly with pathogenic bacteria, for essential nutrients, thereby preventing the growth of such harmful bacteria.

GAS EXCHANGE

Preservation or substantial shelf-life extension can be accomplished by limiting the oxygen supply, or arresting enzymatic or microbiological activity by modifying normal atmosphere in which living tissues, which serve a food, are held. All living organisms adapted to life on earth produce the energy needed to perform their life functions by inhaling oxygen from the atmosphere (except for the anaerobes discussed earlier in this chapter) and exhaling carbon dioxide. Even slaughtered animals, and particularly harvested fruit and vegetable tissues, continue to respire, that is, utilize oxygen to produce carbon dioxide plus energy, using the carbon-containing organic chemicals of which they are composed as the carbon source. For harvested produce, therefore, respiration is a "self-destruct" process in which many naturally occurring, or microorganically introduced enzymes play a key role. In fact, respiration rate is the principal basis for the differences in shelf-life of different products. For example, cabbages and potatoes have a low respiration rate and can be stored for months, while strawberries and papayas keep for just a few days because they respire rapidly.

We have already discussed the benefits of refrigeration in slowing down enzymatic activity and consequently respiration rates, and of heat which inactivates enzymes. Another method of lowering respiration rates is by reducing availability of atmospheric oxygen. Sixty years ago, two English scientists, Kidd and West, discovered that when they enclosed apples in an air tight chamber, the fruit remained fresh much longer. This was of particular importance to those varieties that could not be stored at 31°F, just above their freezing point, because they suffered frost damage unless held at temperatures above 38°F. They found that within a few days or at most weeks, the oxygen within the chamber gradually dropped from the original 21% to 1% or less, while the carbon dioxide increased from the original 0.03% to 20%, while the inert nitrogen gas remained at about 80%. Now, half a century later, we know that every fresh food has its own optimal mix of gases for reducing rate of respiration without causing undesirable side effects. We call this process modified (MA), or controlled atmosphere (CA) storage. Thus the optimal gas mix for certain apple varieties is 3% oxygen and 5% carbon dioxide, while for lettuce oxygen may be reduced to 1% or less, with little or no carbon dioxide accumulation. CA conditions for pears are about the same as apples, and their storage life can be doubled if ethylene, another naturally occurring gas that accelerates respiration, is not permitted to accumulate. Other natural respiration products, such as aldehydes and alcohols, help in extending shelf-life, but cannot be permitted to accumulate because they impart undesirable off-flavors.

Commercial CA storage facilities therefore consist of airtight rooms into which the appropriate oxygen-carbon dioxide and nitrogen mix is introduced, and other gases such as ethylene, acetaldehyde, and alcohol vapors "scrubbed" out of the recirculated atmosphere.

A related process, in which toxic gases that are not natural products of respiration are used, is called fumigation. It is ordinarily used to destroy insects and rodents. Because these toxic gases are lethal and may cause the formation of secondary unwholesome chemicals, their use is carefully controlled and generally discouraged. Some gases commonly used for fumigation are hydrogen cyanide, ethylene oxide, and sulfur dioxide—all powerful oxidants.

An interesting recent research development is preservation of the fresh quality of prepared (peeled and sliced or diced) produce by first evacuating practically all the oxygen not only from the chamber but from within the food tissues as well. The vacuum is then broken by the introduction of an enzymocidal gas, followed by a bactericidal gas. Diced apples and potatoes so treated retain their fresh quality for several months even when stored at ambient temperatures. This "GASPAK" process, like any new food product or process will not be available to the consumer even if it is of superior quality and convenience and lower in cost, until it is approved as safe by the consumer's guardian, the Food and Drug Administration.

CHEMICAL FOOD SPOILAGE

While the changes induced by microorganisms, which we call spoilage, are essentially chemical changes, there are other spoilage transformations which are independent of microbial action. These we may refer to as chemical spoilage. Often these changes may be catalyzed by enzymes, which are natural constituents of the food. All the foods we eat are living, or once living, plants or animals. They all contain a myriad of enzymes which perform essential functions while they are alive. When we attempt to store them for food, these enzymes continue to cause chemical changes, often resulting in spoilage. Pickles become soft and mushy, fruits lose their desirable texture and color, meats develop undesirable flavors, and many other changes take place as a result of natural chemical changes which continue to occur long after consumers would like them to stop. Heating (cooking or blanching) to a high enough temperature will inactivate the enzymes and stop their chemical activity. Some nonenzymatic changes will continue. Refrigerating and freezing will slow most enzymatic reactions to the point where their effects will not be discernible for weeks or months. A few enzymes which were unnoticed at room temperature will remain active at low temperatures (catalases, oxidases, and lipases, for example), though their effects are greatly retarded. Some of these changes may be controlled by heating first, to inactivate enzymes and then freezing.

The most serious non-enzymatic chemical spoilage which occurs is the development of oxidative rancidity. When fats are stored for any length of time, and some form of oxygen is available, they form very unstable oxidized compounds which split to release short-chain aldehydes and ketones, which impart undesirable flavors that are characteristic of what we term rancidity. These changes may be impeded, but not entirely stopped, by the use of antioxidants. These are chemical compounds, or mixtures of compounds, which either absorb the available oxygen themselves or block the combination of oxygen with the fat molecule by attaching themselves to the sites available for oxygen. Some metals such as iron and copper can catalyze oxidative reactions. Many antioxidants include metal chelators which sequester metallic ions to prevent them from entering into the oxidation processes.

Storing fat-containing foods in air-tight containers will limit the availability of atmospheric oxygen and retard rancidity to a considerable degree. This is especially effective in protecting frozen foods. However, many foods are well supplied with compounds which can yield oxygen for combination with susceptible materials; thus atmospheric oxygen is not essential for developing rancidity. In frozen meat products the respiratory pigments which supply oxygen to the muscles in life continue to do so, to a degree, even after cooking, promoting rancid flavors in stored products.

Another type of chemical spoilage that has received much attention from food scientists is non-enzymatic browning. This is a reaction which occurs whenever sugars are heated in the presence of amino acids or some other small nitrogenous molecules. It is sometimes a desirable reaction, as in baking and making French fried potatoes, but is often undesirable where a gradual darkening of the food decreases its acceptability.

MICROBIAL FOOD POISONING

A corollary of food preservation is food poisoning. We preserve food not only so that we will have it available when we want it, but also so that it will be safe to eat when we need it. Not so long ago it was thought that food poisoning was due to protein decomposition products called ptomaines. We now realize that, although there are naturally occurring food toxins, most cases of food poisoning are of bacterial origin.

The principal types of bacteria that cause food poisoning may be classed as: (1) the toxin-producing anaerobes, (2) the toxin-producing aerobes, and (3) the infectious bacteria commonly spread by food. Following is a brief look at each class.

Toxin-producing Anaerobes

Anaerobic bacteria are those that live without atmospheric oxygen, getting their oxygen from chemical compounds. The most spectacular, from the food poisoning standpoint, is *Clostridium botulinum*, a common soil organism which secretes a very powerful poison when it grows in food. A high proportion of botulism cases are fatal. Since it is an anaerobe, it grows only in foods from which air is excluded and in the U.S. is most commonly found in improperly processed canned food. It is very rare in commercially prepared food, but there are usually a score or so of cases each year which are associated with underprocessed home-canned foods. *C. botulinum* is unable to grow and produce toxin at refrigerator temperature (with the exception of one variant known as *C. botulinum*, type C, which can grow slowly at a minimum temperature of 37°F), and it will not grow in the presence of even mild acids. It is usually found associated with foods which might have garden soil adhering to them and which are neutral or slightly alkaline. Underprocessed string beans are the classic example. The toxin of *C. botulinum* is destroyed by vigorous boiling for 10 min.

The other anaerobe of special interest is *Clostridium perfringens*. It has only recently been recognized as an enterotoxin producer. Because large numbers of vegetative cells are needed to produce illness, it was formerly regarded as causing a food infection, but scientists now recognize that the digestive illness it causes is due to an enterotoxin. Meat, particularly if held at temperatures around 90°−100°F for 1−4 hr, is a common vehicle. It is not so fastidious an anaerobe as *C. botulinum* and is likely to grow in deep dishes of food held on steam tables. The importance of perfringens food poisoning has been growing in the United States in recent years. Whether this is a real increase in its incidence or a matter of better diagnosis and reporting is not clear.

Toxin-producing Aerobes

The most prevalent offender in this category is *Staphylococcus aureus*, a common inhabitant of skin, mouth, nose, and throat. When certain strains grow in food they liberate an enterotoxin which produces rather severe gastroenteritis. The enterotoxigenic *staphylococci* have to grow in rather large numbers in the food in order to render it harmful. They will not produce toxin at temperatures below 45°F, but are quite salt-tolerant, and prefer a pH between 6.5 and 7.5. They are most dangerous when they gain access to a food which has been previously pasteurized, because they do not grow well in competition with other organisms. The source of contamination is usually a human handler. Thus, the most dangerous types of foods are ones like sliced, baked, or canned ham; filled bakery products; or some warm desserts. The enterotoxin liberated by *staphylococci* is quite heat-stable and is not destroyed by many cooking procedures.

The Food Infections

The most important infectious disease spread by food is salmonellosis, caused by the many bacteria of the species *Salmonella*. The salmonellae are non-sporeforming organisms whose habitat is the gut of man and animals, where they cause illnesses of varying severity. Although usually a mild upset in a healthy adult, salmonellosis may cause death in infants, the aged, or the infirm. The chain of infection is from man or animals to food and back to man and animals. The chain is perpetuated by rodents, contaminated animal feed, and careless handling which allows contamination of processed foods. An extreme example of how carelessness perpetuates the disease is an incident where pigeons, roosting in the rafters of a milk-drying plant, contaminated the dry milk, resulting in illness among consumers of the product. The salmonellae themselves are not heat-resistant and are easily eliminated by any heat processing.

Other organisms which are rather similar in their habitat and mode of transmission are species of *Shigella*, and abnormal strains of normal intestinal bacteria.

Prevention of Food Poisoning

Prevention measures are dictated by the growth requirements of the organisms concerned. To guard against botulism we must assure ourselves that all processed food capable of supporting toxin formation by the organism is adequately heat-processed to begin with and is subsequently protected from recontamination. When refrigerated, susceptible food must be kept at low enough temperatures to make toxin production impossible. Perfringens food poisoning is best avoided by strict sanitary controls in plants to keep contamination to a minimum, and by adequate refrigeration and avoidance of situations where food is held in the incubator range, 85°−105°F.

Staphylococcal food poisoning can be materially reduced by instituting measures in food-handling establishments which will keep persons with colds, boils, or any suppurating lesions away from food. After this, adequate refrigeration will do much to prevent the proliferation of minor chance contaminants.

Salmonellosis presents a difficult epidemiological control problem. Those who have studied it feel that an important step in breaking the cycle of infection in the United States lies in cleaning up animal feed so that meat and poultry will not be derived from animals with undetected *Salmonella* infections. Vigorous governmental efforts are now under way to improve handling of offal and other waste products that are rendered for animal feed.

Beyond this, better reporting and more follow up by public health authorities of salmonellosis outbreaks will also help. Finally, individuals can do a great deal by maintaining good sanitary practices in kitchens. The justly infamous three f's, fingers, flies, and filth, are mighty perpetuators of salmonellosis and other food infections.

7

Convenience Foods

"A jug of wine, a loaf of bread. . ."
Rubaiyat, XII, 12th Century
. . . are more convenient than a TV dinner

When one thinks of convenience foods these days the usual reaction is to visualize some menu item, or perhaps an entire meal, completely prepared and frozen, so that all the consumer needs to do is "heat and eat." The convenience label is also identified with new foods that have appeared on the shelves in recent years. We need to disentangle our conception of convenience foods from total identification with newly developed frozen prepared menu items, and recognize that the term "convenience" applies to all foods that have been prepared[1] in such a way that they are ready to eat with or without heating. If we accept this definition of a convenience food, it follows that the entire spectrum of processed foods, beginning with the Egyptian inventions of bread and beer, are convenience foods.

After the Egyptians made their great leap forward there were many improvements in bread-making technology of mass production, but only minor improvements in quality and practically no improvements in convenience over the last 5000 years. When the consumer of 3000 B.C. bought or was given his loaf of bread or a jug of beer, nothing was required of him in the way of preparation before eating the bread or drinking the beer—both were prepared processed foods.

Bread and Wine

For bread, from a strictly convenience standpoint, there has been only one advance, hardly an earth-shaking development—sliced bread. Even this small advance in convenience was made possible only after bread

---

[1] Obviously fresh foods eaten as such are totally convenient, but they are not prepared.

was "standardized" to include some harmless additives which prevent mold growth and rapid staling, and water vapor-proof packaging. These technical advances may be considered to add to convenience also, since it is no longer necessary for the consumer to squeeze a well-wrapped loaf of bread to find if it is still soft and warm, and therefore fresh. Oddly enough, maintaining bread freshness is one of the few instances where the refrigerator is not helpful. Certain temperature-related processes that are just now beginning to be understood cause bread to stale most rapidly at the temperature range of 20°–40°F. Bread remains fresher at temperatures higher than 40°F, or lower than 20°F. Bread keeps very well in the freezer for months. If it is placed in an oven, particularly a microwave oven which will thaw and warm the bread quickly and uniformly, the thawed bread will not only taste fresh, but smell as fresh as if it just came out of the oven.

The total convenience of alcoholic beverages is obvious. All the consumer needs to do is lift the cup to the lip and drink. Because of the activity of the very helpful yeasts, these beverages are also free from other microorganisms (some of which may be pathogenic), and in some instances are major sources of nutrients. Throughout history these beverages have been a convenient means of opening up new lands. One of the more recent is the Mississippi Valley. Throughout the 19th century it was a common sight to see rafts floating down the Mississippi loaded with barrels of whiskey. It was most convenient for the settlers of the Great Plains to convert an acre of grain into a barrel of whiskey and float the highly concentrated crop to New Orleans, where it was sold or bartered for tools and other necessities.

Unfermented convenience cereal and fruit products became available only in modern times. True, hardtack and other forms of unleavened bread, dried fruit, and fruit "leather" were available for thousands of years, but were used only because of necessity. No one really liked to subsist on hardtack or fruit leather.[2]

Processed Juices and Drinks

With the advent of pasteurization and canning, all types of beverages became convenience items. All the present-day consumer needs to do is to open the bottle, can, or carton and drink the fresh, unfermented, unspoiled juice of his choice. Since pasteurized foods require refrigeration, frozen juice concentrates may be considered a further advance in convenience. The consumer can purchase one 12-oz container of concentrated juice and refrigerate it until he is ready to consume it, instead of

---

[2]There were of course exceptions such as dates, figs, and olive oil.

purchasing a dozen large oranges and extracting the juice himself. The single strength juice, or less than single strength juice drink, on the other hand, is obviously somewhat more convenient than the frozen concentrate because the juice need not be reconstituted. For this very slight convenience, millions of consumers pay three times as much for the juice they get in a container of drink than they would pay for the concentrated juice. The fruit drink which contains between 25 and 50% natural juice with sugar water added, is not diluted as much as fruit ade (belly wash) which may contain only 5 to 10% juice. But the consumer can do still worse. Undoubtedly his crowning folly is his mass acceptance and purchase of soft drinks made absolutely convenient for him not only in being packaged in easy-to-open bottles or cans, but available at the press of a button from dispensers around the world.

Such purchases are foolish only if the purchaser of the "belly wash" or soft drink believes that he is purchasing nutrients. After all, as was pointed out in Chapter 3, food and particularly drink is selected not for its nutritive value, but for its sensory value. Soft drink manufacturers may imply that their product "is good for you" but they certainly dare not make any claims for nutritive value except for the quantity of calories they may have (or in the case of low-calorie drinks, may not have). What they would normally claim is that "you'll like it" because it tastes good.

Cereal Snacks

The cereal journey down convenience road, in contrast to the soft drink story, is paved with dubious claims to health and nutrition. The ubiquitous crisp breakfast cereals came on the scene before the turn of the century, and became firmly entrenched on the American breakfast table largely on the basis of supposedly imbuing the consumer with health, energy, and vitality. Above all else, they were designed to keep the alimentary track moving (Deutsch 1961). As the science of nutrition developed, it became obvious to breakfast-cereal manufacturers that their products were really not distinguished for their nutritive value; however, when combined with milk and perhaps fruit, they did provide a good all-around source of nutrients. Thus, breakfast cereal manufacturers were among the first to label their products voluntarily for their nutrient content, showing among other things how the proteins in the cereal are balanced by the protein in the milk, etc. Later on, these same foods were fortified with added nutrients.

Although a breakfast cereal such as corn flakes has no greater value nutritionally than corn meal, it is certainly more convenient to use. The grain millers at the same time improved the convenience of the cereal grains by precooking and other means, so that the kernels, or porridge, could be prepared in a few minutes. Much of the rice now purchased by U.S. consumers is of this precooked "instant" type.

The last explosion in cereal-based convenience foods is snack foods. These are as convenient as sliced bread. They are not only ready to eat, but do not even require utensils, since they are "finger food." Many of these snack foods are composed of cereal flour, much as the breakfast foods, to which are added some flavoring, seasoning, and perhaps color components. The mixture is cooked and either rolled, extruded, formed by dyes, or puffed into the desired shape. Here is another line of convenience foods that is extremely expensive from the nutritional standpoint, but consumers may choose to purchase them because they like them. These snack items may also be nutritionally enriched.

The Fried Potato and Other Starches

Along with cereals and other high-starch foods, the per capita utilization of the potato had been showing a downward trend for several decades until convenience items began to appear in great profusion. The process that started the potato on the road to convenience was deep-fat frying. Potato chips and French fries vie with carbonated soft drinks as major representatives of American culture and ingenuity in the culinary arts to the world.

Practically all potato chips—thin slices of potato dehydrated and saturated with oil by deep frying—are commercially prepared, packaged, and purchased by the consumer as convenience snack foods. Similar, but thicker, French fries are also known outside the U.S. as chips. They are prepared in much the same manner as the potato chip, but because they are thicker, they develop a hard crust on the surface but retain a soft center.

It is only in the last generation, with the development of freezing, that French fries have become a truly convenience item. Even today, many restaurants prefer to fry their own instead of purchasing prepared frozen French fries. Preparation in the home has never been common practice, and may have led to the huge popularity that this item enjoys, particularly among young people, since it is associated with "eating out" on special occasions. Thus, when prepared frozen French fries became available to both institutional and home users, they rapidly became the number one frozen vegetable item. Now the cooks in the restaurant and in the home no longer need to peel and trim raw potatoes, cut them to appropriate size and shape, and fry them in deep fat. All they need to do is heat the prepared frozen product and serve.

Potatoes are more or less egg-shaped. When cut into the typical ¼ × ¼ inch strips, many odd-shaped pieces are left over. This material could be used for feed, or the manufacture of starch and alcohol. Although some of the waste from commercial French-frying operations is used for these purposes (and with the search for energy sources, may eventually be diverted entirely for alcohol), it was found more profitable to dehydrate the material into potato flour, granules, or flakes. These dehydrated potato products are sold as another convenience item for use as mashed potatoes. All the cook needs to do is to add water and/or other ingredients, stir, and the mashed potatoes are ready to serve. The same raw material, before or after dehydration, is being used to produce a variety of frozen prepared convenience foods, such as potato puffs and pancakes, or it is compressed and extruded into various shapes, including French fries, as snack foods. The quantity of potatoes used for these many convenience items exceeds that used fresh, despite the fact that raw potatoes hold up well in cold storage and are therefore available the year round at substantially lower prices than the processed product.

Why then should the consumer buy most of his potatoes in the processed form? Obviously, because of convenience. For example, it was calculated that dehydrated potato flakes or granules cost about twice as much as raw potatoes per serving of mashed potatoes. However, when this cost differential was applied to the cook's added labor, it was found that the additional time required to prepare the mashed potatoes would have been worth not more than 25¢/hour (Kramer 1965).

Many other starchy roots, tubers, seeds, and even fruits are being used as major sources of food energy in the form of the cooked vegetable or as a gruel. Although all have been tried in the form of prepared convenience foods, there are few success stories. The sweet potato, richer than the white potato in pro-vitamin A and calories, produces huge yields wherever it is grown in tropical to temperate regions. Although it is sweet and attractive in color, it is widely used in only a few areas of the world, and then usually because of necessity rather than choice. Dehydrated sweet potatoes, or chips, or extruded snacks, have a very limited market. The only convenience sweet potato item that gained considerable acceptability (over 10 million cases per year) is the "candied" sweet potato which is canned in heavy syrup.

Sweet potatoes are a major source of starch, sugar, and alcohol in some parts of the world, notably in Japan and Korea, just as the potato is a major source for these products in Northern Europe. In the United States, however, corn is utilized for these purposes more efficiently. The corn products industry, consisting largely of the items enumerated above, is a billion dollar industry. Cornstarch is used for a variety of food and non-food purposes, while corn sugar and syrup compete favorably as food sweeteners with cane or beet sugar.

Bananas and plantain (cooking bananas) are perhaps the cheapest sources of carbohydrates and calories. In western South America, which supplies more than half the bananas to the world and where sugar cane is produced most cheaply, it was estimated that banana carbohydrates can be produced at a cost of 2.0¢/pound, while cane sugar costs 2.9¢/pound (Watkins 1967). Furthermore, banana solids provide other nutrients, whereas cane sugar provides nothing but empty calories. Yet, with huge quantities of bananas available for practically nothing, it has been very difficult to develop a substantial market for any but fresh bananas, which have penetrated all world markets, undoubtedly in part because of their modest cost compared to other fruits. Canned and frozen banana puree is used largely in the baby food and bakery industries. Limited quantities of dehydrated bananas are also produced and used similarly.

The success story in starches is that of tapioca whose starch forms a smooth creamy pudding. The huge pudding-mix market utilizes tapioca starch. Prepared canned puddings are even more convenient. Since these puddings are prepared by aseptic methods in which very high temperatures are used, special modified starches are used for their formulations.

SOME CONVENIENCE FOODS ARE CHEAPER

Coffee and Tea

It is logical to assume that the buyer pays not only for the commodity he wishes to purchase, but also for any services that were built into the item. Thus, if convenience has been added to a product, the more convenient product should cost more. As we have seen above, this is the case with potato products. There are, however, many instances where the convenience item is in fact less expensive. A prime example is "instant" coffee. Some of us may still remember buying roasted coffee beans in the grocery store. Some grocers provided the use of a grinder without cost so that each buyer could have his coffee ground no earlier than at time of purchase.

Soon after the vacuum coffee can was introduced it became apparent that ground coffee would maintain its flavor in this type of container. Now the consumer was able to purchase ground coffee directly and retain all the flavor until after the can was opened. The coffee was prepared by consumers in a variety of ways, but generally by extracting water-soluble components from the coffee grounds with hot, but not boiling water.

This same process was used on a large commercial scale. The brew was then spray-dried. Since this dried matter contained nothing but water-soluble solids, it was possible to reconstitute it almost instantly simply by adding hot water. And so instant coffee was born. When coffee grounds are brewed in the home about 17% of the coffee solids are extracted. When done commercially, up to 32% of the solids are extracted. Furthermore, the dried extract occupies less space so that packaging and transportation costs are reduced. It turned out that a cup of the more convenient instant coffee cost little more than half the equivalent cup of coffee brewed from the grounds.

Later, when freeze-dried coffee became available, there was no rush to buy it although it presumably had much better flavor than lower priced, spray-dried instant coffee. Are we justified in concluding from this experience that we prefer convenience foods, but are not prepared to pay for better flavor? Perhaps. We might also conclude that most of us don't know or don't care about flavor differences in coffee as detected by a master blender or a professional taste panel. Perhaps we are "hooked" on coffee for other than flavor components, which are present equally in both spray-dried and freeze-dried coffee.

Similar developments with soluble tea were not as successful. Soluble tea has gained a market only for use as iced tea, obviously because of its greater convenience. Soluble tea dissolves in cold water so that instant tea can be obtained without bringing the water to a boil.

Processed Fruits and Vegetables

Practically all canned and frozen fruits and vegetables combine a high degree of convenience with reduced costs. This apparent paradox can be explained by the huge savings that can be made in mass production, and avoidance of spoilage in the processed fruits. Consider for example, the cost of a lb can of tomatoes as against that of a lb of fresh tomatoes. The vines of tomatoes intended for fresh market must be kept off the ground and carefully hand-picked, so their farm price may be 10¢/lb. Tomatoes going to the canner, on the other hand, are mechanically harvested so that their price on the farm is 4¢. Packing fresh tomatoes costs an additional 6¢, and the careful transportation and storage costs raise the price another 5¢. Then 5¢ more must be allocated for spoilage, as tomatoes are highly perishable. Thus, even at the height of the season, the cost of a lb of fresh tomatoes is 26¢. Add to this 7¢ for handling costs and profit to the retailer, and the minimum price for lb of tomatoes at the height of the season is 33¢. As everyone knows, the price is double this and more when tomatoes are out of season and must be shipped in from long distances or from greenhouses.

What are the canner's costs in addition to the 4¢ paid for the raw tomatoes? Five cents more cover his labor and other production costs. He will need to pay 7¢ for the container. Add to this 4¢ for overhead and profit, and the canned, peeled, ready-to-use lb of tomatoes cost only 20¢. Add to this 5¢ for handling and profit by the retailer, and we end up with a cost to the consumer of lb of peeled, ready-to-use tomatoes at a price substantially lower than the cost of the fresh tomatoes at the height of the season.

Cost of frozen fruits and vegetables would be essentially the same as the canned. The freezer would spend less on the container, but more on frozen storage and distribution. It may well be asked why a vegetable, and particularly a fruit, needs to be processed. If a consumer wants to eat a pear or a cherry, how can it be made more convenient for him than simply eating the pear or the cherry? This of course is true if he intends to consume the fruit as is, immediately. However, if he intends to use pears and other fruits in a salad or fruit cup or the cherries in a pie, it would be much more convenient and less expensive to purchase the prepared canned or frozen fruits already diced or sliced and ready to serve. The pitted canned cherries could be most conveniently placed on the pie shell and at a lower cost than freshly purchased cherries which require individual pitting.

If the reader is not yet convinced that more convenient fruits and vegetables can be purchased at less cost, we can look again at the pea situation. At the time of this writing peas in the pod are available if one looks hard enough at 39¢/lb. After some 15–20 min spent in shelling the pods, we will have something less than ½ lb peas. Thus, we are paying 80¢/lb of peas plus ¼ hr labor. At the same time we can purchase the best quality canned or frozen peas for 30–35¢ per pound, with no shelling time involved.

With the recent interest in energy savings, it is interesting to note that energy costs for preparing a serving of fresh, canned or frozen vegetables is about the same, with the least total energy assigned to the frozen product (Rao 1977).

WHAT CAN BE MORE CONVENIENT THAN AN EGG?

Eggs and Egg Products

Nothing is more convenient than an egg if what you want is a raw egg in the shell; if, however, you want just egg yolks or scrambled, or hard-boiled egg slices, there could be some convenience added to the raw egg in the shell so that you would be getting what you want with little or no preparation. Although the quality of dehydrated eggs has been improved substantially since the early 1940s, when this product was a prime source of complaints in the U.S. military, there is still no totally acceptable dehydrated egg product for use as such. Even for further processing, the fresh or frozen product is considered far superior in quality. Entirely satisfactory frozen products are now available not only as scrambled eggs, but fried with yolks intact, and boiled.

The ultimate in convenience and total utilization has been developed recently for the cook who wants prepared egg slices. This product consists of a 12 inch egg. Egg yolks are extruded and simultaneously cooked in the center of a cylinder, with egg whites on the outside. When cut, they produce 75 center-cut egg slices with no waste. One eggroll is equal to a dozen eggs, but yields more center slices than 17 medium-sized eggs. The eggroll is cooked, packaged in a casing and frozen. It may be thawed for use by immersion in boiling water for 7 min or in hot water for 15 min.

An imitation egg product which is cholesterol-free was developed recently. This product utilizes dried egg albumen and combines it with an artificial egg yolk-like formulation of which polyunsaturated safflower oil is the main ingredient.

Bakery and other food processing operations are important users of dehydrated and frozen eggs because eggs in this form are more convenient to use as ingredients in formulations or recipes.

Milk and Milk Products

Milk, along with hens' eggs, was long considered the near-perfect food in the western world. This attitude gained further credence during the first few decades of this century when the newly developing science of nutrition found most of the required nutrients present in goodly amounts in these animal products. The last substantial boost to popularizing universal use of milk was in the mid-twenties, when feeding studies with children indicated that a quart of milk a day was necessary for best growth and development.

Not long after this finding was widely disseminated, some additional information became available, which indicated that milk and eggs were not all good, and that their intake should be moderated. One of the first was the finding that the quart of milk a day was useful only if the total diet included substantial quantities of acid, particularly oxalic acid, which tied up much of the calcium in the milk. Without extensive use of foods high in oxalic acid, such as rhubarb and spinach, there was really no need for more than a pint of milk a day. A little later, in the forties (see Chapter 2) the scientific literature, closely followed by the press, expounded on the relationship between saturated fats, cholesterol, and heart disease.

Thus, by mid-century the steadily rising increase in per capita milk consumption was arrested and reversed. But long before this change in trend of milk utilization, the milk industry developed many new convenience products which expanded milk utilization. Cheese, butter, and sour milk or yogurt production are ancient arts which add to the convenience of milk only from the standpoint that they preserve the product so that all that is produced in a given time need not be consumed immediately. Canned evaporated and condensed milk made their appearance shortly after canning became popular. Because of the cooked flavor, these products were never used widely in the United States as a fresh milk substitute. Sweetened condensed milk, however, is considered a real delicacy (perhaps because of its sweetness) in other parts of the world. Evaporated milk is used widely as an ingredient in further processing and in cooking.

Ice cream and the many frozen milk and cream specialties became perhaps the most popular dessert in the United States, and spread over the world, taking their place along with soft drinks and French fries as major results of the American culinary genius. As the demand for milk was reduced, many states and regions provided legislation to protect milk prices. Dairy farmers received a special high price for a portion of their milk which was marketed as fresh-pasteurized, whole milk. The remainder was sold at lower prices and converted to a variety of other products.

When there was nothing else that could be done with the milk it was dried and stored as whole dried milk or fat-free milk solids, which are used in large quantities as ingredients in the manufacture of all types of food products at a relatively low price. From the early fifties, when it became obvious that the major nutritional problem in many parts of the developing world was inadequacy of protein, huge quantities of milk solids were provided by the U.S. under aid programs, even to some areas in the world where a high proportion of the population could not utilize milk properly. So heavy was this drain on U.S. supplies of milk, that it was being predicted 10 years ago that milk solids of all kinds would soon disappear. Apparently this has not happened.

In recent years the milk industry has finally accepted the fact that there is nothing sacred about milk. In 1923, at the height of its esteem, the Filled Milk Act was passed, essentially prohibiting the use of any other than a milk ingredient in what would be known or appear to be a milk product. It took many years of hard work to make the first break in this solid front, when it became legally possible to add coloring to hydrogenated vegetable fat so that it might resemble butter. Later, frozen desserts similar to ice cream but made of vegetable ingredients made their appearance. Finally in 1973, the Filled Milk Act was declared to be unconstitutional.

The milk industry responded to this change in its preferred status by diverting its activities into the manufacture and distribution of products other than milk. Dairies which bottle and distribute pasteurized milk, for instance, now frequently also bottle (or pack in the same type carton) and distribute pasteurized fruit juices. A satisfactory frozen milk concentrate, however, similar to the highly successful frozen juice concentrate still eludes the milk industry.

The very latest development is the appearance of a completely sterilized aseptically packaged milk that retains pasteurized-milk quality for months even if not refrigerated. This is accomplished by the UHT (ultra high temperature) technique; where milk is heated to a very high temperature, but only for one second or less.

Meat and Meat Products

As with other food commodity groups, man has long preserved red meat, poultry, and fish by sun drying, salting, or liberal use of spices. These, too, were not originally intended as techniques for producing a more convenient product, but were merely attempts to preserve food that could not be utilized immediately. As a result of such efforts, we now have a vast array of cured, smoked and/or dried meats, all with their distinctive flavors and other sensory qualities that are not only acceptable, but cherished by specific groups who have grown accustomed to these flavors. The most widely acceptable, typically American convenience product of this sort is, of course, the hot dog, which is nothing more than a variation of a middle European sausage (wiener or frankfurter). All these products, including the hot dog, are the last word in convenience. When properly prepared and packaged they can be eaten directly even without heating; however their very existence is now threatened because of the suggested link between nitrite-cured meats and cancer.

The modern development in convenience foods again revolves about freezing. As described in Chapter 6, fresh meat spoils very rapidly unless it is refrigerated. If held at 30°–40°F freshly slaughtered meats will retain satisfactory quality long enough to be shipped across a continent and distributed to the consumer, but not much longer. Practically all these meats can be frozen, thereby extending their fresh-like storage life for months or even years. Many seafoods and turkeys are so handled. However, there seems to be a strong prejudice by consumers against purchasing frozen red meats or poultry. Because of economic pressures, the freezing of portion-controlled pieces of meat is gradually gaining momentum. Recent studies indicate a potential saving of 16¢ per pound if meat is centrally cut into portions, frozen, and distributed as such instead of shipping whole carcasses, or even boxed primal cuts, by refrigerated transport. Meats prepared in this manner have some convenience advantage in that the consumer would be buying individual portions which he need not cut or trim further and would therefore not be buying waste. All such waste would be retained in the central processing plants and utilized for by-products.

Seafoods lead the list of meats in prepared frozen items. Breaded fish sticks and breaded butterfly shrimp are two examples of many such products. These products are the ultimate in convenience since all the consumer needs to do is heat and eat. The consumer should know, however, that when he purchases a breaded product, he probably pays as much for a product so prepared as he would for the same weight of nothing but meat. For example, a pound of shelled and deveined frozen shrimp does not cost much more than a pound of breaded shrimp, which consists of little more than half a pound of shrimp and up to a half pound of breading. Apparently the savings in the cost of raw material are utilized by the added work involved in adding the convenience of having the shrimp breaded in advance. Similarly, a stuffed turkey costs as much or more per lb total weight as one that is not stuffed. In all such cases the consumer is paying for the convenience of having a more completely prepared food. The one important red-meat item that is formed and frozen and ready to fry and eat is of course the 2 to 4 oz ground beef patty, the hamburger. But even the hamburger is not cooked before freezing. Thus the only red-meat items that can be canned or precooked and frozen and yet retain acceptable quality are of the stew type. The meat and flavoring industries are still searching for a technique or a flavor that will give a prepared frozen piece of meat the grilled or roast beef flavor and texture so popular today.

COMBINATION FORMULATED FOOD AND MEALS

Prepared Specialties

Much of the drudgery as well as the creative satisfaction of homemakers consisted of elaborate and time-consuming preparation of dishes and recipes favored by her family. With the increased value of labor, it is simply impossible for the many working housewives to put in the time to prepare these specialties. If this is true for the affluent, it is even more true of the poor, where the housewife, more often than in the affluent home, is a major contributor to the family income. A similar situation exists in away-from-home eating. A food service, whether it is in a restaurant, a school, or a hospital, is in the same position as the family. It simply cannot afford the labor involved in preparing meals from raw food materials. It is estimated that a highly efficient food-service operation using conventional raw materials and a minimum of any prepared ready-to-serve foods, will spend up to 40% of the expenditures on food, and much of the remaining 60% on labor. When a food service is converted to utilizing completely prepared ready-to-heat (if necessary) and serve items plus disposable utensils, costs are reversed, so that the food costs go up to 60% of the total. Labor and waste, however, are reduced to such an extent that there is an overall saving of at least 10% by such conversion.

What is the quality of such pre-prepared meals? Like everything else, it varies from poor to excellent. Certainly the average pre-prepared meal compares favorably with the average restaurant meal or even with the average meal prepared at home. Like other mass-produced items, mass-prepared meals are more bland than most consumers would like their foods, and tend to offend no one more than to please everyone. Of course the consumer may add other seasoning to the product as he chooses (Thorner 1973).

It may surprise some to know that many of our fine gourmet-quality restaurants can afford to maintain such a long list of exotic foods, varying from relatively simple products such as roast beef to such intricate foods as crepes Cannelloni, or lobster Canton, only because these products have been processed, packaged, and canned or frozen on a large scale in some central processing plant. The gourmet restaurant can stock these items ready-to-heat and serve as soon as an order is given. In the vast majority of cases, the customer is delighted with this prepared convenience item, although he might have preferred a freshly made entree by a truly gifted chef. In the fancy environment of the fine restaurant, and with gustatory and olfactory senses dulled by the pleasant dimly lit atmosphere and with a couple of drinks under his belt, he would usually not notice the difference. Since the recipes are usually made by gifted chefs under whose supervision the products are manufactured, these prepared products are usually good to excellent, that is, except the roast beef. Best-quality roasts and grills cannot be completely precooked. They can, however, be portion-cut, seasoned and partially cooked. The final searing must be done before serving. The "left-over" off-flavor encountered by air travelers can be eliminated by ultra-quick, cryogenic freezing.

Quantitative as well as sensory quality is of course related to price. When frozen TV dinners first came out in the forties, they usually contained 6 oz of meat, a green vegetable, and a potato product. Raw material cost per dinner was about 18¢. Cost of the aluminum dish, cover, and outer carton was also about 18¢, as was the cost of manufacturing the product, for a total of 54¢. This product was sold for 89 or 99¢, thus making it possible to pay for storage, distribution, and sales costs and yet leave some margin for profit. As more firms entered this market, competition forced prices down so that as of a decade ago, the price of the usual TV dinner was down to 39¢, sometimes 29¢. At such prices, even with more efficient production methods, it was impossible to remain in business without reducing quality of the container and of the product. Cost of container was reduced to some extent, but the major reduction in cost was in the quantity and quality of the food material itself. Thus instead of 6 oz of choice beef, the size of the portion was reduced and the quality as often as not was reduced to utility grade. Instead of a relatively expensive vegetable, such as asparagus with sauce, less expensive peas or greens were used, and instead of lightly fried potato puffs, French fries. At 89¢, the consumer could probably produce his own dinner at a similar cost, but he would still have the labor of preparing it. At 39¢, the consumer could not possibly duplicate such a meal for the price. Yet, apparently because of the poor quality, popularity of TV dinners dropped sharply in the late fifties and early sixties. Only when quality and price were again raised in the so-called "gourmet" dinners, did consumer acceptability rise again.

In recent years, new prepared canned and frozen food items are coming out daily, so that the variety available both to institutional and home buyers is tremendous. In one issue of *Food Engineering*, for example, a manufacturer introduced a line of skillet dinners. All the housewife needs to do is to add 1 lb of ground beef to the contents of a skillet dinner, and in 10 min. have a complete Mexican, Hawaiian, Oriental, Stroganoff, or Lasagna dinner. New developments from another processor requiring only heating and eating are crepes Seville, veal Cordon Bleu, chicken

Kiev, and crepes Cannelloni. A third processor introduced a new line of children's frozen dinners. Only with the aid of such prepared foods can the busy housewife compete with the high-price restaurant in quality and variety of her home-prepared meals, and at a fraction of the cost of eating out.

The big remaining problem is the breakfast meal, but this too is being solved by the introduction of nutritionally enriched complete breakfast drinks. In the same issue of *Food Engineering* (Añon., 1972E) there is a story about "Breakfast squares," which are creme-filled pastries with frosted toppings. Two squares provide all the nutrients in one egg, two strips of bacon, and two slices of buttered toast. They come in chocolate, butter pecan, cherry, orange, and cinnamon flavors.

While many of these new prepared meals or meal items are frozen, it should be emphasized that just as many high-quality prepared formulated foods are canned, as are many of the fancy entree items cited above. One such well-known and popular item, ravioli, has been available as a completely prepared canned food of excellent quality for many years. Although some chefs and housewives can produce ravioli of the same quality and some may even succeed in putting a little special flavor in their "hand-made" ravioli, they certainly cannot produce it at a cost of less than 50¢/lb.

Some dehydrated meals of excellent quality which will reconstitute quickly are also available, but not in the variety and profusion of the frozen and canned. Many of these originated as components of C (combat) rations which were dehydrated to reduce weight and space requirements. To be of high quality, these rations must usually be freeze-dried—an expensive process—so that these dehydrated products usually cost more unless lower transportation and storage cost reductions compensate for the initial higher cost. Thus in the mid-sixties, the A and B (Garrison-type) daily ration allowance was $1.00 to $1.10. This consisted of fresh, canned, and frozen foods. The C ration, consisting almost entirely of dehydrated foods, cost $2.72. Many of the best quality prepared dehydrated foods are fallouts of the military and space research. Although expensive, they provide the opportunity for outdoor campers, hikers, etc., to enjoy excellent quality instantly reconstituted foods. Now that retortable pouches are available as improved cans the Department of Defense will be replacing C-ration items from dehydrated to retorted (sterilized).

Additives

The term *additive* is now frequently suspect, probably because of all the clamor raised by some consumer advocates against any product that is not natural. Practically all the foods we eat contain additives—for example, yeast in bread, or vitamin A in milk. No additives are permitted unless they have been proven to be safe and have some functional purpose, such as preventing rapid staling of bread or vitamin A deficiency in milk. Currently most of the objections are to those additives used strictly for *cosmetic* purposes. But why the objections? Doesn't any cook like to prepare food that not only "*tastes* but *looks* goods"?

As stated earlier, there is little difficulty in preparing boiled, or stewlike canned or frozen convenience items as long as a sauce or gravy or other products containing fat and water mixtures are not included. Heating or freezing cause the water and fat phases to separate, so that in such instances special food materials called *emulsifiers* must be added. These emulsifiers have the property of being partly soluble in fat and partly soluble in water. When added in small quantities to a sauce, or even a cake recipe, they "stabilize" the product by preventing fat-water separation.

Jams and jellies, as well as many prepared foods such as gravies, puddings, pie-fills, stews, require thickening. This is usually accomplished for jellies and candies, such as gum drops, and for gelatin desserts by the addition of pectin, a low-calorie substance found in practically all fruits, or by the use of other gums found in such diverse plants as the carob (St. John's bread) and seaweeds. The most generally used thickener, however, is starch. Ordinary starch may not be satisfactory for thickening products that are subjected to wide temperature changes by canning or freezing. These additives also may not be effective if the recipe is too acid or too alkaline. In these instances special modified starches must be used.

To date the most versatile stabilizer, emulsifier, and thickener is a modified gum called xanthan, developed by the USDA (Rocks 1971) and approved for use in foods by FDA. One of its remarkable features is its tremendous thickening power. Increasing its concentration from 0.5 to 1.5% will increase product viscosity by more than 10 times. It is pseudoplastic and thixotropic, which means that the product to which it is added will continue to get thinner as it is stirred, then when stirring ceases, it will thicken up again. Perhaps the most unusual characteristic is its practically total independence of temperature and acidity. While most products get stiffer as they cool, xanthan is not affected either by heating or by freezing. Its viscosity changes very little across the entire pH (acidity) range. Because of these qualities, xanthan gives excellent shelf-life to salad dressings. As many as 5 freeze-thaw cycles can be experienced without changes in texture or consistency of the dressing. As little as 0.15% in cooked or instant starch puddings will control syneresis (water separation). It is particularly effective in sauces and gravies, protecting them against breakdown resulting from heating or freezing. It will make extra-thick milk shakes, prevent fat separation in canned meat, and oil separation in salad dressings.

Nutrient enrichment of these recipe foods, whether they are Irish stew or doughnuts, can be readily accomplished by the addition of the desired nutrients in the recipe. It should be noted, however, that now there are federal regulations limiting the amount and kind of nutrients that may be added. And, of course, nutrients as well as anti-oxidants, or emulsifiers, must be on the GRAS list before they can be added at all. (See p. 23-24, Chap. 4)

Imitation Foods

Imitation foods are usually foods that resemble natural foods but do not contain the natural food components. An imitation milk has essentially the same chemical composition as cows' milk, but the protein is not casein (the milk protein) but some vegetable protein (most likely from soya); the fat is not butter-fat, but some vegetable fat; and the sugar is not lactose (the milk sugar), but some vegetable sugar (probably glucose). To complete the formulation so that it will resemble milk in sensory quality, an emulsifier (such as monoglyceride), a gum (such as locust or carob), a whitener (such as calcium), and some flavoring must be added. To equal the nutritional quality of cows' milk, some vitamins and minerals may also need to be added (Rusch 1971). Does all this seem familiar, as if we've seen it before? We did, in Chapter 5 when we listed the "chemicals" that made up the coffee whitener.

Why go to the trouble of manufacturing an imitation milk when natural cows' milk is generally available? Surely there are few things more convenient for the consumer than having real milk delivered at his doorstep every other day. We must remember, however, that the milk to which we are accustomed is pasteurized, not sterilized, and it will therefore spoil within a day or two if not refrigerated, and within a week or two even if refrigerated. It would keep much longer if frozen, but we have not as yet learned how to freeze or dehydrate milk without affecting its quality and increasing its cost, particularly energy cost. Imitation milk is far more stable—single strength, concentrated, dehydrated, or frozen and, in this respect, it is more convenient.

The imitation milk is also more convenient in that it can be used by adherents to certain food codes such as vegetarians or orthodox Jews, and by those many millions who cannot digest cows' milk. A soy-milk drink such as the above is now outselling Coca-Cola in Hong Kong, and the use of similar imitation milks is increasing rapidly in other Far Eastern markets.

While imitation milks contain no natural milk components, filled milks usually contain defatted skim milk plus vegetable fat. Other products, not entirely "natural," must be labeled as imitations if they vary from the standardized composition, even if the variation is in the direction of the natural. Strawberry preserves, for instance, must contain ⅓ strawberry fruit solids and ⅔ added sugar solids. Dietetic strawberry preserves to which no sugar has been added so that they contain little besides the natural strawberry solids, must nevertheless be called "imitation" strawberry preserves.

The fruit equivalent of imitation milk is jelly made of an appropriate mix of sugar, acid, pectin, coloring, and flavoring. It is difficult to distinguish such an imitation jelly from the "real" jelly which is made of the same ingredients except that part of the sugar, acid, pectin, and all of the flavoring are derived from fruit juice. In this instance the advantages of the imitation product are more complete control of product quality and lower cost.

Nutritionally Complete Foods

The earliest formulated food that was designed to provide complete nutrients was the dehydrated baby formula which has been serving as imitation mother's milk for several generations. Next came the canned baby foods—another line of convenience items of American invention which were adopted world-wide. These baby foods were among the first food items to be controlled and often labeled for their nutrient contribution. They are totally convenient, since the busy mother can feed her child directly from the can or jar. An additional convenience is that the mother need not be a trained dietician, but can rely on the nutritional adequacy of the prepared baby food.

More recently, with the general availability of home-size blenders and mixers, it has become easier for the mother to prepare her own "natural" baby foods, at times at lower cost than those commercially prepared. These costs, however, do not include labor costs and assume a knowledge of nutrition which many mothers do not have. Although prepared baby foods contain some ingredients for "functional" purposes, these same ingredients also enrich the product nutritionally. Kenda and Williams (1973), for example, ask why it is necessary to add corn, milk, wheat flour, sugar, iodized salt, and onion powder to green beans to be fed to an infant, as is done by canned baby food manufacturers. The answer is that many of the ingredients are added for their "functional" properties and for flavor enhancement, not so much to satisfy the baby as the mother. As pointed out in Chapter 3, baby foods are unique in that their sensory quality is not rated by consumer panels representing the target population, babies, but by their mothers. Thus, flour is added to give the watery green bean slurry a thicker consistency, and incidentally to add protein, carbohydrates and fat. The sugar, salt, and onion powder are added to enhance flavor, and with the possible exception of the iodine in the iodized salt, contribute little to nutritive value. This highly convenient baby food was manufactured to provide nutrition for the baby-consumer, and palatability and convenience for the mother-buyer.

A similar situation was encountered when world-wide efforts were started to eliminate not only hunger, but also "hunger on a full stomach" in populations of entire countries and subcontinents of the developing world, and even in certain population pockets of the developed world. After nutritional deficiencies were identified, it was found that it was not enough to provide the deficient nutrients; it was also necessary to provide them in a form compatible with the tastes, traditions, and mores of the target population. It is now generally agreed that, given enough time, the problem of malnutrition could be solved by providing the nutrients plus mass education in nutrition. To solve the problem more rapidly, "imitation" foods containing all the required nutrients, and at the same time acceptable to the target population, must be devised.

The first and probably best known of these nutritionally complete foods is "Incaparina" which consists mostly of corn flour to which cottonseed flour, vitamin A, lysine, and calcium are added. This product is just beginning to be sold on its nutritional merits, after many years of unacceptability because it was considered a feed rather than a food by the populations of Central America to whom it was offered. A similar product that encountered the same acceptability problem is CSM, which is a mix of corn, soy, skim milk powder, and other nutrients, provided by the United States as part of the AID program. More success was achieved with pasta-type products, primarily because of their universal appeal. Since they are fabricated foods, various types of cereals and other ingredients available in all parts of the world could be used in their manufacture. A product developed and tested by General Foods is called Golden Elbow Macaroni. It is made from a blend of corn, wheat, and soy flours, and contains 20% protein. It has already been approved by the USDA for use in the school lunch program as a 50% replacement for meat. A major advantage cited by Clausi (1971) is that it is less expensive than regular macaroni, but it contains more protein.

The development of nutritionally enriched new and imitation foods was greatly stimulated by the invention of "spun" and otherwise "textured" proteins within the last two decades (Gutcho 1973). By these techniques, proteins derived from vegetable matter can be used to make all types of pasta or bakery products which have the same familiar quality as products made from cereals only, but which are richer in protein and other nutrients.

These textured ingredients are also being used to produce simulated meats and meat products having all, if not more, of the nutritive value of natural meat products. The sensory quality of these imitation meats is also simulated, if not completely, at least to the extent that they are acceptable as meat substitutes. They are already widely used in place of ground beef, bacon, and ham, chicken, and turkey rolls. These products are not only cheaper than the natural, but have practically no waste, are more stable when stored, and as they gain in popularity they may be the answer to the immediate problem of protein nutrient deficiency. Perhaps in the not-too-distant future a soyburger made of textured soy protein and other ingredients will be as available and as popular as the ubiquitous ground-beef hamburger.

8

Packaging and Marketing

*"Do not look at the flask
But what it contains."*
Ethic of the Fathers 4.27

Archaeologists who study the civilizations of prehistoric peoples, gain much of their knowledge from discarded food packages—the potsherds—of ancient man. It is almost impossible to think of a state of civilization where some form of food package or container was not available (Fig. 8.1). Today packaging is an essential part of food processing and

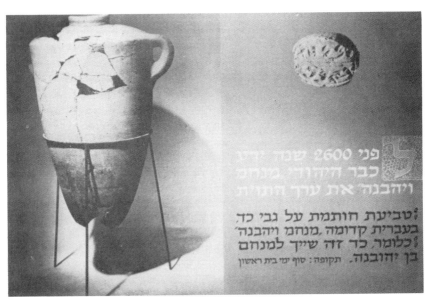

FIG. 8.1. PACKAGING AND LABELING CA 700 B.C. THIS JAR OF OLIVE OIL WAS IN-SCRIBED WITH THE FOLLOWING "LABEL": "THIS JAR BELONGS TO MENAHEM BEN YEHAVENEH."

preservation. Without effective packages, modern systems of food distribution would be impossible.

Packages are often divided into two categories: primary and secondary. We shall be concerned mainly with primary packages—those which contain the smallest unit of the food in question. An example may be made of a "case" of wine. The case is a cardboard or wooden box which contains a dozen bottles of wine. The glass and cork of the bottle comprise the primary package, while the fiberboard, wood, and straw of the case are secondary to preservation of the wine.

The principal materials used for primary packages are metal, glass, paper or other cellulosic materials, and plastic. The primary container has many functions, among which are the exclusion of dirt, microorganisms, oxygen, and/or moisture; the inclusion of oxygen, moisture, flavor, or other volatile constituents of the food; and, of course, the mere holding or containment of the food; and, of course, the mere holding or containment of the food itself. We will look more in detail at several of these factors as they apply to specific materials or special food problems.

PACKAGING MATERIALS

Metal Containers

Probably no single factor has influenced the development of modern food technology as much as the so-called "sanitary" can. About one-third of all primary food packages produced in the United States today are hermetically sealed cans. We are accustomed to referring to them as tin cans, although they are actually made of steel plate. The steel is usually coated with a very thin layer of pure tin. This is because tin is relatively inert, and also because there is a well-developed technology for coating steel with very thin, unbroken, films of tin. Steel cans which are untinned are also used to some extent as food containers, and other metals, largely aluminum, are becoming more prominent. Metal cans are nearly ideal packages for food. They are, either originally or by virtue of coatings, inert to the chemical action of the food. They are good heat conductors (important in processing). They may be made strong enough to resist any strains of filling, processing, and handling. They can completely isolate the food they contain from the surrounding environment, being impervious to gases, liquids, light, and microorganisms. They are light in weight, facilitating distribution.

Perhaps the simplest form of metal container is the biscuit tin, familiar to anyone who has resided in the British Isles or to Americans who can remember a time when minimum price was not a completely paramount factor in food packaging. It is a round or square metal box with a lid held on by friction. Its function is to protect the baked goods it contains from physical damage and to retain their freshness by preventing changes in the original moisture content of the food. It performs this task most admirably and is, in fact, considerably overdesigned. In some laboratories and homes these biscuit tins do service long after they have been emptied of their original contents at tea breaks, as sterilizing boxes for Petri dishes and pipets, and as containers for all manner of valuable gear.

But it is the hermetically sealed can which should occupy most of our attention in thinking of metal containers. As we have seen in Chapter 6, the can plays an essential role in thermal processing. It is made most frequently of thin steel sheet, electroplated with tin. The chemical composition of the steel used to roll the base sheet is carefully controlled to provide a surface that will best resist the corrosive action of the food for which it is used, and to ensure freedom from toxic metals such as arsenic and lead. There are four basic types of steel used for food cans; a fifth is used only for beer. They vary in the amounts of phosphorus, copper, nickel, chromium, and molybdenum. The strength of the can is determined by the thickness of the steel and the heat treatment to which it is subjected. Obviously, a large can which is used for a food sealed under a high vacuum will have to be a good deal stronger than a small can sealed under an average vacuum.

The can is made by cutting the tin plate into rectangles, which are curved into cylinders. The side seams are composed of interlocking hooked ends of the plate which are tightly pressed together ("bumped") and then joined on the outside with silver-lead solder. The can bottom is then attached by a rolling process and the top by a similar process after the can is filled. The attachment of tops and bottoms is accomplished without the use of solder by rolling a double seam in which a rubber-like sealing compound, which has been coated into a flange on the top or bottom, is tightly compressed between double layers of the final seam. This process can be completed while the can and its contents are in an evacuated chamber, thus providing lower pressure inside the can than in the surrounding air. This decreases the strain on the can when it is heated (raising internal pressure) during processing and keeps the ends tight after the can is cooled.

In addition to tin plating, many cans are enameled to protect the metal from corrosion. The enamel is usually applied to the sheet metal and finished by baking in ovens. Enamels, specially designed with food composition in view, are now used on a high proportion of cans, except where the bare tin itself has a desirable chemical effect. In applesauce and grapefruit, for example, tin acts as a reducing agent to prevent darkening of the fruit. In asparagus, it prevents the formation of an unattractive yellow precipitate, so that asparagus "canned" in glass is exposed to some tin, usually in the lid.

Cans are designated by expressing their size in inches and sixteenths with the diameter given first. For example, a 211 × 304 can is 2 11/16 inches in diameter and 3 4/16, or 3 1/4, inches tall. As in many other industries, there has been an effort in recent years to reduce the many different sizes of cans in use. This move toward fewer standard sizes is obviously to the advantage of retailers and consumers as well as to can manufacturers. There are probably still too many can sizes on the market, but additional changes in can dimensions may be coming soon, as the United States adopts the universally accepted metric system.

Although metal cans are nearly ideal food containers they do have some inherent difficulties. One is that if foods, especially acid fruits, are kept for long periods (several years), the tin plating will gradually crystallize and allow the acids of the food to combine with the iron of the steel sheet. This liberates gaseous hydrogen from the acids; as it accumulates, the internal pressure causes the ends of the can to bulge. Such cans are referred to as "hydrogen swells." They are not dangerous in themselves, but the average consumer could hardly be expected to be able to distinguish between a hydrogen swell and a can of spoiled food. Another weakness of cans is the seams, which can occasionally leak and allow microorganisms to enter the can, causing spoilage, or allow the contents to escape. On the whole, however, the metal can surpasses all other packages as a nearly indestructible, trouble-free container for long-term storage of food.

Glass as a Food Container

Glass containers have all the advantages of metal containers except for their greater fragility. To compensate for this, glass is more chemically inert than metal. Glass is not so impervious to light as metal, but it can be colored so as not to transmit harmful light rays and still be sufficiently transparent to allow a clear view of the contents. Glass containers are used in much the same way as metal cans for heat-processed foods. Because of its lower thermal conductivity, glass is not quite as efficient a packaging material as metal in this respect, but the difference is not very great in practice and is compensated for by the superior appearance of glass. Another disadvantage of glass containers is their greater weight for the same size container. Modern glass jars for heat-processed foods are designed so that they can be handled at high speed on filling lines and in closing machines. This was not always the case, and may have been the reason for some hesitancy to use glass containers in some situations in the past.

Glass jars (wide-mouth containers) and bottles (narrow mouths) are made by a combination of molding and blowing to size. The Glass Container Manufacturers Institute has developed a set of standard specifications from which designs may be chosen by the food processor. There are currently about 200 of these containers designed for food use. Some food processors may specify their own distinct shapes, but there is a growing trend toward the use of standard shapes and sizes.

As new glass containers come from the annealing oven they are somewhat subject to breakage because of their tendency to stick to each other when they bump. Hence, new glass is often coated with materials which will reduce the friction of its surface.

The part of the glass container that engages the closure is called the finish, and it must be constructed with a particular closure in mind. At the present time over 65 finishes in hundreds of size variations are commercially recognized.

The closure, of whatever type, is an important part of the food container, since the glass jar or bottle alone would be practically useless without it. Some of the more common closures are screw caps, lug closures (interrupted screw tops), pry-off caps with various types of gaskets (including "crown" seals), and corks or rubber stoppers.

The glass bottle or jar, along with the metal can, comes as close as any material we now have to completely isolating packaged food from the surrounding environment.

Paper and Related Materials

Another packaging material whose history predates written records is paper and its derived product, cardboard. The ancient Chinese are said to have discovered methods for converting cellulose fibers into paper-like materials, but even before this, primitive peoples used leaves (cellulose) to wrap food. The development of means for the cheap production of paper from wood pulp around 1800 may be regarded as the first great packaging revolution.

Paper and cardboard have many advantages for food packaging, including flexibility, low cost, ease of decorating and labeling, variable thickness and strength by manufacturing processes, and the ability to protect food from most external forces other than moisture and gas exchange. By laminating paper with metal foil or certain plastics, its ability to control exchanges of gases and water vapor (moisture) is greatly improved. Today a great many paper food packages incorporate some other material as a coating for paper or as part of the package. A good example is the plastic-covered milk carton, which has virtually replaced the milk bottle. A visit to a supermarket will show a surprisingly large number of items wrapped in paper; and if all packages that incorporate some paper or cellulose fibers are included, a very large proportion indeed of all primary packages will be accounted for. Shipping containers are almost universally constructed of cardboard in today's food industry.

The types of paper are so diverse that it is almost impossible to deal with them in a brief account and, in our role as consumers, we need not be greatly concerned with most. One recent development which certainly does engage our interest is the comparatively recent practice of impregnating paper with antimicrobial agents. In this way we can take advantage of some preservatives without adding them to the food. For example, cheese or bacon wrappers can be treated with propionates, which are mold inhibitors. These will prevent mold from growing on the surface of the cheese or bacon, just under the wrapper, without adding any significant amount of propionate to the food.

Flexible Film Packages

In spite of the excellent properties of glass and metal containers and the flexibility and low cost of paper, there was always a need for packaging materials that could combine light weight and flexibility with transparent, chemical inertness, and low water-vapor transfer rates. Such a need was met in part in 1927 with the invention of waterproof cellophane. This was rapidly followed by the development of many more plastic films, so that today a packaging engineer can find or design a film to supply almost any characteristic of strength, transparency, and gas and water-vapor transfer rates that may be required. This tremendous scope for varying the properties of these films stems from their chemical nature. All belong to a class of compounds called organic polymers. That means that they are made up of many small and identical units linked together chemically (polymerized) to form rather large molecules. By controlling the number of individual units in a molecule and by influencing the types, and hence the tenacity, of the bonds connecting them, the chemist can alter significantly the properties of the polymer. Beyond this the choice of different basic units for polymerization will yield plastics of a wide variety of characteristics.

Some of the polymers which are most useful for making packaging films are polyethylene, polyvinyl chloride, polyvinylidene chloride (saran), polypropylene, and polystyrene. The actual packaging films made with these and other polymers are marketed under many trade names, and it is often difficult to tell what the chemical nature of a particular film is from its name or description.[1]

In preparing a useful packaging film, the pure polymers are frequently coated with other materials which may contribute to better behavior

---

[1] The properties of these and other films are summarized in tabular form in *Encyclopedia Issues of Modern Packaging* (McGraw-Hill, New York).

during packaging operations or may impart special properties to the film. Polymers are also frequently laminated with other polymers or with paper or metal foil. For example, polypropylene in its pure form is a very poor gas barrier, but if it is coated with polyvinylidene chloride it becomes quite a good one. Similarly, when cellulose films (cellophane) were first produced they were poor moisture barriers and were of little use in the food industry. When in the 1930s coatings were developed which made cellophane moisture-proof and heat-sealable, they made possible the display and sale of packaged meat, one of the great revolutions in food merchandising of this century. Since then other films and other combinations have taken over the field, as they were found to have even more desirable properties for specific purposes.

In considering flexible packaging materials we must not lose sight of metal foil. The high ductility of metals makes it possible to stretch and roll them into very thin films. Gold leaf, which has been known and used for hundreds of years, is still one of the thinnest materials man has been able to make. In the food field, lead and silver foil have been used for a very long time. But the really widespread use of metal foil in food packaging came about with the development of aluminum foil.

As used for food packaging, aluminum foil is available in a considerable range of thicknesses from about 3/10 of one thousandth of an inch to about 0.001 inch and thicker. In the very thin grades aluminum foil is actually perforated by many microscopic holes and has a surprisingly high moisture-vapor transfer rate (much lower, however, than for a plastic film of the same thickness). In the thicker grades, especially when laminated with a film like a vinyl polymer or moisture-proof cellophane, it becomes nearly impervious to water vapor and other volatiles. It is now possible to construct flexible packages of aluminum foil—plastic laminates which can be used for thermally processed foods in the same manner as a tin can. As soon as these flexible pouches become less expensive than the conventional "tin" can, they could very well replace it. By their geometry, they need less heating for sterilization, thereby reducing energy costs, and they may prove to be higher in quality than the conventional can. Retortable pouches are already fairly common in Europe and Japan and may soon be readily available in the United States.

Not so new is the pressurized can. The pressurized or aerosol can was first developed as a means of dispensing insecticides. It has now been adapted to some food products, notably whipped toppings and similar creams and pastes. The pressurized can consists of a sturdy metal can—usually with a bursting strength of 150 psi (see Chapter 6)—surmounted by a control valve. The valve is connected to a tube extending to the bottom of the can. The can is filled with the food material and a propellant gas, which is usually a mixture of alkyl chlorides and alkyl fluorides (Freons) which boil well below room temperature so that they generate considerable pressure. By mixing high- and low-boiling propellants, it is possible to obtain almost any pressure desired in the can. When the valve is released, the contents flow from the bottom of the can, while the propellant expands to fill the upper part of the container. A seltzer water siphon is a familiar example, although it is not classed as an aerosol container.

The pressurized container greatly eases the labor of providing whipped cream for ice-cream dishes and other confections, and makes it possible for amateurs to perform easily tasks like decorating pastry, which otherwise require great skill in preparing and handling the toppings.

THE PACKAGE AS A MICROCLIMATE

In describing the various packaging materials we have referred to the ability of the package to isolate its contents from the surrounding environment. Another way to express this is to say that a microclimate is created within the package. It is rather easy to see how this works for the hermetically sealed can, glass jar, or bottle. Within the can or jar the food scientist or packaging engineer can enclose any atmosphere he wishes. He can either admit or exclude light, depending on whether he chooses a metal, or clear or colored glass. He can control temperature by storing the package at a controlled temperature, but he must accept an internal relative humidity temperature determined by the vapor pressure of the food at the storage temperature. Since in the case of the can, bottle, or jar the package is completely gas- and moisture-tight, foods containing substantial amounts of water will bring the relative humidity of the internal atmosphere to 100% in a short time, and it will stay at that level. As indicated earlier, this is very nearly an ideal situation for many foods, particularly those that are rendered sterile by heat-processing. The same sort of package is called for when preserving foods like dehydrated meats, vegetables, and fruits, or dehydrated foods like spray-dried milk, dehydrated soups or other dry foods, like beans, peas, flour, etc. For these low-moisture foods, the purpose of the package is to maintain low levels of humidity so that the food will not cake or become sticky. In fact, desiccants or oxygen scavengers are sometimes enclosed in the package to absorb excessive water vapor or oxygen.

When fresh fruits and vegetables or chilled meat are to be packaged, the requirements are somewhat more sophisticated. Those foods are still actively respiring and, in certain cases may still be considered as being living organisms. For maximum storage life and the preservation of optimum quality, such foods must be packaged with regard for their

respiratory needs. Here the ability to incorporate many different properties into a plastic film has brought about great changes in marketing
and allows us to enjoy fresh foods at seasons when they were unknown 40
years ago. In the case of most fruits and vegetables, the package is
designed to retain water vapor to protect the produce from loss of weight
and turgidity, but to allow for rather free passage of oxygen and carbon
dioxide to permit normal respiration (breathing). For this purpose polyethylene bags (polybags) are used. Polyethylene is a very good moisture
vapor barrier, but a relatively poor oxygen and carbon dioxide barrier.
Sometimes small holes are punched in the polybag to allow for more
complete exchange of oxygen and carbon dioxide.

In other situations, where it is desirable to reduce rate of respiration,
the polybag is sealed tightly and no holes are punched. This allows the
oxygen level in the bag to be reduced, and the carbon dioxide to rise. This
change in the atmosphere within the bag slows down respiration rate and
extends the shelf life of the produce so packaged. For a more detailed
discussion of gas exchange see Chapter 6.

Fresh meats present a similar situation, but for different reasons. The
red color of fresh meat is important to consumers because to them it is an
indication of freshness. The desired bright red color depends for its
maintenance on a plentiful supply of oxygen. The oxygen must be present to keep the pigment myoglobin (a respiratory pigment similar to
hemoglobin) in its red or oxygenated state. If the pigment is reduced (in
the absence of oxygen) it turns a dark, reddish-purple color. Furthermore, if the meat is allowed to dry out it becomes very dark, almost
black. Hence a packaging film is needed which is highly permeable to
oxygen but impermeable to moisture vapor. The film must also remain
transparent so that the purchaser can judge the color fairly. No film
completely answers these needs but many come close. Modern practice
tends to favor oriented polypropylene and some polyvinylidene chloride
(saran) films for this purpose. The latest product to meet this need is
Iolon, which contains oxygen is a form permitting it to escape gradually
thereby extending the red shelf life of freshly cut meats. A similar
product applied to portion controlled frozen meat is not quite entirely
satisfactory because the water crystals in the frozen meat reflect light so
that the frozen meat does not appear to be entirely "natural", although it
really is.

Cured meats, such as ham and bacon, have different needs. In this
instance the red color is due to a fixed compound called nitrosylmyo-
globin which, if oxidized, turns a rather unsightly brown color. Hence a
film which is impervious to both oxygen and moisture vapor is wanted.
This need has been met by many coated polymers, laminates, and some
pure plastics.

Other foods, and some nonfood items like nursery stock and cut flowers, present special problems in atmospheric control which can be met by specially designed packages. All in all, the ability of the package to establish its own internal climate has gone a long way to provide our markets with fresh food of high quality in every season.

THE PACKAGE AS SOLID WASTE

There can be no doubt that discarded packages contribute to the solid waste problem. As indicated at the beginning of this chapter, this is hardly a new problem, but it has certainly been aggravated by time, an exploding human population, more extensive use of packages, and the development of new materials including polymers that are not readily biodegradable. A concern for the proliferation of solid waste is surely justified.

Until recent years many glass bottles were returnable and therefore reused (recycled) many times before they were discarded. As this was not economical, many soft drink bottles are now used once only. The returnable milk bottle is also rapidly disappearing. Other glass containers such as those used for alcoholic beverages never were returnable. Environmentalists and all concerned with the mounting waste disposal problem decry the replacement of the returnable bottle with a one-time disposable container. Discarded glass can be recycled economically provided the glass can be collected and delivered at reasonable cost to the furnace where new glass is made. It has also been suggested that glass be ground and used as a building material.

Discarded metal cans do not constitute very good scrap for remelting. They are, however, readily degraded, so that they do not pose the problem that glass does in terms of waste accumulation. If buried in the ground, steel (tin cans) soon oxidizes and becomes part of the soil. It may be lost as usable iron, but does not then represent an unsightly waste problem, as do undegradable glass and aluminum containers. Perhaps a time will come when it will pay to classify and separate municipal waste so that all discarded tin cans can be collected and compacted for remelting.

Paper and some plastics when burned are converted mainly to carbon dioxide and water. This is the best way to recycle such materials, especially if, on a global scale, reforestation were more vigorously promoted to fix carbon from the atmosphere. Much of the concern which is frequently expressed about the "biodegradability" of plastic packaging materials ignores the importance and simplicity of the carbon cycle.

THE PACKAGE AS A HEALTH HAZARD

Although packaging is indispensable today, and the safety record of packaged foods is far superior to that of any other modern mechanism (automobile, for example), the consumer should be aware that some hazards are associated with every type of package. In this section we shall refer to the hazards of the packaging materials themselves, not the food the package protects, which was discussed elsewhere, particularly in Chapters 4 and 6.

A common misconception among many consumers is that once opened, the unused portion of the can contents must be emptied into another container and refrigerated. Since the can had been sterilized, and remains so until opened, while the dish into which the contents might be transferred is probably not sterilized, there is therefore a margin of added safety in leaving whatever food had not been used in the original can, covering the open end with a piece of film or foil, and returning to the refrigerator where the low temperature will not permit growth of pathogenic microorganisms.

There is some hazard in the opening of the tin cans. Every can should be wiped clean before opening, and the consumer is well advised to use a good, easily cleaned can opener which will not introduce filth or slivers of metal into the food. The only material composing the can which may remotely be toxic is the solder on the outside of the side seam, so that there is little danger of any of the lead in the solder entering the contents. The metal slivers, although nontoxic, may cause mechanical damage if consumed. Both easy-to-open cans and conventional cans may have sharp edges so that it is advisable to remove the contents with a utensil rather than with fingers, and certainly not with the tongue.

Hazards of the glass container are generally similar to those of the can, but since glass is more brittle, there is a greater opportunity for pieces or slivers of glass to enter the food. Besides breakage on impact, the most likely opportunity for glass to enter the product is when the container is opened. The consumer should therefore discard not only an obviously broken or cracked bottle or jar, but also one in which the "finish" and lid appear to be imperfect.

Any containers that are under pressure, intentional or not, have the potential of blowing up. Conventional cans are less of a risk, since cans swell before they burst, and the consumer can discard any cans that begin to swell. Glass, however, is rigid, and on the very rare occasions that it is improperly sealed, the cap can be blown literally into the consumer's face. All pressurized containers, therefore, should be opened with care.

Paper and plastic containers may also be pressurized or evacuated. Some potato chips, for example, are packaged in clear laminated foil with good gas-barrier properties, into which an inert gas such as nitrogen is introduced to "cushion" the chips against breakage. Eventually the gas escapes, but never in an explosive manner that might injure the consumer. Evacuated, "shrink-wrap" techniques are now becoming very common. Their chief advantage is that they remove the air, including the oxygen, from the atmosphere in the package, thereby reducing the chances for oxidation of the contents, which causes rancid off-flavors and color changes. In this situation also, there is no particular hazard to the consumer, except for the extremely remote possibility that some anaerobic pathogens that may have survived an inadequate process would find this anaerobic environment favorable to their growth.

Paper and plastic packaging of itself is inert biochemically, and even if consumed, will do no harm. The only possible hazard from the ingestion of these materials is from the binders, solvents, or printing inks that may diffuse from within the sheets or their outer surface to the inside surface, and from there to the food. All such packaging materials are therefore carefully tested to preclude such a possibility, not only because of possible toxic effects of these substances, but also because of the undesirable effects of such diffusion on the appearance and flavor of the food and the package.

For all packaged foods the consumer should avoid the adage: "If everything else fails, read the directions." Instead he should read the label carefully, and follow the directions—particularly those required to be posted prominently for his protection. Any label statement indicating, for instance, that a package of food should be refrigerated, should be complied with. Usually such products are not sterilized, but only pasteurized, even if they are packed in a can (canned ham or crab meat, for example). If foods so labeled are not refrigerated they will deteriorate rapidly in quality, and may become hazardous to health. Directions regarding dates of expiration should be adhered to for the same reasons.

In the case of most frozen packaged food, directions for thawing and heating should be followed, since most frozen foods are not prepared and packed in a manner that assures their sterility; sterilization to eliminate possible pathogens must be accomplished in the final heating before eating by the consumer.

In general if there is any doubt whatsoever about the continued safety of a packaged food, it should be refrigerated. Refrigeration will rarely do any harm, and in addition to preventing the growth of pathogenic organisms, will also help to preserve the nutrients.

THE PACKAGE AS A SALES PROMOTER

It is usually the package, rather than its contents, that "sell" the product. This is no less true of foods than any other consumer goods. The food packaging engineer therefore designs a package not only to create the appropriate microclimate to maintain the wholesomeness and sensory and nutritional qualities of the food, but also with an eye for sales appeal.

It is a well-established fact that the best and surest way of gaining a market for any food product is to get space on supermarket shelves so that the packages can be prominently displayed to consumers who generally buy on impulse. Thus, an attractive package and label is a "must" for any food manufacturer. Of course, the intelligent consumer should ignore the shape of the container and the artistry of the label, and pay attention only to the real information, which has to do with the quantity and quality of the contents. There are government regulations that protect against excesses in this direction, which go under such names as truth in advertising. A typically food-related label item that is carefully controlled for the protection of the consumer is the "vignette," illustrating the contents. This cannot be shown to be substantially different from the contents as they are in fact.

CONCLUSIONS

Food packaging is an indispensable part of processing, distribution, and marketing. The production of heat-processed, shelf-stable foods, over one-third of all our food supply, would be impossible without metal and glass containers. For retaining freshness in fruits and vegetables and for holding refrigerated meat cuts in salable condition, flexible plastic materials are now also indispensable. Their use has made it possible to buy fresh carrots all year round, to select steaks by personal inspection, and to provide lightweight, durable protection for many perishable or otherwise fragile items. In all these cases we look to the food package to do a few essential things: it must protect the food from dirt; it must exclude microorganisms, insects, or other contaminating agents; it must exclude oxygen and moisture from the surrounding atmosphere when this is important; it must permit gaseous exchange with the surrounding atmosphere when this is wanted; and it must act as a suitable container for holding and viewing the food in the channels of distribution.

9

Waste Disposal and Utilization

*". . . All are of the dust
And all turn to dust again."*
Ecclesiastes III, 20

The ancients recognized that all life springs from the earth and returns to the earth, thereby revealing a basic understanding of a complete life cycle on earth. The soil nourishes plants which in turn nourish animals. The animals then return to earth and are transformed into nutrients for plants. As discussed in Chapter 1, it was only two centuries ago that Malthus first questioned the ability of the earth to sustain unlimited growth. It is only in recent years that we have begun to question the typically American philosophy that the success of any operation is measured by rate of growth, and that no growth at all is in fact an indication of failure. Reports of two recent studies indicate that unless drastic steps are taken to reduce consumption and pollution, this planet is headed for disaster.

The first book, called *The Limits to Growth* (Meadows *et al.* 1972) is the work of a team of engineers and scientists at MIT led by Dennis Meadows, who at 29 was the oldest member of the team. The book, sponsored by the international Club of Rome, was the subject of a press buildup when it was released and has been widely reviewed in the United States and elsewhere, generating a great deal of controversy in the process. As might be expected, it has been widely damned by economists, but also highly praised by well-known amateur ecologists and not-so-well-known professional ecologists.

The Limits to Growth asks whether "spaceship earth" has sufficient resources to survive unlimited economic growth, and answers that pursuit of growth will inevitably lead to cataclysmic increases in death rates and declines in industrial output before the year 2100, no matter which of its assumptions are used. The computer model on which the study is based focuses on four constraints of growth: population, pollution, availability of food, and availability of energy resources. It is assumed that unrestrained growth will continue to increase exponentially. To illustrate the effect of exponential growth: if demand for resources increases at a compound rate of 4% per year, demand by the year 2100 would be about 125 times the current demand; if demand grew linearly by only 4% of current demand, it would reach only 6 times current demand by the year 2100.

In the usual Malthusian manner, the authors assume technologically fixed limits on food supply, indicating that agricultural yield cannot exceed twice that of current levels. This is equivalent only to a 0.6% annual increase to the year 2100. Apparently the authors did not consider such facts as the possibility of a 50% increase in existing food supplies, if all foods were stored optimally—that is, at such temperatures and humidities and in such structures as would prevent them from becoming waste before they are consumed. Thus, the relevant question for future research is whether such factors as improved processing, storage, and transportation, together with mechanical production of food based on new chemical and genetic processes, utilization of formerly unarable land, and farming of the seas can keep food supplies growing at 3–4% per year.

To achieve only 1.7% growth in resources a year, the authors indicate that 75% of resources must be recycled. If this degree of recycling is achieved, resources should not run out by the year 2100. The crash induced in the model was due to pollution or famine. The model assumes that pollution per unit of industrial output can be reduced to no less than one-fourth of current levels. This is equivalent to only about 0.9% annual decline in pollution per unit of output. Although the book gives examples of the sharply rising costs of reducing pollution generated by chemical processes, it tends to ignore the more important declines in pollution available by changing the chemical or other processes involved, such as banning internal combustion engines in automobiles and the use of soft coal for fuel. It is most interesting that energy consumption, the constraint least emphasized by Meadows *et al.*, should have suddenly become *the* limiting constraint just a couple of years later. While the oil embargo of 1974 caused much concern and increased attention to the need to limit growth, we are still floundering on a rational policy for energy conservation.

By assuming absolute limits in agricultural yields, resource availability and pollution control, the authors have stacked the deck. One does not need a computer to know that if demand is growing exponentially and supply is fixed at some level, demand will eventually exceed supply. If that assumption is relaxed, then small changes in the numbers can change the model's results to show that a crisis can be avoided while allowing continuation of growth. The basic question is what technology can do to relax the "limits" to growth. As the *Economist* of London pointed out 100 years ago, a city the size and density of London today would have appeared technologically infeasible because it would be covered in a deluge of horse manure. To cite an example from the food industry, if all freezing were done by immersion in calcium chloride, there would be by now, with the great increase in freezing, a serious pollution and/or waste disposal problem of the calcium chloride. Instead, calcium chloride is rarely used; fluorocarbon refrigerants create practically no pollution problem, since they are recycled to the extent of about 98%.

Meadows *et al.* conclude that the only way to prevent a catastrophe is to stop the growth of both population and industry. Under their "global equilibrium," per capita income would be about half the current U.S. income, but about three times the current world average. The authors recommend that this income be distributed fairly equally among countries, but they do not explain how to convince Americans to cut their living standard in half.

The Limits to Growth was written essentially from the standpoint of developed countries. No consideration was given to the environmental problem of the poor countries which already have the kinds of pollution that are lethal, e.g., cholerapolluted water supplies. *The Founex Report* (International Congress on the Environment, Stockholm, 1972) points out that growth and development are necessary for solving these more serious environmental pollution problems. If one measures the relationship between per capita income and all types of pollution, it is clear that up to a certain point the improved health and sanitation measures outweigh costs of industrial and agricultural modernization. These gains are compounded by declines in fertility that appear to accompany income growth.

The Founex Report, however, also expresses serious concern about growth-induced pollution and recommends steps to control it. There is general agreement that if population and pollution growth continue at past rates, the earth would reach a point of catastrophe sooner or later, if not in the year 2100.

It is clear, therefore, that the big challenge to food technology is to accelerate food production at a faster rate than population growth. At the same time we must recognize that the problem is two-pronged: increasing the food supply on the one hand, and environmental control, particularly pollution control, on the other. Increased utilization rather than disposal of pollutants offers the best opportunity for solving both prongs of the problem. Maximum utilization, particularly of food wastes, would not only reduce waste disposal, but would at the same time increase the food resources available to the rapidly expanding world population.

INCREASING THE FOOD SUPPLY

Before going to the ultimate of returning to the use of night soil and more technical methods of converting human waste into foods (which are being considered seriously in connection with extended space flight), we can increase the availability and utilization of foods that are being produced by less than Herculean efforts and by techniques that offend no one's sensibilities. In approximately the order of ease of accomplishment, the techniques fall into the following categories: (1) improved storage and transportation; (2) manufacture and preservation of by-products; (3) utilization of solid and liquid wastes at the processing plant; (4) total utilization of field crops.

Improving Storage and Transportation

It is conservatively estimated that even before crops are harvested fully, half the potential harvest is lost to infection (fungal diseases), infestation (insects), and depredation (larger animals). The losses are far smaller than if organic farming were generally practiced, when these field losses would probably rise to about 90% of the potential crop yields. Much progress has been made in controlling field losses by the use of effective pesticides. Partly in response to demands of environmentalists who are concerned about survival of wildlife, the current emphasis in plant protection has been in the direction of biological control. This can take two forms. One method is to produce male sterility in the vector so that the population of the offending species dwindles for lack of reproduction. The other is development of diseases that will affect the survival of the offending insect species. A more permanent solution to these problems is changing the genetic structure of the host plant, so that it becomes "resistant" to attack or invasion by the predator.

Further damage can be done to the plant material during harvesting and transportation to storage or market. This can be minimized in the case of grain, for example, to not more than 5%, if the grain is treated properly, dried sufficiently, and put in rodent-proof storage. In many instances, however, particularly in developing countries where much of the storage is done in inadequate structures on the farm, storage losses can be 50% or higher. Such losses can be minimized, and food supply can be increased substantially almost overnight if adequate rodent-proof storages were available where grains could be died and, if necessary, fumigated.

Dr. Mogens Jul (1971), Secretary of UNICEF Protein Advisory Group reported that 11 million of 380 million children living in developing countries suffered from severe malnutrition, and 76 million more from moderate forms of malnutrition. At the same time, out of a total 2.5 billion tons of the world's major foods, well over 1 billion tons were perishable, and needed not only storage, but refrigerated storage. It is known that there is room for less than 1% of the total food supply in refrigerated storage the world over. Thus, if refrigerated storage capacity were to be increased by 25 to 50 times, the food so preserved would provide everyone with a sufficient supply for some years.

Manufacture and Preservation of By-products

The above discussion covered food materials that become waste products even before they can be preserved for consumption. Another huge category of perfectly good foods become waste simply because they are not utilized in the manufacture of the primary food product. Those portions of the plant not suitable for the manufacture of that one product are either left to rot in the field, or to accumulate as waste at the factory site.

It is estimated that only 20–30% of the vegetable plant is utilized directly for human consumption in the United States. If the remaining 70–80% of the material could be converted into nutrients for man, animals, or plants as food, feed, or fertilizer, total nutritional resources could be vastly increased and at the same time the waste disposal problem could be minimized.

Good examples of substantial and successful processing waste utilization already in effect are found in the meat-packing and citrus-processing industries (Ben Gera and Kramer 1969). Yet even in these operations there is much room for improvement. Meat packers do a good job of utilizing "all but the squeal." However, they ship out entire carcasses. This leads to waste when the carcasses are further cut up by distributors and then reduced to consumer-size units by the retailer. Moreover, the greatest proportion of waste is perhaps produced by the ultimate consumer when he prepares and consumes the meat at home. As discussed previously in Chapter 7, much, if not all, of this waste could be avoided if meat packers would in the first place prepare and ship portion-controlled cuts. All the waste could then remain in the packing house, where it could be utilized efficiently for a variety of food and non-food by-products.

The major outlet for citrus processing wastes is in the form of animal feed, although small quantities of peel are utilized in the manufacture of marmalade (which incidentally is an excellent source of vitamin C), candied (sugar-coated) peels, and flavoring oils. A recent development in Europe is the introduction of "comminuted juice drink." Entire fruits or just the peels and pulp, are wet-milled into a paste. This comminuted citrus can be used as a flavoring ingredient as such, or in quantities of

3—5%, can serve as a base for the comminuted juice drink. The paste is not only high in vitamin C and vitamin A, but also contains natural anioxidants that help preserve the product to which it is added from discoloration and off-flavor.

Unfortunately, neither portion-controlled, thoroughly trimmed fresh-frozen meats nor citrus peels have gained wide acceptance in the United States, largely because of the reluctance of consumers to change their buying habits. Thus, again we find that it is the consumer rather than government or industry who stands in the way of expanding food resources. As usual, it will be a good part of a generation before the consumer, influenced by the bargain prices of these new by-products, is persuaded to take advantage of such developments.

Sorting, peeling, trimming, and coring are the major operations in the vegetable-processing industry that result in the formation of vegetable waste. Table 9.1 shows the amount of waste formed in the processing of different vegetable crops. The U.S. Dep. Agric. (1965) estimated for the period of 1951—1960 average annual losses during processing of more than $19,000,000 in edible vegetable material on the basis of the percentage of losses in Table 9.1, the price of the raw material, and the quantities processed. This includes loss of soluble nutrients through leaching during the different steps of processing, as well as losses from excessive peeling and trimming and the removal of culls.

TABLE 9.1. PERCENTAGE OF VEGETABLE CROP LOSSES RELATED TO PROCESSING

Commodity	According to Mercer[1]	According to Dickinson[2]	Other
Asparagus	30	—	50
Beans, green	—	20	5
Beans, lima	—	—	85
Beets	38	40	27
Broccoli	—	—	60
Brussels sprouts	—	—	10
Cabbage	—	—	25
Cauliflower	—	—	50
Corn, sweet	72	—	86
Cucumber, pickling	—	—	5
Peas	—	—	79
Potatoes	—	—	5
Spinach	—	40	40
Sweet potatoes	—	—	15
Tomatoes	25	—	33—66

[1] Mercer (1965).
[2] Dickinson (1960).

Some of the losses are uneconomical to recover. This is mainly the case with nutrients lost by leaching. Other types of waste are not yet fully utilized, mainly because of the seasonal nature of vegetable-canning operations and the perishable nature of the raw waste material (its high moisture content makes a drying treatment necessary if the material is to be utilized over a period of time). The high price of drying is still a major obstacle to economical utilization of vegetable wastes. According to Mercer (1965), utilization of dehydrated solid vegetable waste is largely confined to tomato wastes and, to a limited extent, asparagus and spinach wastes. Sanborn (1961) states that the only vegetable wastes utilized in quantity are pea vines and corn husks and cobs, which are utilized for animal feeding during wintertime. Pea and corn wastes are seldom wasted but are used as livestock feed. Cobs and husks are usually shredded and transported to dairies and livestock establishments, where they are ensiled or utilized fresh.

Problems in utilization of vegetable and fruit processing or production wastes as foods or feeds may arise from the level of residue of chemicals found in them. Yet if and when the need for more food and/or the problems of waste disposal become sufficiently serious, either solutions less expensive than dehydration and omission of pesticides will be found, or new and less expensive recovery techniques will be developed.

Thus, for example, a process for totally utilizing tomato cannery waste was developed, in which the waste was compressed. The presscake containing two-thirds of the solids, 10% protein, was used as cattle feed, and expressed liquor containing one-third of the solids, 60% protein, was precipitated as a tomato protein concentrate. This concentrate can be extracted with acetone to form an 85% protein isolate, plus a tomato flavor and pigment residue (Fig. 9.1). This tomato protein concentrate has unusually good functional properties and a protein efficiency ratio similar to soy protein concentrate (Kramer et al. 1971). It is estimated that for a sufficiently large-scale operation and with the waste provided at no cost, a pound of tomato protein could be produced for about 10¢.

About one-third of the tomatoes delivered to processing plants end up as processing waste. Of the 5,000,000 tons of tomatoes processed annually in the U.S., more than 2,000,000 tons are wasted. With the introduction of mechanical harvesting, the quantity of such waste material is estimated to be doubled. Thus, if the wastes accumulating in U.S. tomato canneries alone could be converted into food fit for human consumption, they would provide all the nutritional requirements for a population of about 3 million people. Similar procedures have been developed for other crops, and more can be expected, so that eventually current food supplies can be increased by as much as 70% to satisfy existing deficiencies, and help feed additional millions yet unborn. All this, provided that these new waste-extracted food ingredients are produced in a safe and sanitary manner, and in a form that is acceptable to the target population.

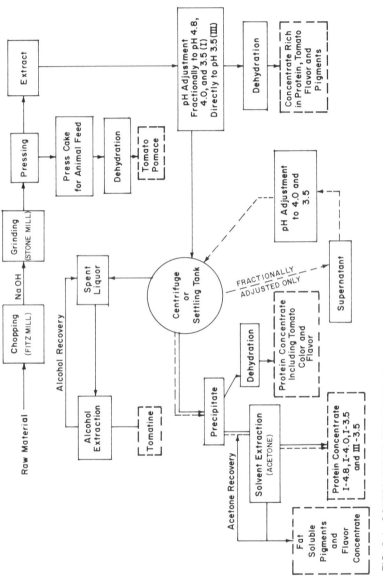

FIG. 9.1.   SCHEMATIC FLOW CHART OF A PROCESS FOR THE TOTAL UTILIZATION OF TOMATO WASTE.

Cheese whey is a sticky waste material. It has approximately the same nutrient composition as tomatoes, and its recovery as dehydrated whey solids, or as a whey protein concentrate and milk (lactose) sugar, is simpler than the processing of tomato cannery wastes. Already perhaps one-third of the whey accumulated in the United States as a result of cheese manufacture is being utilized as a component of many processed foods, filled milk among them. Studies (Kramer *et al.* 1971) have demonstrated that it is not necessary to sustain the cost of drying the whey, but that it can be used "directly from the vat" to produce a variety of highly acceptable foods ranging from filled milk to sherbet to wine and beer. Total utilization of the whey now going to waste could provide an additional 3 million people with their nutrient requirements.

Permitting nutrients in whey to go to waste is not as serious as waste materials lost in other manufacturing. In Southeast Asia, for example, where protein deficiency is common, hundreds of thousands of tons of the mung bean, which contains approximately 25% protein and 50% carbohydrates, are processed into very fine translucent noodles (like vermicelli), highly prized around the world, usually as components of Chinese-type foods. These noodles consist of little more than the mung starch. In the process, the high-quality mung protein is lost as waste. Procedures are now available to precipitate this protein from the mung noodle waste. If only half of this protein were recovered, sufficient protein would be available to provide at least 5 million people with their total recommended protein requirements. If this mung-waste protein were utilized merely to raise the level of protein to a minimal level, it would suffice for at least 50,000,000 people.

Water

Potable water is the nutrient required in the greatest quantity (see Chapter 2). It is also the largest single wasted material during commercial food processing, as well as in the home preparation of food. According to Mercer (1965), about 50 gallons of water are utilized to produce one case containing approximately 30 pounds of canned food. From zero to a maximum of 2% of this water is included in the net weight of the finished product; thus 98% or more of the water must be disposed of as waste. It is common practice for commercial food processors to screen their waste water. A survey of 113 canneries (Wilson *et al.* 1971) showed that only two did not screen their waste water. The screened solids were disposed of as feed in a few instances, but in most cases they were either composted or disposed of by other means providing no recycling of nutrients. Since the screened liquid waste contained substantial amounts of organic matter, it was either discharged into a municipal sewer system or further treated before being returned to field or stream so as not to disturb the ecological balance.

Although there are vast quantities of water-soluble nutrients in such waste waters, it is rarely worthwhile from the economic standpoint to attempt to recover them for use as food or feed. In those few instances where the waste water was spray-irrigated, it did contribute to soil enrichment as a very dilute, but readily available fertilizer.

The big opportunity for water conservation is in the processing plant itself. Most food-processing plants now follow a countercurrent principle. This means that fresh potable (treated or untreated) water is introduced at the end of the processing operation where the product is cleanest and will introduce the least amount of solids into the water. This same water is used over and over again, continuously picking up more solids during the process; it is discharged only after being used for the first preliminary washing of the raw material, which may be contaminated with substantial amounts of soil and other foreign matter.

In most situations, it is not possible to carry the same water, even countercurrent, through all stages of processing. In such cases potable fresh water may have to be added at one or more stages during the processing operation; or the water may have to be partially cleansed after the total solids or microbial counts reach a certain level. This can and is being done by chlorination, or by passing the water through ionization columns, microfilters, or semipermeable membranes. While such in-plant water purification procedures are possible, the economic feasibility of such procedures is questionable. It is likely, however, that in the not too distant future when water supplies become even more limited, such procedures will become necessary rather than optional.

The soluble solids recovered by these means are usually sufficiently concentrated and valuable to deserve further treatment to make them useful as food or feed.

Total Utilization of Field Crops

Only 20 to 30% of the vegetable plant reaches the processing or packaging plant for preparation for human consumption; the rest is wasted. Most of the waste consists of leaves and stems. Efficient utilization of residual plant materials should be directed toward their nutritive value as food or feed. Such a procedure would not only solve a health and pollution problem, but it would also increase the value of the crop and the rate of food production per unit of cultivated farm land.

Ben-Sinai and Kramer (1965), for example, showed that pea plants mowed at a stage of maturity that would grade the peas as minimum fancy (grade A) has a total plant yield of over 6 tons per acre. Yield of peas for human consumption was just a little over 1 ton, or 19% of the total pea plant yield. In terms of nutrients, 27% of the proteins and carbohydrates[1] were found in the peas, 25% in the pods, and 48% in the vines. It is obvious, therefore, that a fourfold increase in food nutrients could be obtained per acre of peas if the entire plant, instead of just the peas, were utilized for food or feed.

Until the early sixties, most pea fields were mowed, and the entire plants were transported to viner stations where the peas were separated from vines and pods. Some pea processors maintained livestock to which they fed the vines and pods. In recent years, however, combine-like mobile viners have come into general use, so that pods and vines are left in the field and only the shelled peas are delivered to the freezing plant or cannery for processing. Thus, where before about one-fourth of the pea crop was used for food, and up to three-fourths for feed, three-fourths of the available pea plant nutrients are now wasted.

It would seem logical to go in the other direction—not only to utilize the nutrients in the entire plant, but to utilize them directly as food rather than feed. This is technically feasible, as demonstrated by Pirie (1966), who developed a pulper, sometimes called the "mechanical cow." This pulper, developed at the Rothamsted Experimental Station in England, is capable of extracting up to 75% of the protein plus other nutrients from leafy crop material fed into the pulper at the rate of about 1 ton per hr.

A very recent development is the stringless pea-pod which automatically doubles edible yield per acre. Preliminary marketing reports indicate high acceptability for pods and peas.

Huge quantities of plant material are available even without considering the tremendous amount of greenery that is not utilized commercially. It has been estimated that if all the soybean cake produced in the United States alone were used in this way as food for man instead for animal feed or waste, enough protein would be produced to supply the entire protein deficiency of the world at this time. Some beginnings in this direction have been initiated (see Chapter 7). A general utilization of such products as foods or food ingredients will not come about until the sensory qualities of foods produced by these methods are acceptable to the consumer.

The transformation of a part of an agricultural crop or product from discarded waste into a by-product, a co-product, and finally into the main product is a lengthy process, influenced and regulated by accumulated know-how, needs, economics and legislature on a worldwide or

---

[1]Peas contain negligible amounts of fat, and the vitamin and mineral nutrients weigh very little.

on a local basis. The relative value of different fractions may change from time to time, depending on the methods by which an agricultural commodity is broken down, as a result of harvesting, sorting, or processing procedures and techniques.

The relative values of the different fractions of the agricultural commodity change as their importance and potential change. Prices of cotton and cotton production by-products show this trend. During less than a century, cottonseed, which had been a problem waste material, became a source of edible oil and animal feed and a promising source of low-cost, high-quality proteins for humans as well. With cottonseed increasing in value, it was not economically advisable to develop mobile cotton gins which would leave the seeds in the field and bring only the deseeded raw cotton to the mill. In the case of peas, however, it was not economical to bring pods and vines to the processing plant.

Since more complete utilization of the entire vegetable plant is based primarily on economic considerations and consumer acceptance, it would appear that techniques for total utilization of plant crops will be adopted more readily in developing countries. This is not the case. There is more, rather than less, waste of this sort in connection with practically every crop grown in tropical developing countries. Maximum attention is given to the exportable fraction, and the remainder of the plant materials goes largely to waste.

Bananas are a major article of international trade. Total world exports of bananas approximated 5,000,000 tons annually in recent years. It is estimated that less than one-third of the bananas produced are exported from South America, Central American, and African countries; approximately one-third are utilized for food or feed locally, and the remainder is wasted (Watkins 1967). There have been some attempts at utilization of bananas other than as fresh fruit for export. An increasing market is canned or processed as frozen banana purée used mostly in baby food, bakery goods, and ice-cream mixes.

Some effort has been directed toward the production of dehydrated products. Since the cost of the raw material can be low, it is possible to produce a banana flour. This would provide a very cheap source of food energy. A number of schemes have been proposed for the utilization of banana peels, stems, and leaves.

Among other products that could be produced from these huge quantities of waste are furfural, pectin, wilted stock feed, paper, and wall board. It has even been proposed to form the containers for bananas by compressing stems at high pressures. With the exception of some pilot plant operations for producing paper and pelletized feed, nothing has yet been accomplished in this direction. As with other wastes, the major obstacle in the utilization of banana stems is the cost of removing water.

World exports of cocoa beans have been exceeding 1 million metric tons annually, the majority of exports originating in central African countries. The usual practice is to remove the cocoa fruit from the tree when it reaches an appropriate stage of maturation, wrap a number of fruits in plantain, palm, or other suitable leaves, and allow the fruits to ferment until the mucilage surrounding the beans is sufficiently decomposed for the beans to be removed easily. The beans are then dried and bagged for shipment from the farm. This process wastes the entire fruit except for the beans. Forsyth and Quesnel (1963) developed an enzymatic process for separating the beans from the placental mucilage. Such a process would permit harvesting the entire fruit, including several million tons of nutritious fruit for feed and perhaps food uses.

Many tropical regions have an abundance of papaya, avocado, and mango that are used to only a very small extent. High-quality oil resembling olive oil could be extracted from avocados if a method were available for removal of the bitter principle. There are even possibilities of utilizing parts of the coffee plant other than the bean (Barbera 1965).

SHORT-CUTTING NATURE'S CYCLE

It was pointed out in Chapter 5 that all living plants and animals, their foods and their wastes, are a part of the natural life cycle. In current management terms we would call this cycle "life support system," which may be more or less complex. It is always more complex for the support of animal life than plant life because only chlorophyll-containing plants are able to produce organic foods photosynthetically; this means that chlorophyll-containing plants utilize the inorganic substances on the earth's surface—carbon dioxide in the air, as well as water and minerals in the soil—to manufacture food with the aid of solar energy. Animals, including man, then feed on these organic plant materials. To complete the cycle, all plants and animals and their waste products are decomposed by enzymes released by a host of different microorganisms to their original inorganic state, where they can be reutilized by plants.

It is generally assumed that the simplest life support system is the most efficient. Thus in searching for the most efficient life support system for space flight of long duration, much attention was directed to the use of one-cell chlorophyll-containing plants called algae. Theoretically, algae could provide all the nutrients required by men, and the men could provide all the nutrients required by algae. As yet, such an algae-based life support system has not been perfected, and when it is, it will not be nearly as simple as originally hoped. The major problem is not that algae do not contain all the essential nutrients for man, but that they also produce substances that are unwholesome; thus other organisms must feed on the algae before man can consume them safely in sufficient quantity. Another problem requiring solution is that the sensory quality of algae as such or of the organisms that feed on them is not acceptable.

Most of the foods we eat are products of a much more elaborate life cycle. Let us consider cows' milk as an example. Plant food is harvested and delivered to the calf for about two years before any milk is produced. Then, when the cow begins to produce milk, only a fraction of the plant food is converted to milk, the bulk being used for the life support of the cow itself, and the production of solid and liquid wastes. Thus by consuming cows' milk, man obtains only a fraction of the nutrients he would have received had he consumed the plant material directly. It should be pointed out, however, that much of the raw plant food that is digestible by the cow and therefore provides it with nutrition, is not available, or only partially available, to man. In this respect, therefore, the cow serves as a food-processing factory that converts raw food materials into a form that can be digested by man.

However, man has learned to perform many such functions himself without the aid of other animals. Whenever man succeeds in short-cutting a stage in the life cycle of a food, he improves the efficiency of producing that food, and reduces waste.

Reduction in the number of animals that compete with man for the food supply is another means of increasing food supply and reducing waste. Elimination of draft animals was completed in the first half of the 20th century in the United States and other developed countries. When this is accomplished in the developing countries (not only further replacement of work and transportation animals with machinery, but also reduction of the numbers of "unemployed" animals that compete with man for food instead of serving as a source of food), the overall deficiency of food in the developing countries could be reduced materially.

Channeling of sources of energy and proteins from livestock feeding to human consumption, which involves both education and technological and scientific research and development, may help to minimize the food shortage, but will create difficult problems, too. According to Szebiotko (1966), 50% or more of the potatoes produced in Poland and the U.S.S.R. were utilized for animal feeding. More than 17,000,000 tons of oilseeds meal and mill feeds of a high potential nutritive value for humans were used in the United States during 1964 for animal feeding. Peru, the world's largest producer and exporter of high-protein fish meal which is utilized mainly as animal feed, experiences the tragedy of food shortage and malnutrition. Overcoming this wastage of valuable nutrients is essential as part of a total effort to improve overall world food supplies. It will require a successful and economical substitution of today's potential foods that are presently animal feeds, with other feed materials. The possibility of replacing animal feeds by synthetic mixtures free of proteins was demonstrated successfully by Virtanen (1966) in feeding trials with dairy cows. Utilization of urea as a nitrogen source was not found to have any adverse effect on the cow or on the milk produced; this opens the road to further developments leading to the release of materials presently fed to livestock for human consumption.

The most efficient way of utilizing plant materials is directly as food. Failing this, the material should be used as feed, or if this is also not possible, as fertilizer (plant food). The least efficient technique is not to utilize it at all, but to bear the expense of disposing of the material as waste. The greatest success achieved thus far in transforming waste, fertilizer and feed material to food has been with the oilseeds.

New products from soybean and cottonseed, comprising together more than 20,000,000 tons of protein (more than enough to cover present world protein deficiencies), have now reached that stage of development where high-protein foods are becoming increasingly available for use by humans around the world. Peanuts, the third major oilseed, are consumed, either roasted or boiled, by humans in many parts of the world. Removal of the peanut oil results in a meal containing 50 to 55% protein, but deficient in lysine, methionine, and threonine. Peanut meal is used as food only to a limited extent, although its potential is an important tool in combating malnutrition is well recognized. It is estimated that 80% of the peanut meal produced in India, which produces more than a third of the world peanut crop, is used as manure. More than 14,000,000 tons of peanuts, with 27% protein content and 48% fat, were produced in 1965 and used mainly for crushing for oil. The high-protein meal is potentially an important ingredient in mixes with other protein sources, where it can be supplemented and save valuable proteins of animal origin (Altschul 1967).

Problems of high fiber content exist in coconut, safflower, sunflower, and other meals, and present problems in using these meals as foods for humans.

Future use of several meals as feed for livestock and humans will depend on the development of reliable procedures for detoxification. Examples are rapeseed meal, castor bean meal, and tung seed meal, with a combined annual production of more than 5,000,000 tons. Sesame seed meal and linseed meal, produced from more than 4.5 million tons of raw material in 1966, are potential important sources of good-quality protein that are as yet almost untapped for human consumption.

DISPOSING OF RESIDUAL WASTES

The raw food materials that are not utilized for food, feed, or other by-products must be disposed of in a safe, sanitary manner, so as not to disturb the natural ecological system. Practically all food-processing plants screen waste water to remove larger-particle solids (0.02 in. or larger). These screenings, together with other solid waste, are hauled away to designated garbage dumps. The screened water is usually discharged into municipal sewer systems. In large urban areas, therefore, the food-processing plant contributes only a small part of the total organic waste that must be removed.

Some of the larger plants require in excess of 4000 gal./min of fresh water for blending products, washing ingredients, cleaning equipment and cooling. The waste water from these plants is high in Biological Oxygen Demand (BOD) and solids. Municipal facilities in smaller communities are incapable of properly treating the large quantities of water involved. The treatment systems of these plants are currently designed to reduce the BOD of the waste water to less than 30 ppm so that it can be released to local streams and rivers. Without question, the greatest waste problem that the food processor has faced has been the treatment of this waste water. This results not only from the large quantities, but also from the very limited number of places in which to dispose of it.

In general, food-processing waste does not transmit disease; but its presence is nonetheless objectionable in public water, since organic matter is a source of food for microorganisms which reduce the dissolved oxygen in the water while breaking down the organic matter. Such pollution of water is of great concern to the public and especially to federal and state water pollution control agencies. Local regulations and conditions prescribe treatment and disposal practices. Areas of major concern which are often regulated include waste strength as measured by BOD, dissolved oxygen concentration in the receiving water, and thermal pollution.

The preliminary screening, even with the finest practical mesh and vibration does not materially reduce BOD or suspended solids. Further treatment is therefore required before the screened waste water can be released into public waters. The treatment methods generally used are: (1) lagooning, (2) land spraying, (3) chemical treatment, or a combination of the above (Green and Kramer 1979).

Lagooning consists of holding the waste effluent in shallow ponds which accomplish treatment in five ways: biological action (aerobic and anaerobic), sedimentation, soil absorption, evaporation, and dilution. Biological action involves several steps including the breakdown of large organic molecules into their constituent units (i.e., simple sugars, amino acids, fatty acids) by bacterial enzymes. These products are further decomposed by the microorganisms present to the final aerobic products carbon dioxide and water (ammonia, hydrogen sulfide, and mercaptans are often developed from anaerobic decomposition due to "incomplete"

Courtesy of Environmental Protection Agency

View of Mount Trashmore—an above-grade sanitary landfill built up with municipal solid wastes compacted and covered each day with a six-inch layer of earth. Top soil, when the project is completed, will be added to the slopes and covered with vegetation. In the foreground are maintenance buildings.

breakdown). To maintain an aerobic system, approximately 1 ppm of dissolved oxygen is required at all times.

Spray irrigation serves as an economical and unobjectionable waste-disposal method when land is available. It is limited only by the capacity of the spray field to absorb the waste water. A vegetative cover crop is used to increase rate of absorption and transpiration and to prevent soil erosion. Waste waters can also be applied to shallow beds or furrows, and the water follows ground contours for gravity flow.

A spray system with a "polishing" pond can be considered as a combination of spraying and lagooning. Perforated drainpipes carry off the sprayed water after it filters through several feet of top soil to the polishing pond, where treatment is completed.

Chemical treatment is accomplished by use of coagulants such as lime followed by ferrous sulfate or alum, the operation being conducted by batch or continuous flow system. Chemical precipitation, at best, removes from 25 to 50% of the BOD. Because of this partial removal, its value would be as a pretreatment.

Land application of all organic wastes, including food-processing wastes and consumers' wastes, appears at long last to becoming official United States policy. More and more high-placed government agencies are condemning the practice of dumping sewage sludge in the ocean. By a process of elimination, the land is the alternative. Initial recommendations call for finding land that is federally or state owned, of low value, and using wastes to reclaim such land. There certainly is credit to these recommendations, but it must be realized that such a philosophy is a most modest step to the long-range societal needs of recycling wastes. What is truly needed is an overall plan of relating waste management to agriculture. Once this relationship is clearly established, other beneficial results will follow.

These results include: (1) The maintaining of farms around cities so that waste hauling costs are minimized; presently, urban and industrial development are eliminating farms rapidly. (There are obvious advantages other than recycling wastes cheaply to such local farms—fresher foods, better quality foods, open space, etc.—all from having farms closer to cities.) (2) The transference of waste disposal expenditures to help pay for applying such wastes to farmland. (3) The obvious need "to clean up" wastes and to keep toxic elements from getting into the waste stream in the first place.

10

Food of the Future

*"Study the past if you would
Divine the future."*
                    Confucius

We can confidently predict a continued introduction of thousands of new foods every year. These new foods will be similar in appearance, taste, and texture to existing foods, but will be more convenient, more completely prepared, and produced from less expensive raw ingredients. They may or may not be more nutritious, but will be even safer than present foods. Although more foods will be concentrated so that they will weigh less and occupy less space than today, we will never reach the science fiction-predicted food pill. All the vitamin and mineral and perhaps even the amino acid daily requirements could be packed into 2 or 3 reasonably sized pills. But to obtain an adequate supply of energy in the most concentrated form available would require the ingestion of well over a half pound (or half pint) of food, mostly in the form of fat, which is hardly a reasonable size for a pill.

It is difficult to imagine people anywhere, past, present, or future, satisfying their appetites by swallowing a few pills and a few globs of blubber, even if pelletized like much of today's feed. Although these could satisfy all nutrient requirements, it can be safely predicted that at no time in the foreseeable future will people change drastically enough to eat what they need instead of what they like. Of course in famine situations people will eat anything, and if Meadows *et al.* (1972) are correct perhaps some time before the year 2100 men will of necessity be reduced to surviving on a few pills and globs of oil or converted petroleum. But they won't like it.

At this time, in the United States one farmer produces food for more than 40 people. We might assume, therefore, that about 2.5% of disposable income is spent for food. The actual percentage of income has been approximately 20% for many years. Thus people have been spending about 7 times what they need to spend on food. Put in another way, we could say that only ⅐ of the total spent on food is for nutrients while ⁶⁄₇ are for preparation, packaging, and other food-related services that consumers are willing to pay for.

THE PAST AS PROLOGUE TO THE FUTURE

A good basis for predicting changes in food consumption for the next decade or two is to see what change has occurred during the past 10 or 20 years. Garner and Mountney (1970) discuss the effect of the continuously increasing food product development research done by government, universities, and the food industry itself on changes in consumption of food commodities. They show that over the decade 1956-1966, many fresh agricultural products have increased in civilian consumption only very slightly, and that in fact some products, such as citrus fruit, butter, and pork, have shown a loss in consumption. The big increases have been in prepared frozen foods, particularly frozen potato products which lead the list with an increase of 822% over this decade, followed closely by non-caloric sweeteners. Ice milk, low-fat milk, and shrimp sales also more than doubled during this period. Among the products that showed gains of more than 50% are cheese, margarine, shortening, salad oils, fish sticks, soluble coffee, poultry, and frozen vegetables. Beef sales increased by 47%, canned juices by 43%, confectionery by 37%, bakery products by 30%, and canned vegetables by 27%. Frozen fruits and juices, ice cream, canned and frozen fish, whole milk and dry milk, fresh fruits and vegetables, wheat flour, and regular coffee made modest gains of less than 25%. They conclude that agricultural commodities will serve more and more as "ingredients" in new fabricated foods.

Similar data from the U.S. Dep. Commer. (1970) and U.S. Dep. Agric. (1970) confirm the fact that per capita consumption has declined over the last two decades for milk and milk products (including butter, but not cheese), eggs, flour and cereal, sugar and sweets, potatoes, beans, and fresh fruits and vegetables. Substantial gains were noted for vegetable fats and oils, red meats and fish, canned fruits and vegetables, bakery products, and soups and other mixtures. Spectacular gainers were prepared chicken, frozen fruits, vegetables and juices, and prepared frozen foods in general.

At first glance it would appear that new (not necessarily confirmed) information about diet and health may have been responsible for this trend. Milk and egg consumption may have declined because of the possible relationship between cholesterol and heart disease; but why the increased consumption of cheese and shrimp? The decline in consumption of cereals, sugar, potatoes, fruits, and vegetables might be attributed to the currently popular low-carbohydrate high-fat and protein diet; but why the increased consumption of frozen fruits and vegetables and bakery goods, which are high-carbohydrate foods?

Apparently the real reason behind these changes in food consumption patterns is convenience. The general conclusion that emerges from these data therefore is similar to that of Garner and Mountney (1970) which is that we can expect a continued increase in consumer demand for fabricated prepared convenience foods, and that raw agricultural commodities will serve as ingredients, or components, of these prepared foods. Although many consumers talk as if they would walk many miles to get peas in the pod, or fresh unhusked corn, or tree-ripened apricots or tomatoes, their money isn't where their mouths are. Why? Because of the added convenience and lower price of the processed foods.

Red meat is the outstanding exception to this trend; consumers are demanding ever-increasing quantites of fresh unfrozen meat, particularly beef. But even here there are visible cracks in the solid front of consumer resistance to retail purchase of portioned fresh-frozen meat, so that we can anticipate a substantial increase in centrally prepared portioned and packaged red meats within this decade. The acceptance of frozen red meat will come about largely because of the opportunity for cost reduction.

Here is the clue to what is in the future, at least for the developed nations: increasingly palatable and convenient foods at lower costs. This can be accomplished by reducing labor costs and making more complete and efficient use of our food resources, while at the same time minimizing waste and pollution.

In the great world beyond the limits of the continental United States this situation differs only in degree—not in kind. Thus, although in this country we spend a smaller proportion of the cost of food and related services on the food itself, and we tend to overeat rather than undereat, we are today spending only about 18% of our disposable income for food (approximately the same amount as we spend on defense), as compared to about 30% in Western Europe and Japan, 50% in the U.S.S.R., and over 50% in the rest of the world (Farrall 1973). There are indications that the proportion of our expenditures on food and food services is leveling off. Under favorable political economic and social conditions and with farsighted planning on a global scale, the rest of the world should catch up to us if not in the next generation, then within the next century.

REDUCING THE MARGIN BETWEEN PRODUCTION AND RETAIL COSTS

Less than 25 years ago a benevolent ruler of a developing country, in his concern for the health and welfare of his people, decreed that foods that might carry disease should be sterilized in hermetically sealed containers—in other words, canned. He then proceeded to construct the finest and most modern canning facility money could buy. A number of vegetable, fruit, and animal canned products were produced in this plant and placed on the market. Although the products were invariably of high quality and the package had a high sales appeal, the effort as conceived originally failed miserably. People simply were not prepared to pay 24¢/lb for some vegetable that grew like a weed and could be obtained for the picking in the countryside or for less than 4¢/lb in the urban market.

To this day, the greater part of this magnificent facility remains largely unused. The part that is operational produces some military rations and canned foods such as pineapples and mushrooms for export, because these products are not available at low cost in the importing countries. Eventually this food factory may be utilized for its original purpose. At this time, however, it stands as a monumental example of the folly of arbitrarily increasing the margin between cost of production of a food product and its price to the consumer, where the added cost involves services the consumer does not need and/or is not prepared to pay for.

Reducing Farm Costs

In looking ahead, there is no particular reason to find opportunities to reduce the margin between cost of production (that is, price on the farm) and price on the retail food shelf. It is more reasonable to seek a reduction in price to the consumer at all stages of crop and animal production, processing, packaging, storage, transportation, food preparation and service, and distribution.

For over a hundred years there have been increasingly accelerating cost reductions in food production by means of judicious selection of mutations or purposeful cross-breeding, supplementation of plant foods (fertilizers), and plant and animal protection against pests. For example, in the 1930s 4 tons of tomatoes per acre was the average yield, and a farmer who succeeded in raising 10 tons per acre was honored for this remarkable feat by election to the elite "10-ton club". Now 20 ton acre yields are common. Before the U.S. civil war, Edmond Ruffin wrote that it was uneconomical to use slave labor to raise 5 bushels of corn per acre, the usual yield for that time. Now 100 is common, and 200 is not unheard of. In the thirties it took 6 lb of feed to produce 1 lb of chicken. Now the ratio of feed to weight gain is close to 1:1. In general it is estimated that the American farmer has increased food production in just the last 15 years threefold, twice the rate of increase of all U.S. industry (Anon. 1972F). All this was done on reduced, not greater, acreage.

The so-called "miracle" rice and wheat varieties developed in Mexico and the Philippines are simply another recent advance in this same chain of events, which not only increase our total food supply, but reduce its cost.[1] There is no reason to assume that such improvements in efficiency of agricultural production will now come to a sudden stop, although further advances may not be as rapid. If Meadows *et al.* (1972) are correct, agricultural yields cannot exceed twice the current levels.

Further economies in food production and marketing can be achieved by reduction in labor costs, largely through automation. Sowing, reaping, and all manner of farming operations in between are no longer being done in the United States by back-breaking manual labor, assisted by animal power. Instead this work is done by complex machinery propelled on or over the crops by land or air. To take full advantage of such mechanization, farm units must be enlarged. Thus the average farm size has increased from over 100 acres to over 500 acres during the last 40 years. Those crops that do not lend themselves to mechanization, particularly to mechanical harvesting, are rapidly declining in the United States and are imported from abroad where labor costs are lower.

Thus U.S. exports of automated crops such as corn, wheat, and soybeans are increasing, while imports of small fruits and other labor-intensive crops are also increasing. But this cannot be considered a permanent solution. Undoubtedly the rest of the world will follow the U.S. lead, so that certain natural foods will eventually price themselves out of the market. At this time, for instance, although locally grown raspberries may be obtained by the food processor, he can obtain frozen raspberries from Eastern Europe for one-third of the cost. It will not be too long before rising labor costs in Eastern Europe, or competition for the limited quantities produced, will raise the price of all raspberries to the point where the U.S. consumer will not be able to afford the luxury of the natural raspberry, particularly in the form of a jam, jelly, or drink ingredient, when he can get a much cheaper imitation.

There is no going back to the old homestead—not now in the United States, nor eventually elsewhere in the world. We might as well overcome our nostalgic yearning for farming as an idyllic way of life and recognize farming for what it always was and will be—an industrial operation whose end product is mainly food or feed. Like any other industrial operation, it may be a family-owned and operated unit, but for optimal size and efficiency more than "pop and mom," or father and son are needed. There is no holding back the farm "corporation," whether it is individually, cooperatively, or state-owned.

---

[1] It costs a little more, but not nearly twice as much, to produce 4 tons of "miracle" rice than to produce 2 tons of another variety of rice from the same acreage.

Transportation Costs

Economies in transportation and storage which eventually result in lower cost to the consumer can be realized only with large farm units. The man farming an acre or two may carry his sack of grain or goose or pig to market on his back or on his wife's head. At best he may have the use of an animal-drawn cart. The fully mechanized corporation farm operator, on the other hand, will bulk-load 10 to 40 tons into a container direct from the combine. The bulk container can go by trailer truck on a flat-bed rail car, or on shipboard to the grain elevator, or directly to the food or feed miller.

Movement of perishable foods and other products is expected to increase both in volume and in distance as transportation techniques become automated. Containerization, that is, shipments in units that are $8 \times 8 \times 20$ to 40 ft in length, reduces transportation handling costs appreciably. The introduction of large transport is expected to make air transport less expensive than rail. Some huge planes can transport 6 carloads of material across the country in a matter of hours at a cost somewhat less than rail transport. Such inexpensive air transport airplanes should greatly stimulate the importation of perishable foods, particularly tropical fruits, from overseas. We may soon see papayas competing successfully with melons; mangoes and many other exotic tropical fruits competing with temperate-zone fruits for the consumer market in the developed countries. These new bulk transportation techniques will not only reduce consumers' costs, but will also provide them with the opportunity of experiencing new adventures in eating without traveling to the ends of the earth.

Automation of Processing and Warehousing

Automation of warehousing and storage operations has made tremendous strides in recent years. Some computerized, fully automated warehouses are already in operation, and are undoubtedly harbingers of the future. Incoming and outgoing palletized units are picked up by a crane whose motion is controlled by a computer.

Similar total automated techniques are being introduced into food-processing plants. In fact, a milk pasteurization plant in which one not very busy man can handle over 40,000 lb/hr is not uncommon. In a recently completed cheese-processing plant the process involves automatic inoculation of pasteurized, cold-ripened, and pre-heated milk with starter culture and rennet. The curd is mechanically cut in vats, transferred to a whey-draining station, and is then automatically molded and stacked. The stacks are immersed in brine, and pneumatically transferred for ripening and storage. This automation is stated to have reduced labor requirements by 70%, so that only 3 or 4 persons are needed to process 9000 qt of milk per hour.

A number of new continuous processes for the automated handling of doughnuts are now available (Anon. 1972E). Microwave proofing is stated to require only half as much dusting flour, and microwave-assisted frying reduces scaling; since the doughnuts fry faster, they absorb 25% less frying fat.

Continuous fermenters are now available where the ingredients are continuously incorporated into a dough, which is deposited in ribbon form on slow-traveling fermentation belts; it is then pumped into horizontal mixers, from which it is discharged as a continuous ribbon into a hopper feeding a six-pocket divider. A double unit operated by one man will handle 15,000 lb/hr.

Packaging Costs

The indispensability of packaging in modern food economy was discussed in Chapter 8. It has also been noted that frequently the package costs as much or more than its contents. It would appear, therefore, that there is plenty of room for cutting costs by reducing packaging costs. Since the packaging engineer is well aware of cost problems, whenever he designs a package, he attempts not to overdesign so that the package will do the job for which it is intended at least cost.

Not much more can be done to reduce costs of the tin can. The last substantial advance in cost reduction was in the forties when in rapid order, the weight of tin was reduced twice and weight of steel sheet once. The first reduction in thickness of tin was made possible by replacing the hot-dip process with electroplating, which made it possible to cover the steel sheet thoroughly with a thinner coating of tin. The second reduction in tin weight followed the realization that the tin coating on the outside of the can need not be as thick as on the inside, which is in contact with the food. A reduction in weight of the steel sheet came about as a result of improvements in the preparation of the sheet and also by adding one or more corrugations around the body of larger cans to give them added resistance to denting.

Little has been accomplished in reducing the cost of glass containers. The major introduction of the non-returnable bottle reduced the cost per bottle, but actually increased the cost of the container per use.

The big saving in packaging cost came with the introduction of plastic, or plastic-coated containers. In addition to providing heretofore unavailable flexible packaging, these materials are usually considerably cheaper than metal or glass. The replacement of the milk bottle with the plastic-coated carton was a real cost saving. There are many other opportunities for replacing metal or glass packaging with plastic.

The big question today is whether plastic packaging can replace metal or glass for heat-sterilized foods. The problem is not whether the plastic container will withstand the high temperatures required for sterilization, but whether the much more complex and costly equipment needed to form, fill, and seal the pouches at relatively slow speeds will not raise costs to equal or exceed those of the can.

Marketing and Distribution

Undoubtedly the big revolution of modern times in the food industry, which has already occurred in the United States, is in the area of marketing and distribution. The self-service chain-store supermarket has reduced retail cost to the consumer by 15 to 25%. Labor reduction through self-service, increased sales volume, and more rapid turnover are by no means the only factors responsible for the cost reductions. By purchasing in large volumes, supermarket firms have effectively eliminated all but the two ends of the marketing chain. When a manufacturer can sell all, or a substantial part of his output directly to the retailer, there is no need for commission men, brokers, jobbers, and wholesalers. A good part, if not all, of the promotion and sales costs of the manufacturer can be eliminated. Cost reductions are also made possible by large-volume operations in transportation, storage, and distribution.

Large-scale retailing has economic advantages similar to those of large-scale farming, and has resulted in analogous occupational changes, though at the opposite end of the food chain. Just as the small, marginal farmer was forced to leave his farm and seek employment on a larger, more prosperous farm or elsewhere, so were the neighborhood grocer, butcher, and the like forced to leave their shops and seek employment in the supermarket. In both instances overwhelming economic forces (giving the buyer as good or better quality product for a lower price) made the change inevitable, despite powerful social-political counterpressures.

Now that the changeover has been largely accomplished, it may be anticipated that some further savings will be made, largely at the expense of the profit margins of the retailers, since they are no longer competing with the small-scale independent grocers, but with each other.

Many of the western European and other developed countries are now in the midst of the supermarket retailing revolution, realizing similar cost reduction benefits and undergoing similar personnel displacement traumas. In the developing countries this revolution is just beginning, or is yet to come. In the more rigidly regimented countries this changeover may be considered to have already occurred with state ownership of retail outlets; where it has not occurred, it could be accomplished very quickly. Small stores could be combined into fewer large stores just as easily as small farms could be converted into collective farms.

COMPETITION FOR THE FOOD SUPPLY—SURVIVAL OF THE FITTEST

Animals depend entirely on chlorophyll-containing plants for their primary source of food and nutrition. Although animals and their products provide man with highly nutritious and palatable food, man could survive without them by eating only vegetables. Until recent times man carried on a constant struggle for survival against other animals larger, stronger or fleeter than he. To this day he shares the food supply with his animal cohabitators of this earth.

Fish and Wildlife

Neither at this time, nor in the foreseeable future is it anticipated that fish and other sea animals will compete with man for food. There are vast untapped opportunities for "fish farming" that could be developed before man will need to resort to direct utilization of plankton, the major plant life of the sea.

Animal wildlife of the land, however, is directly competitive with man, so that in some instances their numbers must be reduced while in a few instances there is even a serious attempt at extermination. One of the more recent candidates for extermination was the rabbit in Australia, which multiplied so rapidly that he became a threat to the survival not only of man but of other animals. Managers of wildlife and game preserves recognize that it is necessary to have an "open season" on deer and other animals not so much to reduce their inroads on the food and feed supply, as to provide the survivors with a better opportunity to avoid hunger and starvation.

The most serious and effective competitor and enemy of man among the mammals is without doubt the rat. One or more species is present wherever man is, often in far greater numbers than man himself. Estimates of man's food supply that is consumed or spoiled by rats vary from 25% to more than 50% of the total. The rat has few friends, perhaps because he not only spoils so much good food, but is a carrier of deadly diseases. Complete eradication of the rat would be opposed by very few. Thus far man has failed to eliminate rats completely, although he has done so in some designated areas so constructed that rats could not gain entry, those already in the confined area being killed by poisoned baits and/or traps. Rat poisons must be used with great caution, since they are also poisonous to other animals, including man.

The easiest way of solving the rat problem is to use them as food. We can anticipate shudders of horror by consumers at the very thought of such a practice. Yet primitive man and some aboriginal tribes hardly touched by the food habits and mores of our civilization eat rats, reptiles, and insects with relish, and in some instance owe their survival to the consumption of these species held in contempt and therefore taboo by "enlightened people." We should therefore not expect to increase our food supplies by using rats as food or even as feed. We do, however, anticipate substantial reduction in losses of food resources to rodents.

It is interesting to note that reptiles, among the most effective enemies of the rat, are also held in contempt and feared by modern man. Snakes, particularly poisonous snakes, although eaten by some, are exterminated with even greater passion than are rats.

Birds are the other family of larger animals that seriously damage food crops. Unlike rodents and reptiles, however, birds have a favored position in the eyes of men. A few species such as chickens, ducks, turkeys, have been domesticated and are important sources of highly acceptable, nutritious food. Some serve as pets, but most bird species exist in the wild, protected by naturalists and wildlife enthusiasts to the point that even a flock of crows despoiling vast acres of grain cannot be summarily executed, but may be driven away by scarecrows. This tolerant attitude to destructive birds may be permitted during fat years, but if "lean years" come as predicted, crows and the like will be destroyed or eaten.

Insects, Diseases, and Other Pests

While rodents may be the great despoilers of food after harvest, the major competitors for man's food supply while it is still growing in the field are insects and pathogenic plant microorganisms (diseases). Their food-destructive activities do not stop in the field, however. Insect-infested and disease-infected raw food materials will suffer further spoilage, and in some cases will develop toxins in storage. These added losses may be controlled by chemical means (fumigation), heating, refrigeration, or a combination of these. Since the use of chemicals is frowned upon particularly when other methods of control are available, and heating may have a deleterious effect on the functional and nutritional quality of the stored foods, refrigerated storage alone or in combination with drying and/or fumigation remains as the most acceptable and eventually the least costly means of protecting foods in storage. At temperatures below 40°F neither insects nor any pathogenic organisms will grow or produce toxins.

Insects take an enormous toll of practically all foods while they are in the field. Estimates of annual losses in the United States alone due to insect infestation vary, but they are well in the billions of dollars. During the first third of this century and before, highly toxic substances such as arsenic and lead compounds were used liberally. These insecticides are now all but forgotten; they were replaced with organic chemicals that were not generally toxic to all animals, but selectively toxic to insects. A long list of theses substances was introduced about mid-century. Quite a few of these new insecticides belonged to a class of chemicals known as chlorinated hydrocarbons. The first of these, developed in the early years of World War II and used with gay abandon was dichlorodiphenyltri-chloroethane, which was promptly shortened to DDT. For the next 10 years the use of DDT spread to control of insects on tremendous acreages of crops. It was used on still larger areas of swamp and marsh land to eliminate mosquitoes and the diseases they carry, and on vast tracts of forest to prevent timber from being attacked by insects. By the mid-fifties practically every person in the world had measurable quantities of DDT in his system; but this was of no concern, since it was demonstrated that DDT had no harmful effect on at least three experimental animals, even if they consumed food containing many times the amount of DDT it could possibly carry. At the same time, disturbing reports began coming in, suggesting that indiscriminate use of this powerful insecticide may have a deleterious effect on beneficial insects such as bees, birds, and fish. Thus, although no harmful effects were ever demonstrated on humans, a low tolerance (7 ppm) was imposed. Later this tolerance was reduced further, until now DDT cannot be used at all. On the other hand insecticides based on organic esters of phosphorus, which are far more toxic to humans than DDT, are permitted in some areas, since they are biodegradable, which DDT is not.

Most plant diseases are caused by fungi, which can be controlled by less toxic organic salts of metals such as copper, iron, zinc, or by organic acids or their salts. These chemicals have not aroused as much concern as the insecticides. Still, the general public's concern over the use of chemical pesticides in general has been aroused to such an extent that there is a reluctance to use any chemicals for purposes of plant protection. The methods that are now being explored that may eventually replace pesticide chemicals are biological control.

One form of biological control is to find a microorganism that will be pathogenic to the insect or a virus that will be pathogenic to a microorganism. A good example of what has already been accomplished in this direction is the control and practical elimination of the Japanese fruit fly by spreading a bacterium which produces the "milky spore disease" in the adult fly. It may be difficult to understand why such biological control is acceptable to self-appointed naturalists and ecologists, and some chemical harmless to man is not. If the concern is for welfare of existing wildlife, how do we know that these bacteria or viruses that are highly pathogenic to a specific insect or microorganism which is a pest, will not also be harmful to other desirable and beneficial wildlife?

The other biological control that is not new, but is sure to be utilized more intensively now that chemical controls are being de-emphasized, is the use of molecular biology, the term now used for genetics, that is, breeding of new breeds and varieties of animals and plants that will be inherently resistant to insects and diseases. Although this technique is preferred by those naturalists who abhor the use of chemicals, there is now a serious doubt raised as to whether such genetically derived resistance is not due to the presence of some chemical toxic to the invading organism, which may also be toxic to other forms of life, including man. Remember the "great potato debate"? (See Chapter 4.)

Pets and Sacred Cows

Many of us have animal pets whom we love as if they were human. Some of us believe all animal life to be sacred and recognize their right to live out their lives, although they may serve no practical purpose to mankind. We should recognize, however, that such animals compete with us for limited food supplies even more directly than wildlife, since they live with us and share our food, while the wild creatures subsist only on the fringes of settled and cultivated areas.

There are areas in the world today where man and beast alike are chronically hungry and on the verge of starvation. This situation could be changed overnight if the animals were used as food for man instead of sharing the food with him. With our current concern about population growth, is it not reasonable to consider zero growth if not reduction in numbers of unproductive animals?

INCREASING THE FOOD SUPPLY

With so many opportunities for developing new food supplies, and initiating others yet untapped, it is obvious that Meadows et al. (1972) did not equate increases in agricultural yields with increases in food production. These opportunities lie mainly in controlled farming of the seas and irrigating the earth's vast deserts.

Farming the Seas

Even with our present crude methods of capture, it is estimated that man is hauling in about 50 million tons of seafood per year and could increase this to 400 million tons. With the total world food supply estimated at 2.5 billion tons, such an increase in the fishery haul would increase total world food supplies by about one-sixth. Since fish are highly nutritious, particularly rich in protein and unsaturated fat, this alone could eliminate malnutrition in the world for many years.

But the potential of exploiting the seas by farming is vastly greater. The seas, containing all the mineral nutrients required by plants, and with the upper 75 ft exposed to light energy of sufficient intensity, can produce about 10 tons of plant material per year per acre. This is not too different from yields of plant material from arable land. Without even considering the fact that most of the land is not utilized for food production, but simply on the basis of the fact that the sea area of the earth's surface is more than twice the land area, it may be concluded that potential for food production from the sea is more than double that from the land, or something over 5 billion tons per year. To accomplish this, the seas would need to be farmed rather than hunted.

Irrigating the Land

On the land also tremendous increases in food production could be accomplished. The limiting factor, again, is water management. If only all the irrigation and draining systems of former civilizations, and all the terraces so laboriously constructed in ancient times were repaired and improved upon with techniques available only in modern times, total world food production would probably double. The big opportunity, however, will come when the oceans serve as the water reservoir for the entire globe, and when evaporation and condensation of water are accomplished with precision, mainly by solar energy. Under such a system of water management, all the deserts would bloom. We have made the first feeble efforts in this direction by way of cloud seeding and desalination of sea water. Surely such a worldwide scheme is not beyond the capability of man in this age of the spaceship. Mineral nutrients need not be of concern. For the immediate future, huge deposits of minerals collected in dry inland water basins could be utilized, and before these are exhausted, additional supplies could be recovered from the oceans.

Substitution of Ingredients

We have already discussed in Chapters 1 and 9 the probability of major increases in production of nutrients from plant, sea, and microorganic materials. At this time we cannot predict with any certainty that we will be producing microorganisms that will have the appearance, flavor, and texture of roast beef. What we can safely predict, however, is that in the foreseeable future there will be a great expansion in production of protein, fat, and vitamins directly from plants and microorganisms, and that these nutrients will serve as ingredients in new foods that will be quite similar to those we are now consuming with pleasure.

GLOBAL STRATEGIES

What we have just been suggesting is that the entire environment of the earth's surface be controlled in such a way as to maximize food resources. At the same time waste matter should be controlled, largely by recycling; population levels of man and his cohabitators of the earth should be controlled so that all may enjoy a full life; and all this can be accomplished mainly by the judicious control of solar energy. If such a global strategy can be put in effect well before the year 2100, we may succeed in delaying doomsday indefinitely.

At this time global strategies for survival seem doomed. What small efforts are being made in this direction are overwhelmed by international monopolistic practices which would burden the food producer not only with production of bread, the staff of life, but also liquid fuel. Can we make the transition of diverting a large share of the available biomass from food to energy without causing mass starvation? Will low-cost solar energy come to the rescue in time?

Certainly a global plan will not be accomplished overnight, and perhaps not within a century. In the meantime, while striving for worldwide cooperation towards such a goal, we can plan and execute more limited programs on a local basis. We could begin by making rather minor changes and extensions in planning our new model cities. These plans now usually call for a pleasant blend of residences, commercial centers, and industrial parks, all surrounded by manicured lawns and recreational areas, and untouched wilderness. All this is well and good. Undoubtedly all solid and liquid wastes and other pollutants are trapped, treated, and hauled away. If instead of, or in addition to, the recreational and wilderness areas, active operating farms were maintained around these urban communities, a fairly complete microcycle could be established. The wastes from the city could be sprayed or spread on the farm land, and the farm land thus enriched would provide high yields of fresh food for the urban dweller. There is nothing really revolutionary about this concept, and it seems just too simple to work. Let's give it a try; perhaps it will work.

References

ALBRIGHT, F. and REIFENSTEIN, E.C. 1948. The Parathyroid Glands and Metabolic Bone Disease. Williams & Wilkins Co., Baltimore.

ALTSCHUL, A.M. 1967. Food proteins: New sources from seeds. Science *158*, 221.

ANON. 1967. Lathyrism—A preventable paralysis. Nutr. Res. Lab. Bull., Hyderabad, India.

ANON. 1968. Manual on sensory testing methods. Am. Soc. Test. Mater. Spec. Tech. Bull. *434*.

ANON. 1969. Iodized salt. Nutr. Today *4* (1) 22.

ANON. 1970. The Dietary Management of Hyperlipoproteinemia. National Institutes of Health, Bethesda, Md.

ANON. 1971. Hereditary defect in intestinal iron transport. Nutr. Rev. *29*, 47.

ANON. 1972A. Highlights from the ten-state nutrition survey. Nutr. Today *7* (4) 4.

ANON. 1972B. The dietary iron controversy. Nutr. Today *7* (4) 2.

ANON. 1972C. Recommendations on diet and coronary heart disease. From a joint statement of the Food, Nutr. Board, NAS/NRC, and Am. Med. Assoc. Counc. Foods Nutr. Nutr. Today *7* (4) 21.

ANON. 1972D. Food facts can be fun. Food Nutr. *2* (3) 8.

ANON. 1972E. Engineers report innovations. Food Eng. *44* (8) 125.

ANON. 1972F. New developments in process control. Food Process. (Chicago) *33* (7) 41.

ANON. 1973. The great potato debate. A special report on a new hypothesis for neural tube defects. Med. World News *14* (7) 29.

ANON. 1976. Energy Use in the Food System. GPO, Washington, D.C.

ASHRAE. 1971. Applications—Guide and Data Book. Am. Soc. Heat. Refrig. Air Cond. Engrs., New York.

ASSOC. OF OFFIC. ANAL. CHEMISTS. 1970 Methods of Analysis, 11th edition. Washington, D.C.

BARBERA, C.E. 1965. The utilization of coffee residues. Cafe, Cacao, The *9*, 206. (French)

BEDNARCZYK, A.A. and KRAMER, A. 1971. Practical approach to flavor development. Food Technol. 25 (11) 24.

BEN-GERA, I. and KRAMER, A. 1969. The utilization of food industries wastes. Advan. Food. Res. 17, 77.

BEN-SINAI, I. and KRAMER, A. 1965. The food and fodder value of pea plant parts as related to harvest time and variety. Food Technol. 19, 856.

BERG, G.L. (Editor). 1972. Master manual on molds and mycotoxins. Farm Technol. 28 (5) 19.

BORTHWELL, P. 1969. Food in Antiquity. Praeger Publishers, New York.

CARSON, R. 1962. Silent Spring. Houghton Mifflin Co., Boston.

CHILDERS, N.F. and RUSSO, G.M. 1977. The Nightshades and Health. Somerset Press, Somerville, N.J.

CLAUSI, A.S. 1971. Cereal grains as dietary protein sources. Food Technol. 25 (8), 63.

COHEN, A.M. 1971. Lessons from diabetes in Yemenites. Isr. J. Med. Sci. 7, 1554.

CUATRECASAS, P., LOCKWOOD, D.H. and CALDWELL, J.R. 1965. Lactase deficiency in the adult. Lancet 15 (1) 14.

DAMON, G.E. 1973. Primer on food additives. FDA Consumer 7 (4) 10.

DAVIS, A. 1970. Let's Eat Right to Keep Fit. Harcourt Brace Jovanovich, New York.

DESROSIER, N.W. and DESROSIER, J.N. 1977. The Technology of Food Preservation, 4th edition. AVI Publishing Co., Westport, Conn.

DESROSIER, N.W. and TRESSLER, D.K. 1977. Fundamentals of Food Freezing. AVI Publishing Co., Westport, Conn.

DEUTSCH, R.M. 1961. The Nuts Among the Berries. Ballantine Books, New York.

DEUTSCH, R.M. 1971. The Family Guide to Better Food and Better Health. Creative Library, Des Moines.

DICKINSON, D. 1960. Treatment of food processing waste waters. In Waste Treatment. P.C.G. Isaac (Editor). Pergamon Press, New York.

EDWARDS, C.C. 1972. FDA today: An interview with the Commissioner. FDA Consumer 6 (10) 8.

EDWARDS, C.C. 1973. Nutrition labeling. Fed. Regist. 38 (13) Part III, 2125.

FARRALL, A.W. 1973. Food engineering—a look at the future. In Food Engineering Forum Proceedings. Dairy and Food Industry Supply Assoc., Washington, D.C.

FILBY, F.A. 1934. A History of Food Adulteration and Analysis. Allen and Unwin, London.

FORSYTH, G.C. and QUESNEL, V.C. 1963. The mechanism of cocoa curing. Advan. Enzymol. 25, 457.

FRIEND, B. 1967. Nutrients in U.S. Food supply. A review of trends 1909–1913 to 1965. Am. J. Clin. Nutr. 20, 907.

GARN, S.M., ROHMANN, G.G. and WAGNER, B. 1967. Bone loss as a general phenomenon in man. Fed. Am. Soc. Exp. Biol. Proc. *26*, 1729.

GARNER, R.G. and MOUNTNEY, G.J. 1970. Food product development research. Coop. State Res. Serv. USDA, Agric. Sci. Rev. *8* (2) 9.

GREEN, J.H. 1979. Food Processing Waste Management. AVI Publishing Co., Westport, Conn.

GUTCHO, M. 1973. Textured Foods and Allied Products. Noyes Data Corp., Park Ridge, N.J.

HAAGEN-SMIT, A.J. 1972. Man and his home. Chron. Hortic. *12* (1) 1.

HANSEN, R.G., WYSE, B.W. and SORENSON, A.W. 1979. Nutritional Quality Index of Foods. AVI Publishing Co., Westport, Conn.

HOBBS, B.C. and GILBERT, R.J. 1978. Food Poisoning and Food Hygiene. Food and Nutrition Press, Westport, Conn.

HORWITT, M.K. 1960. Vitamin E and lipid metabolism in man. Am. J. Clin. Nutr. *8*, 451.

JACKSON, H. 1758. An Essay on Bread. Jackson, London.

JACOBSON, M.F. 1972. Eater's Digest—The Consumer's Fact Book of Food Additives. Doubleday & Co., New York.

JENSEN, L.B. 1953. Man's Foods. Garrard Publishing Co., Champaign, Ill.

JENSEN, M.W. and FOLKES, T.M. 1973. A new era in consumer safety. FDA Consumer *7* (1) 10.

JUL, M. 1971. The role of refrigeration in our world food supply. ASHRAE J. *12* (8) 32.

KAPLOW, M. 1970. Commercial development of intermediate moisture foods. Food Technol. *24* (8) 889.

KEHR, A.E. 1973. Naturally occurring toxicants and nutritive values in food crops. J. Hort. Sci. *8* (1) 4.

KENDA, M.E. and WILLIAMS, P.S. 1973. The Natural Baby Food Cookbook. Nash Publishing Co., Los Angeles.

KEYS, A. 1957. Diet and epidemiology of coronary heart disease. J. Am. med. Assoc. *164*, 1912.

KLINER, I.S. and ORTEN, J.M. 1966. Biochemistry, 7th edition. C.V. Mosby Co., St. Louis.

KRAMER, A. 1966. Food industry developments in the next twenty years. Md. Process. Rep. *12* (3) 1.

KRAMER, A., KING, R.L., SOLOMOS, T., and WHEATON, F.W. 1980. The GASPAK PROCESS - I. Maintenance of like-fresh quality of prepared raw fruits and vegetables at ambient temperatures. Paper presented at IFT 40th Annual Meeting, New Orleans.

KRAMER, A., MATTICK, J.C., LEFFEL, E.C. and AXLEY, J.A. 1971. Utilization of wastes formed during the manufacture of vegetable and dairy products. DHEW, Bur. Solid Waste Manage., Final Rep., Proj. *5R01*, Cincinnati.

KRAMER, A. and TWIGG, B.A. 1970. Quality Control for the Food Industry. Vol. 1, 3rd edition. AVI Publishing Co., Westport, Conn.

KRAMER, A., and TWIGG, B.A. 1973. Quality Control for the Food Industry, Vol. 2, 3rd edition. AVI Publishing Co., Westport, Conn.

LABUZA, T.P. 1977. Food and Your Well-being. West Publishing Co. and AVI Publishing Co., Westport, Conn.

LABUZA, T.P. and SLOAN, A.E. 1977. Food for Thought. 2nd edition. AVI Publishing Co., Westport, Conn.

MALTHUS, T.R. 1798. An Essay on the Principle of Population.

MARGOLIUS, S.K. The Great American Food Hoax. Walker, New York.

MARTIN, P.S. 1973. The discovery of America. Science *179*, 969–973.

McINTIRE, J.M. 1972. Formulated meals—foods of the future. Food Technol. *26* (4) 34.

MEADOWS, D.H., MEADOWS, D.L., RANDERS, J. and BEHRENS, W.W. 1972. The Limits to Growth: A Report for the Club of Rome's Project on the Predicament of Mankind. Potomac Books, Washington, D.C.

MERCER, W.A. 1965. Canned foods. *In* Industrial Waste Water Control. C.F. Gurnham (Editor). Academic Press, New York.

MERCER, W.A. and ROSE, W.A. 1968. Integrated Treatment of Liquid Wastes from Food Canning Operations. Nat. Canners Assoc., Washington, D.C.

NAS/NRC. 1966. Toxicants occurring naturally in foods. Publ. *1354*.

NAS/NRC. 1980. Recommended Dietary Allowances. Revised. Food Nutr. Bd., Washington, D.C.

NAS/NRC. 1978. Postharvest Food Losses in Developing Countries: a Bibliography. Washington D.C.

NAT. CANNERS ASSOC. 1960. Modern Labels for Canned Foods. Washington, D.C.

NAT. RES. COUNC. WORLD FOOD AND NUTRITION STUDY STEERING COM. 1977. World Food and Nutrition Study: the Potential contributions of Research. Nat. Acad. Sci., Washington, D.C.

PAINE, F.A. 1967. Packaging Materials and Containers. Blackie, London.

PANGBORN, R.M. 1968. Interrelationship of odor, taste and flavor. Food Prod. Dev. *4*, 74–81.

PARRISH, J.B. 1971. Implications of changing food habits for nutrition educators. J. Nutr. Educ. *2*, 140.

PAULING, L. 1970. Vitamin C and the Common Cold. W.H. Freeman, San Francisco.

PINNER, S.H. 1967. Modern Packaging Films. Plenum Press, New York.

PIRIE, N.W. 1966. Leaf protein as human food. Science *152*, 1701.

PRENTICE, E.P. 1939. Hunger and History. Harper & Row, New York.

RAO, M.A. 1977. Energy consumption for refrigerated, canned and frozen peas. J. Food Process Eng. *1* (2) 149–165.

REIMANN, H. 1969. Food-borne Infections and Intoxicators. Academic Press, New York.

ROCKS, J.K. 1971. Xanthan gum. Food Technol. 25 (5) 476—477.

ROE, D. 1979. Alcohol and the Diet. AVI Publishing Co., Westport, Conn.

ROE, D. 1976. Drug-induced Nutritional Deficiencies. AVI Publishing Co., Westport, Conn.

RUSCH, D.T. 1971. Vegetable fat based dairy substitutes. Food Technol. 25 (5) 32.

SACHAROW, S. 1979. Packaging Regulations. AVI Publishing Co., Westport, Conn.

SACHAROW, S. and GRIFFIN, R.C., JR. 1970. Food Packaging. AVI Publishing Co., Westport, Conn.

SANBORN, N.H. 1961. Canning, freezing, and dehydration. In Industrial Wastes—Their Disposal and Treatment. W. Rudolfs (Editor). Library of Engineering Classics, Valley Stream, N.Y.

SIMOONS, F.J. 1961. Eat Not This Flesh. Univ. Wisconsin Press, Madison.

STOCK, A.L. and YUDKIN, J. 1970. Nutrient intake of subjects on low-carbohydrate diet used in treatment of obesity. Am. J. Clin. Nutr. 23, 948.

STUMBO, R. 1965. Thermobacteriology in Food Processing. Academic Press, New York.

SZEBIOTKO, K. 1966. Total utilization of potatoes. In International Symposium on Utilization and Disposal of Potato Wastes, Proceedings. New Brunswick Research and Productivity Council, Fredericton, N.B.

THORNER, M.E. 1973. Convenience and Fast Food Handbook. AVI Publishing Co., Westport, Conn.

TRESSLER, D.K., VAN ARSDEL, W.B. and COPLEY, M.J. 1968. The Freezing Preservation of Foods, Vol. 1—4, 4th edition. AVI Publishing Co., Westport, Conn.

UCKO, P.J. and DIMBLEBY, G.W. 1968. The Domestication and Exploitation of Plants and Animals. Aldine-Atherton, Chicago.

ULLENSVANG, L.P. 1970. Food consumption patterns of the seventies. Vital Speeches 36, 240.

U.K. DEP. HEALTH SOC. SECURITY. 1969. Recommended Intakes of Nutrients of Nutrients for the United Kingdom. Panel on Recommended Allowances of Nutrients, Rep. Public Health Med. Subjects (London) 120.

U.N. CONFERENCE ON THE HUMAN ENVIRONMENT, STOCKHOLM, 1972. Report. New York, United Nations.

U.S. CONGRESS. HOUSE. COMMITTEE ON AGRICULTURE. SUBCOMMITTEE ON DOMESTIC MARKETING, CONSUMER RELATIONS AND NUTRITION. 1977—1978. Hearings, Pt. 1—2. 95th Cong., 1st & 2nd sess.

U.S. CONGRESS. OFFICE OF TECHNOLOGY ASSESSMENT. 1979. Open shelf-life dating of food. GPO, Washington, D.C.

U.S. CONGRESS. SENATE. COMMITTEE ON AGRICULTURE, NUTRITION AND FORESTRY. SUBCOMMITTEE ON NUTRITION. 1978. Nutrition Labeling and Information. Hearings, Pt. 1. 95th Cong., 2nd sess.

U.S. CONGRESS. SENATE. SELECT COMMITTEE ON NUTRITION AND HUMAN NEEDS. 1975. Nutrition and Health, with an Evaluation of Nutritional Surveillance in the U.S. Committee Print, 94th Cong., 1st sess.

U.S. CONGRESS. SENATE. SELECT COMMITTEE ON NUTRITION AND HUMAN NEEDS. 1977. Diet Related to Killer Diseases, Parts I—VIII. Hearings. 95th Cong., 1st sess.

U.S. CONGRESS. SENATE. SELECT COMMITTEE ON NUTRITION AND HUMAN NEEDS. 1977. Dietary Goals for the U.S. Committee Print. 95th Cong., 1st sess.

U.S. DEP. AGRIC. 1939. Regulations Governing Inspection and Certification of Processed Fruits and Vegetables and Related Products. USDA Agric. Mark. Serv. *155.*

U.S. DEP. AGRIC. 1960. Composition of foods—raw, processed, prepared. USDA Agric. Handb. *8.*

U.S. DEP. AGRIC. 1965. Losses in Agriculture. GPO, Washington, D.C.

U.S. DEP. AGRIC. 1968. Food Consumption of Households in the United States, Spring 1965. USDA Agric. Res. Serv. Mark. Res. Rep., Washington, D.C.

U.S. DEP. AGRIC. 1970. Agricultural Statistics. GPO, Washington, D.C.

U.S. DEP. COMMER. 1979. Statistical Abstract of the U.S. GPO, Washington, D.C.

U.S. DEP. HEALTH, EDUC, WELFARE. 1972. Ten-State Nutrition Survey 1968—1970. Rep. Center for Disease Control, Washington, D.C.

VAN ARSDEL, W.B., COPLEY, M.J. and MORGAN, A.I. 1973. Food Dehydration, Vol. 1—2, 2nd edition. AVI Publishing Co., Westport, Conn.

VIRTANEN, A.I. 1966. Milk production of cows on protein-free feed. Science *153,* 1603.

WATKINS, R.J. 1967. Expanding Ecuador's Exports. Praeger Publishers, New York.

WHITE, H. 1972. The organic food movement. Food Technol. *26* (4) 29.

WILSON, J., TWIGG, B.A. and KRAMER, A. 1971. Completion *Report A-005-Md.* Water Resources Res. Center, College Park, Md.

WILSON, J.M. and TWIGG, B.A. 1973. Water and waste control. *In* Quality Control for the Food Industry, Vol. 2. 3rd edition. A. Kramer and B.A. Twigg (Editors). AVI Publishing Co., Westport, Conn.

YUDKIN, J. 1972. Sugar and disease. Nature *239,* 197.

YUDKIN, J. and CAREY, M. 1960. The treatment of obesity by the "high fat" diet. Lancet 10 (2) 939.

Index

A$_w$, 120, 128−130, 138
Acceptability, measurement of, 54−59. *See also* Palatibility
Acceptance inspection, 63−66
Accusations, 16−17
Acids, acetic, 119
aliphatic, 119
amino, 26−28, 30
arachidonic, 26
ascorbic, 31. *See also* Vitamin C
folic, 31, 37
linoleic, 26
oxalic, 99, 150
pentothenic, 30
propionic, 119, 135
sorbic, 135
Addiction, 110−111
Additives, 3, 80, 90, 103, 109, 119, 156−158
distrust of, 115
emulsifiers, 157
inhibitors, 134−135
reducing A$_w$, 157
stabilizer, 157
Ade drinks, 143−144
Adulterants, 57, 66, 70
Adulteration, 58
Aerobes, 119, 139
Aerosol, 168
Agriculture, 2
extension service, 62
marketing service, 99−101
Air transport, 198
Alcohol, 108, 110−111, 143
Algae, 187−188
Alimentum, 18
Allergens, 88−90
Aluminum, 124−125, 163, 168
American contributions to diet, 106, 144−145, 151−152, 159
Amino acids, 26−28, 30
Anaerobes, 120, 139
Anemia, 28−29, 31, 36−37

Antibiotics, 135
Antioxidants, 29, 131, 138
Appearance of food, 46−48, 54−55
Appert, 5, 122, 124
Apples, 115
Aquaculture, 14
Aroma, 56−57. *See also* Odor
Aseptic canning, 68, 124
Asparagus, 180
Atherosclerosis, 40
Atomic power, 126
Automation, 197, 198−199
Aviden, 30
Avocado, 187
Aztecs, 111

Baby foods, 54, 125, 147, 159−166, 186
Bacteria, 105, 119, 121, 122, 129, 134, 139, 190
Baked goods, 120, 147, 164, 187, 194
Bananas, 147, 186
Beans, 46, 122, 194
Beef, 52, 72
sales, 194−195
Beer, 107, 120, 125, 142, 183
Beri-beri, 30
Beverages, 47, 53, 111, 142−143
Biltong, 130
Biodegradability, 171, 203
Biological control, 178, 203
Biotin, 30
Bird, damage, 202
migrations, 118
Birth defects, 89−90
Biscuit, 107, 164
Black pea disease, 90
Blanching, 132, 138
Blintz, 109

BOD, 190−192
Botulism, 63−64, 68−69, 122
Bread, 8, 107, 120 130, 142−143
Breading, 153
Breakfast foods, 47, 156
Broker, 69
Butter, 58, 151
Buyers specifications, 59−61
By-products, 179−183, 186

Caffeine, 110−111
Calcium, 20−21, 27, 106
Cannibalism, 18, 105−107
Canning, 51−53, 66−68, 122−125, 148−
   149, 151, 156, 183, 186, 194, 196
Cans, 163−165, 168−169, 171−172, 199
   closing, 67−68
Carbohydrates, 23−26, 38−39, 185, 194
Carbon dioxide, 170−171, 187
   liquid, 131
Carcinogens, 84, 135
   Delaney Amendment, 84
Cardboard, 166−167
Carson, 16
Cellophane, 167−168
Cereals, 130, 194
   snacks, 144−145
Chapati, 109
Cheese, 81, 119, 130, 151, 194
Chemical changes, 126
   definition, 112−113
   inhibitors, 120, 134−135
   insecticides, 202−203
   residues, 64, 181
   spoilage, 137, 139
   waste treatment, 190−191
Cherries, 149
Chinese eggrolls, 109
   noodles, 183
   tea, 110
Chlorination, 184
Chlorine, 27
Chlorophyll, 187
Chocolate, 111
Cholesterol, 26, 40, 98, 150, 194
Chromium, 29
Citrus, 179
   Commission, 49
Clostridium botulinum, 68, 83, 122, 124
   125
   Cl. sporogenes, 122
Coca Cola, 158

Cocoa, 111, 187
Coffee, 98, 110−111, 147−148, 187, 194
   whitener, 115
Cold storage, 13. *See also* Refrigeration
Color of foods, 55, 60, 63, 65, 170, 181
   off-color, 131, 138−139
Competition for food, 201−204
Confectionery, 157, 194
Consumer, advocates, 16, 94, 97, 102−104,
   109
   education, 58, 115
   inspection, 71−74
   preference, 46−57. *See also* Convenience
      foods
   Products Safety Act, 94
   programs, 93−94
   protection, 16−17, 75−104
   taste panels, 54−53
Consumerism, 93−94
Consumers Union, 49
Containerization, 10, 198
Containers. *See* Packaging
Controlled atmosphere storage, 137
Convenience foods, 51, 142−167, 195
Copper, 28, 37
Corn, 46, 51, 84, 146, 181, 196−197
Costs, 14, 195−201
   farm, 196, 197
   labor, 8−9, 197
Cottonseed, 186
Crust freezing, 126
Cryogenic freezing, 133, 154
CSM, 160
Cycle, carbon-nitrogen, 112−113
   life, 175
   nature's, 187−189

Dates, 130
Dating food packages, 71, 173
DDT, 114, 203
Defects, 63−65, 66, 71
Dehydration, 2, 130−132, 150, 156, 188,
   216
Dental health, 33, 39
Desalination, 13, 205
Desiccants, 169
Detoxification, 189
Developed countries, 8−12, 188
Developing countries, 8, 12−15, 187, 188
Diabetes, 40−41
Diet, 19, 29, 116
   adaptation, 75

carbohydrate, 38—39
  selection, 45—46
  RDA, 20—22
  vegetarian, 116
  Zen, 117
Dietetic foods, 159
Disease resistance, 178
Distribution, 69, 200—201
  automated, 198—199
DNA, 121
Drinks, 110—111, 143. *See also* Beverages
Drip loss, 132
Drying, 120, 130—132, 148, 152, 181

Ecological system, 190. *See also* Cycle
Eggs, 73, 130, 149—150, 194
Egypt, 107, 142
Electron beam, 126
Emulsifiers, 157
Enchilada, 109
Energy, applications, 121—127
  costs, 9, 149
  expenditure, 23
  food, 20, 23, 108
  ionizing radiation, 126—127
  nuclear, 126
  policy, 176
  radiant, 120
  resources, 176
  solar, 187, 206
Environment, 6, 6—7, 115
  Protection Agency, 6, 93
Enzymes, 10, 121, 126, 132, 138, 187—188, 190
Exports, 186—187, 197
Extermination, 107

F_o, 122
F_t, 122
Fads, 54, 61, 108, 110, 111—112
Famine, 18
Farm, costs, 196—198
  inspection, 62—63
  quality control, 60—62
  size, 197—200
  way of life, 197
Fats, 26, 58, 98
  saturated, 26, 40
  unsaturated, 26, 29, 37

Favism, 89
Federal Register, 96, 100
Feed, 193, 196
Feel, sense of, 46—47
Fermentation, 2, 107, 121, 135—136, 199
Field crops, 184—185
Filled, eggs, 150
  milk, 150—151, 158
  Milk Act, 94
Fish, 152
  canning, 122
  fads, 111
  farming, 201, 205
  frozen, 133
  meal, 188
  protein concentrate, 13
  radurization, 127
  runs, 118
  sticks, 153, 194
Flavor, 10, 56—57, 63, 65, 119, 151, 153, 156, 158, 179
  off-flavor, 157, 126, 131, 138, 154
Flexible packaging, 167—169
Flour, 107—108, 186
Fluidized-bed freezer, 133
Fluorine, 28
  in water, 42
Fly eggs, 67
Folic acid, 31
Foods, acceptability, 3, 42—57
  addiction, 110
  availability, 176, 178—187
  codes, 105—117, 158
  competition for, 201—204
  consumption changes, 194—195
  costs, 195—201
  dietetic, 159
  energy, 108
  fads, 54
  formulated, 153—156
  future, 193—206
  habits, 105—117
  imitation, 95, 158—159
  inspection, 63—72, 99—102
  new, 9, 59
  nutritional, 159
  organic, 112—116
  packaging, 10—12, 120—133, 162—174
  pills, 193
  plant food, 187, 196
  prepared, 153—156
  preservation, 2, 5, 9, 118—141
  production, 8—10
  quality, 72—80
  service, 154
  spoilage, 16—17, 119—120, 134, 137—139
  standards, 91—93

Food and Drug Administration, 59, 94−99, 113
Formulation, 55
Freeze drying, 131, 148, 156
Freezer, 50
Freezer-burn, 133
Freezing, 9, 132−134, 150−151, 152−154, 186, 199
  bacterial growth, 120
  preservation, 120, 127
Freon. See R-12
Fresh, 50−51
Frozen, concentrates, 173
  desserts, 55
  milk, 151
  peas, 53
  prepared foods, 153−156, 194
Fruits, 58, 73, 119, 126, 130, 134−135, 138, 148−149, 194, 197
Fumigation, 137
Functional properties, 159

Health, foods, 112. See also Organic, foods
  hazards, 115, 172. See also Toxins
Hearing, sense of, 46−47
Heart disease, 26−28
Heat, bacterial resistance, 120
  exchange, 124−125
HTST, 125, 152
  mold resistance, 119
  penetration, 122
  protein denaturation, 121
  yeast resistance, 120
Heat and eat foods, 142−153
Hedonic scale, 55
Heptachlor, 83
Honey, 112, 130
  fermented, 110
Hot dog, 152
Hunger, 160
Husbandry, 2−3
Hydro cooler, 128
Hydrogen swells, 165
Hydroponics, 114
Hypercholesteremia, 26

Gamma rays, 146
Gas exchange, 136−137
Gaspak, 157
Gelatin, 157
Genetics, 196−197, 204
Ginger, 82
Glass, 124, 165−166, 172, 199−200
Global strategies, 206
Grades, 49, 100−102, 184. See also Specifications, Standards
  official grading, 70−72
Grains, miracle, 6, 197
GRAS list, 97−98
Greece, 18, 107, 111
Green Revolution, 114

Ice Age, 118
Ice cream and Specialties, 79−80, 151, 186
Imitation foods, 59, 95, 150, 158−159
Imports, 196−197
Incaparina, 160
India, 109, 189
Industrial revolution, 3, 19
Infection, 140, 177
Infestation, 178. See also Insects
Ingredients, 195. See also Additives
Insecticides, 202−203. See also Pesticides
Insects, 202−204
  fragments, 84−87, 92
Inspection, 55−56
  acceptance, 61−62, 63−66
  certificate of, 71
  consumer, 72−74
  finished, 61−62, 68−70
  official, 70−71
  on-line, 61−62, 62−68
Instant foods, 131, 144, 147−148
Institutional foods, 59, 69−70
Intermediate-moisture foods, 132
Iodine, 21, 28, 34
Ionizing radiation, 126−127
Iron, 21, 28, 34
Irradiation, 13, 126−127

Habits, 105−107
  cultural, 109
  ethnic, 109
  neo-environmental, 110
  religious, 108
  tradition, 108
Ham, canned, 125
HACCP, 67−68
Hamburger, 152−161

Jams and jellies, 130, 135, 157, 159
Jerkey, 130
Juices, 49–50, 143–144, 179, 194

Khesakidal, 90
Kiln drying, 131
Kola nut, 111
Kwashiorkor, 27

Labeling, brand, 47, 73–74
  descriptive, 74, 102
  grade, 72–73
  nutrition, 58–59, 95–96
Labor costs, 8–9, 52–53
Lactase, 108
Lactose, 43, 108
Lagooning, 190
Land Grant Colleges, 8
Lathyrism, 90
Lavoisier, 20
Liebig, 20
Life cycle, 175
  support systems, 187
Limits to growth, 175–176, 194, 197
Lyophilization, 131. *See also* Freeze drying

Magnesium, 21, 27
Male sterility, 178
Malnutrition, 36–43, 59, 114, 178
Malthus, 45, 176
Mandatory regulations, 60, 92–93, 99. *See also* Standards
Manganese, 28
Mango, 187
Maple syrup, 130
Margarine, 194
Mariculture, 14
Marketing, 61–72, 162–174, 200–201
Master taster, 47–48, 55
Maturity, 184
Mead, 110
Meat, 72–73, 111, 119, 127, 130, 133, 138, 152–153, 160, 179, 194–195
  Inspection Act, 94

Mechanical cow, 185
Mesophiles, 120
Metal containers, 163–165
Metrication, 165
Microbial, food poisoning, 139–141
  spoilage, 119–121, 125
Microclimate, 169–171
Microorganisms, 14–15, 64, 119–121, 135–136, 187, 190
Microwave, 9
Military rations, 156
Milk, 26, 58, 108, 125, 127, 150–151, 158–159, 183, 188, 194, 198
Minerals, 21–22, 34, 113
  macro, 27–28
  micro, 28–29
Modified atmosphere storage, 137
Molasses, 112
Molds, 66, 119–120, 129, 135
Molecular biology. *See* Genetics
Molybdenum, 28
Mouthfeel, 47–48
Mung, 183
Mycotoxins, 119. *See also* Molds
Myoglobin, 170

Nader, 16, 93–94
Napoleon, 118, 122
National Canners Association, 102
Natural food,
  preference for, 50
  scheme, 112–114. *See also* Cycle
Neanderthals, 106
New products, 51–54
Niacin, 30
Nitrates, 134–135
Nitrites, 134–135
Nitrogen, liquid, 126, 131
Nitrosamines, 134
Non-enzymatic browning, 138
Nucleic acid, 121, 126
Nutrients, analysis, 57–58, 65–66, 106
  loss by irradiation, 126
  loss by refining, 107
Nutrition, 18–44, 115
  education, 115
  labeling, 58–59, 77–78, 96
  plant, 114
  quality, 57–59
  selection, 45–46, 75, 78, 107
  surveys, 32–36
Nutritive value, 75–77

Obesity, 35, 36, 37−39, 46
Objective testing, 55−57
Odor, 46−48, 57
Oil, olive, 82, 187
  salad, 194
  seeds, 186, 188−189
Open-dating, 51
Orange juice, 49−50
Organic, 112, 187, 190
  farming, 178
  foods, 110, 112−116
Origins of food, 105−107
Overrun, 79−80
Oxidizers, enzymatic, 119, 138
  non-enzymatic, 138
Oxygen, 169−170, 190−191
Oysters, 80−81

Packaging, 10−12, 51−53, 120, 162−174
  costs, 199−200
  cushion-pack, 173
  dating, 173
  freezer-burn, 133
  gas barriers, 138
  plastic laminates, 12
  produce, 51−53
Palatability, 3, 45−47, 75. *See also*
  Acceptability, measurement of
Pantothenic acid, 30
Papaya, 187
Paper, 166−167, 186
Pasteur, 5
Pasteurization, 125
Peaches, 46−47
Peanuts, 189
Pears, 149
Peas, 49, 53, 72−74, 102, 149, 180, 184−185
Pectin, 157, 186
Pellagra, 30
Permissive regulations, 60
Peroxides, 126
Pesticides, 178, 196
  Miller Amendment, 95
Pet food, 130, 132, 204
pH, 119−121
Phosphorus, 20, 27, 112
Photosynthesis, 187
Pickling, 130−138
Pitta, 109
Pizza, 53, 109
Plant diseases, 203−204
  food, 187, 196

Plantain, 147
Plastic, 12, 167−170, 199−200
Pleistocene hunters, 107
Polishing ponds, 191
Pollution, 6, 114, 175−177, 190
Polyethylene, 167, 170
Polyvinylidene chloride, 167, 170
Population, 5−6, 8, 15, 29, 175−176, 206
Pork, ?
Portion control, 53, 152−153, 179
Potassium, 27−28
Potato, debate, 89−90, 98, 204
  products, 145−146, 127, 152, 194
Poultry, 50, 53, 73, 127, 152, 194
Precooked foods, 133
Preference, 3
  natural foods, 46−50
Preservation, 118−141
  canning, 122−125
  chemical, 120. *See also* Additives
  cold, 120. *See also* Refrigeration
  definition, 118
  heat, 120
  ionizing radiation, 126−127
  pasteurization, 125−126
  water availability, 120, 132. *See also*
    Drying, Freezing
Preservatives, 119
Processing. *See* Canning
  automation, 198−199
  quality control and inspection, 61−68
  times, 122, 124−125
Processor, 69
Propionates, 119, 135
Protein, costs, 14
  deficiency, 27
  denaturation, 121
  milk, 58, 151
  mung, 183
  oilseed, 189
  plant, 14, 185
  textured, 160
  yeast, 120
Psychrophiles, 120
Ptomaines, 139
Pudding, 147−156
Pyridoxine, 30

Quality, control, 59−72
  hidden, 57−59
  sensory, 54−57

R-12, 133, 168
Radiation, ionizing, 126−127
microwave, 9
Radurization, 127
Rancidity, 57, 138
Raoult's law, 129
Rations, 76
RDA, 19−21, 29, 43
Recycling, 13, 15−16, 176, 192
Reducing agents, 131
Refrigeration, 50, 126, 127−128, 152, 172−173, 179, 202
Refrigerator, 50
Relative humidity, 129
Reptiles, 106, 202
Research, 103−104, 194
Respiration, 169−170
Restaurants, 154
Retortable pouch, 125, 156, 168
Revolution, agricultural, 2
industrial, 3, 19
Riboflavin, 30, 35, 43
Ritual, 111, 108−109
Rodents, 106, 178, 201−202
Rome, 18, 107

Safety, 64, 90−91, 98, 103. See also Wholesomeness
GRAS list, 97−98
Salad, dressing, 157
greens, 112
Sales promotion, 173−174. See also Marketing
Salmonella, 83, 127, 140
Salt, 28
Salting, 130, 134, 152
Sampling, 70, 71
Saprophytes, 120
Scandinavia, 107
Science,
role of, 3−4
School lunch program 33, 36, 160
Seafood, 13−14, 153, 201, 205. See also Fish
Selection, See also Acceptability
learned, 46−47
natural, 45−46
Selenium, 28
Sensory properties, feel, 46
odor, 47
sight, 46
sound, 47
taste, 47. See Flavor

Sensory quality, 45−74, 64, 75, 81, 188
mandatory, 92−93, 99
voluntary, 91−92, 99
Shigella, 127
Shrimp, 153
Shrink-wrap, 133, 173
Silicon, 28
Skillet dinners, 155−156
Smell, 46−48
Snacks, 144−145
Sodium, 27−28
benzoate, 134
chloride. See salt
sulfite, 134
Soft drinks, 111, 143−144, 171
Solar energy, 187, 206
Solids, 58, 60, 63, 65
Soy, burger, 161
cake, 186, 189
milk, 158
production, 197
protein, 110
Space foods, 157, 187
Specification, 55, 60, 61. See also Grades, Standards
Spices, 3, 10, 109, 134, 152
Spoilage, chemical, 119, 137−139
claims, 67
enzymatic, 119
meat, 152
microbial, 68, 119−121
Spores, 119, 120, 121
Spray drying, 131, 148
Spray irrigation, 191
Stabilizers, 157
Standards, 91−102. See also Grades, Specifications
fill, 79−80
government, 60, 94−101
identity, 80−82, 95
industry, 102
mandatory, 92−93, 99
voluntary, 91−92, 99. See Permissive
wholesomeness, 82−87
Staphylococcus, 83, 127, 140
S. aureus, 129, 140
Starch, 145−147, 157
Sterilization, 2, 125, 127. See also Canning
Sugar, 24, 55, 111−112, 130, 134, 146, 194
Sulfur, 27−28
Sulfur dioxide, 134
Sun drying, 131
Supermarket, 113, 200−201
Survival, 17, 201
Sweet potatoes, 105
Sweeteners, 194
Synthetic foods, 59, 110

Taboos, 105, 108
Tactile, 46. *See also* Texture
Tapioca, 147
Taste, definition, 56
  panel, 54–55
  sense of, 46–50
Tea, 110, 148
Temperature, exhaust, 67
  for preservation, 119–125
  for refrigeration, 127–128
Teratogenicity, 89–90
Texture, 52–56, 119, 138. *See also* Feel,
  Mouthfeel
Thermal, death times, 122, 139
  pollution, 190
  processing, 163
Thermophiles, 120
Thiamine, 20, 30, 35
Thickeners, 157
Tobacco, 105
Tomatoes, 47–48, 52, 60, 61–72, 148,
  181–182, 196
Toppings, 168
Tortilla, 109
Toxicants, 87–91
Toxins, 45. *See also* Health, hazards
  aerobes, 140
  anaerobes, 139–140
  botulism, 64–68
  mycotoxins, 119
  storage, 202
Transporation, 10, 178–179, 198
Trichinosis, 108
Tryptophan, 30
Turkey, 52, 106, 153
TV dinners, 78, 155
(Twelve) 12-D process, 122, 124

United States, costs, 195
  diets, 32–36
  exports, 197
  imports, 197
  official grading and inspection, 70–72
  production, 118
  standards, 99–102
Urban development, 3, 206

Vacuum, cans, 67, 147
  coolers, 128

drying, 131
Vegetables, 14, 51, 55, 73, 127, 133, 148–
  149, 180–183, 194–195
Vegetarians, 105, 107, 109, 117, 158
Vendor specifications, 60–61
Vitamins, 29–31, 33–36
  A, 29, 34, 42
  B, 29–31, 107, 112
  B$_1$, 30. *See also* Thiamine
  B$_2$, 30. *See also* Riboflavin
  B$_6$, 30. *See also* Pyridoxine
  B$_{12}$, 31. *See also* Cobalamin
  Biotin, 30
  C, 31, 34, 43, 58, 65–66, 87, 131
    See also Ascorbic acid
  D, 29, 106
  E, 29, 37, 43
  excess, 87
  fat-soluble, 29
  folic acid, 31
  K, 29, 43
  niacin, 30
  pantothenic acid, 30
  water soluble, 29–31
Volstead Act, 78

Warehousing automation, 198–199
Waste disposal, utilization, 12–13, 15,
  175–192
  liquid, 189–192
  recycling, 110, 206
  solid, 171
Water, activity, 120, 128–130
  adulteration with, 66
  bacterial growth, 120
  balance, 32
  desalination, 13, 205
  managment, 205
  waste, 183–184, 190
Weights and measures, drained, 61, 66–67,
  69, 79
  net, 66–67, 78
  overrun, 79–80
Wheat utilization, 107–108, 197
Whey, 183
Whips, 80
Whiskey, 47–48, 111, 143
Wholesomeness, 60, 72. *See also* Consumer,
  protection, Mandatory regulations
Wildlife, 114, 178, 201–204
Wine, 47, 81, 110–111, 120, 142–143, 183

X-rays, 126
Xanthan, 157
Xargue, 130

Yeasts, 107, 112, 118—120, 129
Yogurt, 151

Zen diet, 117
Zero population, 7
Zero tolerance, 82—87
Zinc, 28

Other AVI Books

ALCOHOL AND THE DIET
  Roe
CARBOHYDRATES AND HEALTH
  Hood, Wardrip and Bollenback
CONSUMER BEHAVIOR: THEORY AND APPLICATIONS
  Redman
DIETARY NUTRIENT GUIDE
  Pennington
DRUG-INDUCED NUTRITIONAL DEFICIENCIES
  Roe
EVALUATION OF PROTEINS FOR HUMANS
  Bodwell
FOOD AND ECONOMICS
  Hungate and Sherman
FOOD AND YOUR WELL-BEING
  Labunza
FOOD, PEOPLE AND NUTRITION
  Eckstein
FOOD PROTEINS
  Whitaker and Tannenbaum
IMMUNOLOGICAL ASPECTS OF FOODS
  Catsimpoolas
MENU PLANNING
  2nd Edition   *Eckstein*
NUTRITIONAL EVALUATION OF FOOD PROCESSING
  2nd Edition   *Harris and Karmas*
NUTRITIONAL QUALITY INDEX OF FOODS
  Hansen, Wyse and Sorenson
PROGRESS IN HUMAN NUTRITION
  Vol. 1   *Margen*
  Vol. 2   *Margen and Ogar*
SCHOOL FOODSERVICE
  Van Egmond